Alexandar Alexandrov

Revolution and Transition

MISCELLANEA BULGARICA

herausgegeben vom

Verein „Freunde des Hauses Wittgenstein
Österreichisch-Bulgarisches Wissenschaftsforum“

Band 24

LIT

Alexandar Alexandrov

Revolution and Transition

Cultural Policy in Bulgaria, 1989 – 2012

LIT

Cover illustration: *Carmina Burana*, oil painting by Stoimen Stoilov, 2005

With the support of Austrian Science Fund (FWF):
[PUB-307-G16]

Der Wissenschaftsfonds.

With the support of the Institute of Culture Management and Culture Studies, Vienna

Institut für Kulturmanagement
und Kulturwissenschaft

Translated from the German by WordWorks / Neil Perkins

Bibliographic information published by the Deutsche Nationalbibliothek
The Deutsche Nationalbibliothek lists this publication in the Deutsche Nationalbibliografie; detailed bibliographic data are available on the Internet at http://dnb.d-nb.de.

ISBN 978-3-643-90814-8

A catalogue record for this book is available from the British Library

Klosbachstr. 107
CH-8032 Zürich
Tel. +41 (0) 44-251 75 05
E-Mail: zuerich@lit-verlag.ch http://www.lit-verlag.ch

Distribution:

In the UK: Global Book Marketing, e-mail: mo@centralbooks.com
In North America: International Specialized Book Services, e-mail: orders@isbs.com
In Germany: LIT Verlag Fresnostr. 2, D-48159 Münster
Tel. +49 (0) 2 51-620 32 22, Fax +49 (0) 2 51-922 60 99, e-mail: vertrieb@lit-verlag.de

In Austria: Medienlogistik Pichler-ÖBZ, e-mail: mlo@medien-logistik.at
e-books are available at www.litwebshop.de

Contents

Foreword by
Franz-Otto Hofecker
Institute for Culture Management and Culture Studies
at the
University of Music and Performing Arts Vienna

I.

The analyses provided by Alexandar Alexandrov in *Revolution and Transition. Cultural Policy in Bulgaria, 1989–2012* represent a long overdue appraisal that will not only aid an academically descriptive approach, but also support the development of analytical instruments for fact-based decision-making in the action field of cultural policy in Bulgaria. Against the background and paradigm of cultural institutions studies and supplemented by comprehensive analyses of characteristics of Bulgaria's cultural industry specific to that country, the end result is an impressive account of the "state of the cultural nation Bulgaria". Academic work generally takes places in specialist disciplines. The present work, however, breaks with this convention by adopting a transdisciplinary approach which is pursued with as much consistency as success and also combines theory and practice. Only in this way can the present research field be examined in a way that befits its complexity. Anyone wishing to understand and interpret the cultural industry in modern-day Bulgaria needs must become acquainted with the country and its historical specifics, and must make an in-depth study not only of the development of the cultural industry in Bulgaria since 1989, but also of the preceding eras.

The hardships suffered by the cultural industry in Bulgaria, but also its opportunities, can be adequately portrayed only with the aid of various perspectives that exhibit complex interconnections. Formulation of useful recommendations for measures to support the cultural development of Bulgaria in general is only possible with recourse to and acknowledgment of comprehensive, keenly analytical in-depth studies covering the entire spectrum of the present-day cultural industry. In cultural institutions studies, the action field of cultural policy has a method of analysis specific to that discipline and bound by its own values. Only in this way can effects be triggered that will have a sustainable, long-term and positive impact on the dynamics of the development of the cultural industry. In the project presented here, cultural institutions studies as a set of analytical instruments and informed consideration of Bulgaria's specific characteristics are presented as an inseparable synthesis and always appear as connected in the practical discourse. They are shown to be interrelated, and only thus are scenarios for action developed for shaping the future. Alexandar Alexandrov is an agent and a protagonist in both the world of thought that is analysis of the cultural industry and in the appropriate application of this method to the real world, in this instance his case study of Bulgaria. From this stem the resources of his own potentiality, and this is also the strength of the publication itself.

Introductory remarks to this book must not fail to mention Alexandar Alexandrov's far more extensive study – or better, confrontation – with the cultural policy and, by association, the future of his homeland, Bulgaria. The publication of PhD projects in the specialist field of cultural institutions studies is important as a matter of principle. The primary legitimation of cultural institutions studies as an academic discipline lies in its voice at the intersection of theory and practice, in its power to transform and shape the activities of cultural institutions. The publication of Alexandar Alexandrov's PhD project *Revolution and Transition. Cultural Policy in Bulgaria 1989–2012* is a medium and an instrument that provides the Bulgarian cultural industry with a basis for discussion which is meticulously constructed, comprehensible in its presentation of the subject matter and on a sound theoretical and empirical footing. Alexandar Alexandrov has the ambition and has built up sufficient contacts in networks to enable him to propound the evaluations and recommendations elaborated here in the centres of cultural policy decision-making themselves. Consequently, it is through acting astutely under the eye of a broad public, in specific expert groups and in direct contact with the organs relevant to decision-making in Bulgaria's cultural institutions that Alexandar Alexandrov's PhD project ultimately fulfils its object. It makes a contribution and plays a role at the point where the examination originated many years ago: in the evident concern and attachment that Alexandar Alexandrov has with cultural activity in Bulgaria.

II.

Any analysis and appraisal of the way a cultural identity evolves and stabilizes is *per se* a complex undertaking and in every case transdisciplinary. In the examination of the subject of cultural identity conducted by cultural institutions studies, a further consideration is that it is an extremely young scientific university discipline, first introduced only two decades ago and still striving to establish itself in the research landscape and find its identity and cogency, as it were. The present work focuses on the problems and challenges faced by cultural policy in countries in transition after 1989, represented and explained by the specific example of Bulgaria. And yet, Alexandar Alexandrov had, by originally calling the work *Wende und Aufbruch*, expressed considerably greater optimism. The euphoria of the new beginning expressed in this title was subsequently replaced by the neutral term "transition". Furthermore, the work concludes with this finding: "The principal objective of this investigation is to provide the basis for further discussions in the field of cultural policy. If politicians claim that culture is important for Bulgaria, this study set out to scrutinize the reality of this 'cultural industry' and how it is reflected in legislation and life. The information on this, which was hitherto lacking, was gathered in the course of this study and can serve as the basis for further research."[1] That is good, and should by no means be taken as understatement. It quite simply characterizes the informed and realistic view of how difficult and laborious it is to achieve processes of change. It is also good and encouraging when such a finding is put forward by someone with the knowledge and empathy that Alexandar Alexandrov possesses. Long years of intensive research, meticulous scientific work and immersion in a research topic that ends by yielding approximately 450 pages of text correspond to and stand for nothing more than a basic framework for further discussion. A further circumstance that must be considered in order to gauge this work's importance with some degree of accuracy is that in its findings someone is speaking, thinking and analysing to whom the country and the people of Bulgaria are important because he himself is part of them, who therefore plainly sees the artistic potential of "his" country and its concomitant future viability as a personal challenge and equally as an opportunity to test his professional mettle, which is also how he presents it to himself and to others.

For Alexandrov, the analyses presented here are only the tools and master plan required to see more clearly and are ultimately only an instrument to reach the objectives (his own objectives) set out here, to focus more clearly as a means of raising awareness of them as a possibility (for personal action), as a means of locating and keeping them in view as a focal point on a horizon which is still far distant. Alexandar Alexandrov's final conclusion is that all the data gathered so far is still piecemeal and provisional. The defining work is still to be done, should the foundations for changes in Bulgaria's cultural industry really be laid for whose developmental stage the term "new beginning" may subsequently turn out to be fitting after all. Instructive arguments for this can be examined in Alexandrov's work. When standpoints and feelings of this kind mark the end of work on a dissertation, it is undeniable that a tremendous amount has been accomplished in the PhD project itself, more than can generally be expected. With this, he has placed himself in the service of achieving the objectives set out here and made himself an instrument for doing so.

III.

Conducting an examination with approaches used in cultural institutions studies implies a certain notion of the definition of cultural industry. Cultural institutions studies always and synchronously locates cultural industry in its micro- and macro-perspectives. The concepts of "industry" and "institutions" in cultural institutions studies begin with individual projects, with the skills and aspirations of an individual artist and can extend as far as systematic analysis of cultural policy in a particular country. Alexandrov's work investigates the cultural industry in Bulgaria in both senses. The small series of readings in one of the 3,000 *chital-*

[1] Alexandrov A., 2016, p. 215

ishta[2] in Bulgaria is just as much a topic for investigation as the identification of underlying trends in cultural industry from 1989 to the present day. In addition, the observations and analyses relate to a period that was difficult, since developments during that time were as turbulent as they were promising: in culture especially, the period of Bulgaria's transformation after 1989 is associated with great ambitions and hopes. It is significant that the original title of this work paired the terms *Wende* and *Aufbruch* instead of the pairing ultimately chosen, *Wende* and *Übergang*. From the outset, a greater proportion than might be expected of those involved in the transformation that was ultimately to change the entire political system came from the cultural industry: in only a few decades a country of the former "Eastern Bloc", previously governed centralistically and controlled with ideological rigour, transformed itself into a member of the European Union, its economy and politics now determined by a liberal, democratically pluralistic conception of society. The aim of this work is to document the transformation processes in the field of art and culture in concentrated form.

Besides its focus on the processes of change in Bulgaria itself, this publication also includes the possibility of extending the discourse to other specific countries in transition in Southeast Europe. Alexandar Alexandrov's investigation supplies valuable approaches for this, too, which are an inducement to conduct a succession of follow-up projects. The majority of the countries in Southeast Europe have also been members of the European Union for approximately ten years: Croatia joined recently and other countries are preparing for accession. In every case, membership of the European Union also entails a change in society and a repositioning of the cultural industry in each country. Alexandar Alexandrov's work develops solid theoretical and empirical foundations for observing and evaluating the process of integration into the European Union. Besides the focus on analysis of the countries themselves, study of the European Union's programmes relating to cultural policy and cultural sciences and of other European (Council of Europe) and international (UNESCO) organizations is a prerequisite.

Comparative research and analysis in a transnational context first requires intensive and detailed study of cultural policy and the perspectives for development in the nation state itself. Alexandar Alexandrov's work on *Revolution and Transition. Cultural Policy in Bulgaria* is an inducement to carry out similar projects in other Southeast European countries. This will lead step by step to frameworks for transnational comparative cultural research. However, conducting qualified transnational comparisons requires measures and definition frameworks at international level into which national findings are incorporated. Investigations such as Alexandrov's into cultural policy or Demerdzhiev's into music schools in Bul-

[2] A *chitalishte* is a public institution in Bulgaria that fulfils several functions at once, such as community centre, library and theatre.

garia are impressive examples of how this can be achieved from a technical point of view. Within the European Union, the Eurostat project aims to provide the member states with a framework for cultural statistics that is binding across national borders. Only when this Eurostat project is accepted and applied at national level will it become a transnationally helpful instrument. In the Council of Europe it is the Compendium Project in which comparative observations and indicators are already available for forty-seven countries. For a first approach, data sets are being developed which are genuinely comparative because they are collected in the participating countries according to a framework of definitions developed together at international level. In both projects, representatives from Bulgaria were involved, also in designing the concept. It is to the credit of Alexandrov's present publication that reference is made to both projects and the methods they produced, and that the methods they lay down are integrated into it.

The Compendium Project is run by the European Institute for Comparative Cultural Research (ERICArts) and the Council of Europe. In key sections of his investigation, as well as in his own delineations, Alexandrov refers to the framework of definitions provided for the fields of culture and cultural industry. By incorporating the Compendium Project's basic structure of methods for reaching definitions he has created a solid basis for transnational comparison, and not only in his own investigations. This fundamental decision is especially important from the point of view of pragmatic research because his work is the first of its kind to be done at the Institute for Culture Management and Culture Studies. With this publication, Alexandar Alexandrov invites the use of similar procedures in subsequent projects on other countries. This will have hitherto unforeseeable consequences, specifically for the formation of discussion forums on particular topics and the further exploration of Bulgaria's cultural policy, for instance. They will have consequences whose effects will last longer the more analogous studies are conducted with the aim, for example, of making direct comparisons of the transformation processes in other Southeast European countries, but also when they lead to in-depth direct comparisons with all the other member states of the European Union, for example with Austria.

Lazar Koprinarov

CONTRIBUTION TO THE CULTURAL POLICY DISCOURSE IN BULGARIA AND ON BULGARIA

At the end of the previous century and in the first decade of the twentieth century, interest in interpreting and improving cultural policy grew significantly in every European country. Why did a widespread discussion of the aims, priorities and sources of cultural development emerge apparent during this period in particular? In each European country there was a different configuration of the factors that triggered the debates in the field of cultural policy. Even though it is risky to do so, several causes can be identified that prompted these debates and determined their character.

Firstly, a growing necessity for increased "economic rationality" in culture emerged. In the second half of the twentieth century, similarities between cultural and material production began to spread. On the one hand, the dimensions of the circulation of intellectual values. On the other hand, the technology used for the creation, distribution and reception of art became more complicated and more expensive. This increased the role played by market criteria in cultural activity. Society's reaction to the necessity for increased economic rationality in the culture sector was expressed by growing political pressure to use those state resources sparingly and selectively that were allocated to cultural activities. In present-day society, the importance of culture is growing, but at the same time the expenditure required to maintain cultural life is growing, too. Culture is becoming more necessary, but at the same time its cost is rising. And the more obvious the relationship between the increased social need for cultural activity and its rising cost becomes, the more urgent it becomes to discuss the question of the amount of state resources, the criteria for assessing whether they are being used rationally and the order of priorities for this expenditure.

Secondly, it became more necessary to interpret present-day European societies in their current form of multicultural societies and, in this context, to guarantee in the best way possible the rights of minorities in cultural policy. Mass immigration has drastically reduced the existing homogeneity, whether hoped for or imagined, of European societies and turned them into a complicated and conflict-laden multicultural mosaic. In past eras, foreigners were the exception, but now they are a regular sight in today's European societies. In traditional society, a correlation existed between physical and social distance. One's neighbours in the locality were also "neighbours" in one's value system. Similarly, those geographically distant were also distant in terms of values. In today's societies, the criteria applied to proximity and distance have shifted – our great mobility, the decreasing importance of territorial demarcation, the large number of immigrants and modern means of communication mean that "near" and "far" cease to convey information about space. It is not just the immigrants who feel "distant" in their new environment; the "local" population also feel distant because their social setting is filled with alien customs. The neighbours in a locality are, in reality, often far apart from one another. In this way, tension between people who are physically close, but far apart in terms of their values, is produced naturally. The French intellectual of Bulgarian descent, Julia Kristeva, predicted years ago when reflecting on this topic that the touchstone of the twentieth century would be the answer to the question of how to live with aliens without rejecting them, but without assimilating them either. This strategic societal task sparked a lively debate about cultural policy in a multicultural society.

Thirdly, during the past decades – particularly following the fall of the "Iron Curtain" – the necessity emerged with ever increasing urgency to develop and implement a policy for maintaining European identity. In this connection, the British historian Hugh Seton-Watson posed the question: "What connection is there, or should there be, between a movement for European economic and political unity, and a sense of a European cultural community?" His answer was: "The second cannot exist without the first: it did for more than 200 years. But can the first exist without the second? It can, but at a high cost and probably not for long. Let us not underrate the need for a positive common cause, for something more exciting than the price of butter ...". This perspective makes it clear why cultural policy in Europe in the second half of the twentieth century, and especially in the last two decades, became a topic of intensive debate, comparison and assessment. That which is beyond the power of even the best economic policy is one of the possibilities offered by "good" cultural policy – that a consciousness of the common European identity is restored and strengthened that is capable of uniting and fostering efforts towards a common future for the continent.

Fourthly, another factor existed alongside the abovementioned reasons that created the conditions for lively debates on cultural policy – the fall of the "Iron Curtain" – and the dramatic transition of Central and Eastern Europe from totalitarian regimes to democratic societies with a market economy. The transition of these countries – their "return to Europe" – could not help but lead to a paradigm shift in cultural policy. The cultural transition was expressed by the efforts undertaken to make management of cultural activities democratic and to decentralize them by creating a market-oriented infrastructure of cultural values, by establishing a new legal basis, by abolishing the ideological monopoly, by overcoming cultural isolation, by becoming open to the West, by changing the way culture was funded and so on. All of this heightened the need for an exchange of ideas, for mutual assistance with the search for suitable legal solutions to promote cultural development, the study of the experiences of institutions in other countries, the joint development and improvement of theoretical instruments for the analysis, comparison and appraisal of cultural policy in Europe.

Bulgaria accomplished its transition of cultural policy under extremely difficult circumstances. The extraordinarily tight state control exercised by the totalitarian regime left deep impressions on the administration of the culture sector, and in the community of creators as well. The changes took place in a highly unfavourable economic climate that inflicted serious damage on the status of artists and led to destructive processes in the patrimonial and extensively developed cultural infrastructure. At the same time, the first years of transition were marked by political instability, and this prevented the development of a long-term strategy for the development of Bulgarian culture. All this hampered not just the implementation of the transition, but also the theoretization of cultural policy.

In this context, Bulgaria's participation in the European Review Programme of National Cultural Development Policies run by the Council of Europe in the years 1996–1997 was highly productive and beneficial. As part of this involvement, a comprehensive report on the situation and development of cultural policy in the period from 1990 to 1995 was produced. This report was adjudged to be a "valuable document" by a group of European experts headed by Charles Landry because, for the first time, it presented an exhaustive and accurate picture of cultural life and cultural policy in Bulgaria during the first five years of transition.

Alexandar Alexandrov's book *Revolution and Transition. Cultural Policy in Bulgaria 1989–2012* is the successful continuation of these efforts that were included in the national report compiled fifteen years ago. Although studies of particular aspects of Bulgarian cultural policy appeared in the years following publication of the report, it is only with Alexandar Alexandrov's investigation that a new and decisive step has been taken in this direction. By covering the period from the beginning of the transition until the present day, *Revolution and Transition. Cultural Policy in Bulgaria 1989–2012* significantly broadens the scope of analysis of Bulgarian cultural policy.

The period from 1989 to 2012 studied by Alexandar Alexandrov was, from the point of view of the cultural policy changes that were implemented, remarkably dynamic. However, the momentum was not evenly distributed. The path of cultural policy was complicated. The changes in the objectives of cultural policy, in various sectors of cultural life, at various levels of cultural policy did not take place at the same time or with the same rhythm. Consequently, the author made the right decision when he chose to proceed with his investigation chronologically. He conducted a diachronic analysis of the changes in the objectives of the instruments, the funding schemes and the normative basis of cultural policy, and revealed those moments that were of critical importance for changes in cultural policy.

The approach adopted in Alexandar Alexandrov's investigation is predominantly descriptive and analytical. He is an author with first-hand knowledge of the realities of Bulgarian culture policy. He is adept at finding his way through its manifold guises. Alexandar Alexandrov considers the programme and objectives side of cultural policy, the institutions and their modus operandi, the various cultural sectors, the financial resources and available personnel, the normative basis, the forms and standard of access to culture, policy in the field of cultural heritage and so on. To accomplish this task, he collected and processed a large amount of data. When one considers that the discipline of cultural statistics remains underdeveloped in Bulgaria, the data collation performed by Alexandar Alexandrov and the generalizations he makes are extremely useful. He collected and processed the data on the situation of cultural policy at various stages of its development and presented it in an appropriate manner. He worked with key figures that will make monitoring of the processes he analysed possible in future. In that respect, this book is not simply a summary of what has happened in Bulgarian cultural policy, but also an inducement to continue the work in new investigations.

At the start of the book, Alexandar Alexandrov sets himself the aim of making his investigation "a contribution to the cultural policy discourse, both in general and in the country itself. It is intended to be the starting point for an evaluation and analysis by means of which Bulgaria defines its position within the European Union." Reading this book gives cause to believe that his aim has been successfully achieved.

Peter Bachmaier

THE INFLUENCE OF THE WEST ON BULGARIAN CULTURAL POLICY, 1989–2013

The Revolution of 1989: from East to West

Following the *coup d'état* of 1989, the institutions that had previously been funded by the Committee for Culture changed both in terms of their structure and their activities. The programmes for the reorganization of society and culture were drawn up by western institutes and consultants. The theories espoused by these experts were strongly influenced by neoliberalism which was at that time becoming the dominant ideology in the West.[3] The aims of the Washington Consensus, which was reached at a conference of the IMF and World Bank in 1990, were the abolition of protectionism of states by means of liberalization, privatization and deregulation. The first programme, drawn up by Jeffrey Sachs for eastern Europe in 1989, was given the name "Shock Therapy".[4]

In the new paradigm of the Bulgarian economic model, cultural policy was not a national priority and no longer a public political category. On the foundations of political pluralism and civil society, new subjects of cultural policy emerged – non-governmental organizations, private institutes and international foundations.[5] The status of the creators also changed, as Alexandrov shows: from a central to a peripheral status, and many found themselves with no work and no social support.[6]

The programme of economic reforms drawn up by the American economists Richard Rahn and Ronald Utt in October 1990 on behalf of the Bulgarian government called for the replacement of national culture with "universal values". This programme formed the basis of the neoliberal project that was put into effect in Bulgaria.[7] In 1991, a first attempt was made to decentralize and de-ideologize culture by creating "centres of the arts" which, however, remained under the control of the Ministry of Culture.

In the first years after the end of communist rule, Bulgarian society and culture was in an intermediary state between socialism and liberalism, and culture remained essentially a state responsibility and centralized. The Ministry of Culture continued to support traditional culture and prevented any cooperation with the Western foundations.

---

3 Müller, K. Post-Washingtoner Consensus und Comprehensive Development Framework. Neue Perspektiven für Transformationsforschung und Transformationstheorie. In: *Osteuropa Forum* 16, p. 5. *Totalitarismus, Modernisierung und Transformation*. Opladen, 2001.

4 Williamson, J. *What Washington Means by Policy Reform*. Washington D. C., 1990.

5 Riedel, S. Bulgariens Kulturpolitik nach 1989: Ein Spiegelbild der wirtschaftlichen Krise. *Südosteuropa*, 45th year, 6–7, 1996, p. 508.

6 Alexandrov, A. *Revolution and Transition. Cultural Policy in Bulgaria, 1989–2012*. Vienna, 2016.

7 Rahn, R. and Utt, R. Bulgarian Economic Growth and Transition Project. Washington, 1990.

The Liberal Shift of 1997

However, in 1997, following the "Blue Revolution", the Ivan Kostov government (1997–2001) started to implement radical changes in society and culture. At the suggestion of the Council of Europe, and based on a report by the British culture manager Charles Landry, a new law relating to culture was drafted which provided for a radical decentralization and a new form of funding.[8]

Landry criticized the "uniform perspective of culture" in which modern artistic movements are unable to find any room and the disengagement of Bulgarian culture from international cultural trends. He suggested a new system of funding with the aid of sponsors instead of the state.

The national commission that discussed these suggestions separated into two factions: seventeen members supported the neoliberal Western system of legislation, while fourteen advocated the traditional cultural policy of the state. At the end of this debate, the new law on the protection and development of culture was passed in 1999 in accordance with the ideas of the first group.[9]

The new law *stipulated that 70% of funds for cultural institutions were to be provided by the Ministry of Culture and 30% by municipalities and private sponsors.* National arts centres based on the British model were established that were funded by the state but free to decide how to use the money. The work done by the arts centres was assessed on the basis of their economic result. For this, new forms of sponsorship and marketing were required. *This law was the prerequisite stipulated by the European Union for the inclusion of Bulgaria in its cultural programmes. The EU gave priority to the "third sector", i.e. the organizations of civil society between the state and the market.*[10]

The government led by the GERB party under Prime Minister Boyko Borisov (2009–2013) cut the entire national budget, and consequently also the budget for culture, by 15%. More and more cultural institutions were privatized and assessed according to their economic success. The Minister of Culture, Vezhdi Rashidov, declared: "It is time for culture to enter the market!" ("Vreme e kulturata da izleze na pazara!")[11]

---

8 Landry, C. *Bulgaria's Cultural Policy in Transition: From the Art of the State to the State of the Art.* London, 1997, p. 3; Koprinarov L. *Balgarskata kulturna politika 1990–1995 (Bulgarian Cultural Policy, 1990–1995).* Sofia: Institute of Culturology, 1996.

9 Zakon za zakrila i razvitie na kulturata, Darzhaven vestnik no. 50, 1.06.1999. (Protection and Development of Culture Act, State Gazette no. 50, 01.06.1999.) Stoyan Dencev, Sofia Vasileva. *Darzhavna politika za kul-turno-istorichesko nasledstvo na Balgariya, 1978-2005* (Cultural heritage policy of Bulgaria, 1978–2005). Sofia, 2006, p. 177.

10 Policies for Culture. Workshop dossier, Bistritsa, Bulgaria, 18–20 January 2001. Co-financed by the European Culture Foundation, Amsterdam, 2001, p. 66.

11 *24 Chasa*, 05.09.2009.

Since joining the EU in January 2007, Bulgaria has reorganized its cultural policy according to the European model and participated actively in all relevant EU programmes. The Bulgarian laws pertaining to audiovisual media and intellectual property were brought entirely in line with the EU. Since then, Bulgaria has regularly taken part in the biannual meeting of the Education, Youth, Culture and Sport Council which is chaired by the Commissioner and Directorate General responsible for Education and Culture. At these meetings, the EU programmes Culture 2007–2013 and Audiovisual Media 2007–2013 were discussed, which aim to secure financial support for joint projects in every sector of the arts and culture. In May 2008, the Contemporary European Art exhibition was opened by Commissioner Ján Figel in the European Commission building in Brussels. Works by Bulgarian artists were also shown at this exhibition.[12]

During the French presidency of the EU from 1 July to 31 December 2008, Bulgaria took part in the European Cultural Season and, in April 2009, staged a large-scale exhibition of mediaeval Bulgarian icons in the Château de Vincennes and a concert of the Orthodox male choir in La Madeleine Church in May that same year.[13]

The aim of the EU is the establishment of a multicultural society, officially called "Culture and Diversity", because according to this view all cultures are of equal value and should intermingle. The instruments used by the EU to achieve this are the Culture programme, the Europe-wide Cultural Contact Points, the Television Without Frontiers Directive and many more besides.

One sector of particular importance for culture is the media.[14] The EU directives provide for the possibility of establishing private television and radio stations and the privatization of state broadcasters. This makes it possible for the large international media concerns to take over such private stations.[15] The media policy of the EU aims to create an open audiovisual zone in Europe, and the Television Without Frontiers Directive of 1989 was the basis of this. In November 2007 a new directive was passed by the EU media ministers and the European Parliament that established the conditions necessary for the free exchange of media services within the EU.[16]

The MEDIA Mundus programme (2011–2013) assumes growing interest in global cooperation on the part of the audiovisual industry. It aims to give con-

---

12 Ministerstvo na kulturata, novini (Ministry of Culture, news), 12.11.2008.

13 Ministry of Culture. Portal of the European Union, 2009.

14 Müller, H. Die Vierte Gewalt: Medien und Journalismus kritisch betrachtet. In: *Österreichische Landsmann- schaft, Eckartschrift* 189.Vienna, 2008; Schachtschneider, K.A. Freiheitliche Aspekte der Demokratie. *Zeit- Fragen*, 26, 28.06.2010, A. 3.

15 Balgarska televiziya, Za BTV 2009 (Bulgarian television). www.btv.bg/content

16 Kultur wird Chefsache. *Der Spiegel*, 13.02.2007.

sumers more choice by bringing a wider assortment of products onto the international market. The EU directives provided for the possibility of establishing private television and radio stations and the privatization of state broadcasters. This made it possible for the large international media concerns to take over such private stations.

In the year 2000, Rupert Murdoch's News Corporation concern took over the Bulgarian national television channel Efir 2. It was turned into Bulgaria TV (bTV), the first private television station in Bulgaria, and is now the most-watched television station in the country with an audience share of 37%. In 2010, bTV was taken over by Central European Media Enterprises (CME), owned by Ronald Lauder and Time Warner. The television station bTV also includes the channels bTV Action, bTV Comedy, bTV Cinema, the women's channel bTV Lady and the pay-TV internet portal for films and videos http://voyo.bg. bTV introduced series and reality shows such as *Desperate Housewives*, *Survivor* and *Strictly Come Dancing* to Bulgarian viewers.[17]

After 1989, the newspapers and periodicals in Central and Eastern Europe had new owners, usually from abroad, such as the German WAZ Group, today the biggest publishing concern in Southeast Europe, which makes 40% of its total turnover in the region. In 1996, the group took over three daily newspapers, six weeklies and eleven periodicals in Bulgaria.[18]

In the Culture Article of the Treaty of Lisbon (2009) the EU committed to preserving Europe's cultural diversity and supporting activities undertaken by member states to protect the common cultural heritage and promote contemporary artistic work.

Intercultural dialogue and its promotion were cited in the EU Commission strategy "European agenda for culture in a globalising world" (2007) as an instrument that can aid relations between the various cultures in society. This item of the agenda is also supported by the new EU programmes for culture and by Europe for Citizens (2007–2013). International institutions such as the Council of Europe, the OECD and UNESCO list intercultural dialogue among their priorities, as do various non-governmental organizations.[19]

The Culture 2000 programme that began in the year 2000 was one of the EU's most important initiatives. In the years 2007 to 2013, EUR 400 million was available for cultural activities through this programme. The programme aims to promote transnational mobility for creators and intercultural dialogue with a view to engendering a "European citizenship".[20] The Cultural Contact Points such as

17 Balgarska televiziya, Za BTV 2012 (Bulgarian television). www.btv.bg/content

18 Hillard, P. *La fondation Bertelsmann et la gouvernance mondiale*. Paris, 2009, p. 57.

19 European Institute for Comparative Cultural Research (ERICarts). *Sharing Diversity: Kulturelle Vielfalt gemeinsam leben*. Bonn, 2008.

20 The European Union portal www.europa.eu/pol/cult/index-de.htm, 02.07.2012.

Kulturkontakt Austria received funding from the EU's Culture 2007–2013 programme.[21]

Above all, regulation of the cultural market is the most important element of cultural policy. Cultural policy is not merely the work of the EU Commission, but also the indirect management of these sectors by the European Parliament, the Council of Europe, the Conference of EU Education and Culture Ministers and by non-governmental organizations such as the Fundamental Rights Agency and the European Cultural Foundation which are, however, closely linked to these bodies.[22]

A special role in modern arts and culture is played by Gulliver Clearing House (now Gulliver's Connect), founded in 1987 after an idea of Günter Grass's by the Felix Meritis Foundation, an independent centre for the arts, culture and science in Amsterdam that aims to promote the cultural harmonization of Europe. The Foundation's work is based on the Council of Europe's European Cultural Convention.

The board at the time consisted of Andrey Bitov, György Konrád and Heiner Müller. Promotion of cooperation with Eastern European countries was a particular objective, with a view to contributing to the process of cultural change.[23]

The role of the "third sector"

Today, however, Bulgarian culture is no longer shaped by public cultural institutions alone, but also by the "third sector", i.e. non-governmental organizations (NGOs) which are generally funded by international foundations.[24]

In June 1995, the Institute of Contemporary Art (ISI) in Sofia was founded by Iaroslava Boubnova, Lachezar Boyadzhiev, Kiril Prashkov, Nedko Solakov, Maria Vasileva and Ivan Mudov. The Institute pursued the principal objective of promoting informal arts and collaborated with institutions from other countries that were represented in Sofia such as the British Council, the Goethe-Institut, the Institut Français, the Kulturkontakt Austria organization and the Soros Centre of the Arts.

Of particular significance was the Sofia City Art Gallery, founded in 1952, which had been a focal point for new trends in Bulgarian art since the 1970s.

---

21 www.ccp-austria.at, 02.07.2012.

22 Obuljen, N. *Why we need European cultural policies: The impact of EU enlargement on cultural policies in transition countries*. Amsterdam: European Cultural Foundation, 2005, p. 4. See also: Erhard Busek's speech "Bigger... better... beautiful? The impact of EU enlargement on cultural opportunities across Europe". Budapest, February 2002.

23 Felix Meritis Foundation. Newsletter, 12/2012.

24 Roth, M. Erziehung zur Demokratie: Amerikanische Erziehungs- und Kulturpolitik in Deutschland nach 1945 und in Bulgarien seit 1990. In: P. Bachmaier, A. Schwarcz and A. Cholakova, eds. *Der Transforma tionsprozess in Bulgarien und der Beitritt zur EU*. In: *Miscellanea Bulgarica* 18, Vienna, 2006, pp. 153–168.

In 2004, the new Department of Contemporary Art and Photography was established.[25]

The Open Society foundations created by the American billionaire and philanthropist of Hungarian extraction George Soros played a prominent role in the value shift in the Bulgarian population. The national Open Society Foundation Sofia was established in Bulgaria on 5 April 1990 with the approval of the Bulgarian government.[26]

From 1997–2004, Open Society (including its programmes for culture, media, libraries, women and Roma) spent a total of USD 9,792,000, of which USD 3,918,000 was spent by the Soros Arts Centre alone. Other sponsors who supported projects in the field of culture were the European Cultural Foundation, the Pro Helvetia Foundation and the Rotary Club. The lion's share of these subsidies went to modern art. The Soros Arts Centre set itself the target of documenting unconventional art which had until then been neglected and included installations, happenings, performances and assemblages.[27]

A particularly important role was played in modern arts and culture by The Red House Centre for Culture and Debate in Sofia (motto: Voi che entrate qui lasciate ogni cattivo pensiero), a project initiated by Gulliver Clearing House (now Gulliver's Connect).[28]

The Red House in Sofia was built in 1996 by Desislava Gavrilova with the aim of promoting contemporary art and aesthetic pluralism. It was conceived as a place for experimentation and innovation. Additional support came from the Dutch Ministry of Foreign Affairs, the American Center in Sofia, the European Cultural Foundation in Amsterdam and the USA Dance Theater Workshop. The Red House collaborated with the Centre for Liberal Strategies in Sofia, the Balkan Trust for Democracy and the Open Russia Foundation in Moscow (established in 2001 by Mikhail Khodorkovsky), the Central and Eastern Europe Trust for Civil Society, the István Bibó Society in Budapest and the American Research Center in Sofia. The Transeuropa Festival in Sofia fostered the spread of Bulgarian culture beyond its national borders. The Red House presented modern dance, alternative art, experimental theatre, LGBT festivals, documentary theatre, new music (John Cage), installations, rock music, the theatre of the absurd and electroacoustic music.[29]

---

25 Vasileva, M. *Sofiyska gradska chudozhestvena galeriya*. Sofia, 2009.

26 Roth, M. Erziehung zur Demokratie: Amerikanische Erziehungs- und Kulturpolitik in Deutschland nach 1945 und in Bulgarien seit 1990. In: P. Bachmaier, A. Schwarcz and A. Cholakova, eds. *Der Transforma tionsprozess in Bulgarien und der Beitritt zur EU*. In: *Miscellanea Bulgarica* 18, Vienna, 2006, p. 78.

27 Tsentar za izkustva "Soros", godishnite izlozhbi 2013 (Soros Arts Centre, annual exhibitions).

28 Felix Meritis Foundation. Newsletter, 12/2009.

29 Chervenata kashta (The Red House) Centre for Culture and Debate. Monthly programmes 2008–2013. Sofia.

After the fall of communism in 1989, and especially after 1997, Austria began to cooperate intensively with Bulgaria. The organization Kulturkontakt Austria was tasked by the EU with presenting contemporary art from Southeast Europe in Austria and Western contemporary art in Southeast Europe.[30] Since 1998, it has staged an annual exhibition in Sofia. At the same time, exhibitions of works by contemporary Bulgarian artists were organized in Vienna in association with the Institute of Contemporary Art in Sofia and the Open Society foundations. Among these was an exhibition featuring works by the head of the Institute, Maria Vasileva. For its part, the Institute for Contemporary Art (ISI) exhibits Austrian concept artists in association with Kulturkontakt and the MuseumsQuartier Wien, such as the exhibition Double Contact in 2002 and the exhibition featuring the Gelatin group in 2008.[31]

Kulturkontakt invited numerous Bulgarian artists to Austria for exhibitions and lengthy visits as part of the artist in residence programme, including Nedko Solakov, who came to Vienna on a scholarship in 1993 and exhibited in the Museum moderner Kunst (Stiftung Ludwig) and the Kunstforum. He lectured at the Academy of Fine Arts (2000) and the O.K. Zentrum in Linz (2005). In 1999, Iara Boubnova and Lachezar Boyadzhiev lectured at the Generali Stiftung in Vienna. In the year 2000, Hermann Nitsch held a talk and a workshop on the Orgien Mysterien Theater at the Sofia City Art Gallery. In 2002, Peter Weibel (Graz) spent some time at the Institute of Contemporary Art with an exhibition titled "In search of the Balkans".[32]

The painter Lachezar Boyadzhiev, now one of the most famous artists in Bulgaria, exhibited at the Kunstforum Wien in 1992, 1996, 1997 and 2007 and worked as "artist in residence" at the MuseumsQuartier Wien. In the autumn of 2008, the author and playwright Yuri Dachev spent some time in Vienna at the invitation of the Kulturkontakt organization as "writer in residence" where he held a reading of his works with the aid of his translator, Alexander Sitzmann.[33]

The Bulgarian Cultural Institute in Haus Wittgenstein in Vienna, founded in 1977, continued its cultural activities in the fields of literature, visual arts, theatre and music after 1989. In the years before and after Bulgaria's accession to the EU on 1 January 2007, a series of events was organized dealing with contemporary Bulgarian literature, visual arts and cinematic art with the aim of persuading the Austrian public of Bulgaria's European character: the Elias Canetti Week (2005), exhibitions of prominent artists such as Svetlin Rusev (2006) and Stoimen Stoilov

30 Kulturkontakt Austria. *Junge Kunst aus Bulgarien*. Galerie Art Point. Vienna, 2007.

31 Institut za savremeno izkustvo, Sofia (Institute of Modern Art, Sofia), 2008.

32 Institut za savremenno izkustvo Sofia (Institute of Modern Art, Sofia), annual reports 2008–2013.

33 *Springerin, Hefte für Gegenwartskunst*. Museumsquartier Vienna, 4/2006.

(2009), the exhibition “The Cyrillic Alphabet – the new Alphabet in the European Union” (2006) and the major exhibition “Fire and Spirit – 1000 Years of Bulgarian Icons” (2007) in the Dommuseum which was opened by Stefan Danailov, the Bulgarian Minister of Culture. Examples of Bulgarian cinema included important films from the past such as *The Goat Horn* (*Koziyat rog*) after a story by Nikolay Haytov and films by directors who, prior to 1989, had often fallen foul of the censors, such as Binka Zhelyazkova (1923–2011). In January 2009, a retrospective of her films and a documentary about her life were shown.

The crisis of Bulgarian culture during the “transition”

The reforms after 1989, and especially after 1997, have had lasting consequences for Bulgarian culture. The state largely relinquished its responsibility for culture. Many cultural institutions were closed and the employees laid off. The remaining cultural institutions could only pay meagre salaries and could not afford to carry out any new projects or productions.

The share for culture of GDP fell from 1.1% (1990) to 0.6 % in 2012, or 0.4% if expenditure on television and radio is deducted.[34] Of all EU countries, Bulgaria spends least on culture.[35] The artistic intelligentsia that, in the second half of the 1980s, had become the mouthpiece of the changes that subsequently ensued suffered most from the cutbacks and the loss of their status. The ideology of socialism was replaced by liberalism and consumerism.

Despite this, culture continued to play an important role. The population developed a great interest in their own past. A series of significant archaeological discoveries in recent years has led to an increase in domestic tourism, as people flock to the sacred sites of Bulgaria’s history. After all, the state-run cultural institutions – the theatres, opera houses, concert halls, art galleries, film studios and *chitalishta* – are still able to produce significant artistic accomplishments despite the difficult economic conditions, and to gain international recognition for them. Today, Bulgaria needs a change of system, a new orientation of the national elite and the restoration of the sovereign state. The concepts of the last few governments have already cited the following as the most important aims and principles: turning culture into a national priority in order to preserve the unity of the nation; maintaining traditional values; and strengthening the role of Bulgarian culture in the European context. It is to be hoped that this concept does in fact determine the path that cultural policy in Bulgaria takes in future.

34 Alexandrov, A. *Revolution and Transition: Cultural Policy in Bulgaria, 1989–2012*. Vienna, 2013.

35 Statisticheski godishnik na Republika Balgariya (Statistical Yearbook of the Republic of Bulgaria), Sofia 2011.

1. INTRODUCTION

The period of the so-called "transition to democracy" in Bulgaria has proved to be an extraordinarily dynamic turning point. It evolved under considerable external influences. It began in 1989, and many authors date the end of the transition at 2001, whereas others hold that it is still in progress. What is undisputed among researchers is that the nature of society changed from a totalitarian form of government to a pluralistic democracy. When the first democratically elected president, the philosopher Dr. Zhelyu Zhelev (1990 to 1997), came to power, the crisis of government ended. This also led to a temporary propitiation of the intellectual elite, thanks to a shift in the previous understanding of the term "culture" and the end of censorship.

The year 1989 was an *annus mirabilis*, a caesura in European history, but the change from a planned to a market economy initially caused a serious crisis, with production falling by over 50% in some sectors and unemployment rising accordingly. The welfare state system collapsed, and the country was plagued by hyperinflation. The years immediately following 1989 therefore entail a dramatic loss of prosperity, purchasing power and social security. It was to take more than ten years for the gross domestic product of 1989 to be equalled. One indication of the uncertainty, but also of the incipient shift in values towards individual self-fulfilment, was the dramatic drop in the birth rate. The revolution of 1989 had demographic consequences the like of which had never been seen before in the recent history of Bulgaria. Another factor was unemployment, which was between 37% and 57% in large parts of the country. The post-communism of the 1990s also led to the establishment of criminal structures within the economy. These succeeded in privatizing state structures and exploiting them for their own ends. They created a new hierarchy. The outside world did nothing to prevent this criminalization of the Bulgarian economy, since that would have meant interfering in the country's internal affairs, and consequently lent indirect support to these processes. Organized crime had yielded huge profits to the detriment of the country's development and the state reserves. The terms of a treaty signed with the International Monetary Fund after the years of hyperinflation were dictated by hopelessness and the threat of the country's financial collapse. The programme of economic reforms drawn up by the American economists Richard Rahn and Ronald Utt on behalf of the Bulgarian government in October 1990 called for the replacement of the country's national culture with "universal values". This programme formed the basis of the neoliberal project that was subsequently put into effect in Bulgaria.[1] On the country's territory a veritable war was under way to

[1] Rahn, R. and Utt, R. Bulgarian Economic Growth and Transition Project. Washington, 1990.

determine the redistribution of influence and interests within the economy. Before the end of communism, artists in Bulgaria were organized in artistic collectives, legitimized by the government and with the task of defining, through the various committees, what art is and what it is not. In this situation the only producer and buyer of art was the state. The state was happy because it saw that the hierarchy that had formed among the artists was more flexible than the one the state had imposed and that artistic freedom was not recognized as art anyway. The artists were happy because they were being well enough "looked after" and had no need to submit themselves to the vagaries of the market. And the general public was happy because people had no idea how much they were paying for the culture and artworks that had been placed before them and that they were silently filing past. The myth of the joys of life as an artist was a kind of reward of destiny, as Iara Boubnova puts it.[2] This myth and the undisputed loyalty of the artists themselves left an impression in both the West and the East. Material prosperity "liberated" Bulgaria's Socialist art from alternative, dissident tendencies; all such attempts were nipped in the bud. There were some artists who felt unable to become part of this status quo of a Garden of Eden and sought ways of leaving the country. Examples of these are the now famous graphic artist and wrapping artist Christo Javacheff (Christo), the twentieth-century operatic bass Boris Christoff, the director Mara Mattuschka, the philosopher Julia Kristeva and the writer Iliya Troyanov, who now ranks as a German writer, but whose Bulgarian family fled to Germany in 1971 via Yugoslavia and Italy and was granted political asylum there. The list of artists and scientists who have fled Bulgaria is very long.

In 2005, the then prime minister proclaimed the "end of the transition". The term was starting to contradict palpable reality, was being overused and ultimately lost its ability to mobilize. The value shift towards neoliberalism also lost out to the model of culture that had been in place up to then. The purpose of the new model is maximizing profits and not social relevance. What happened in Bulgarian culture in the 1990s should serve as a warning to western European countries, to the effect that neglecting art and culture has serious consequences for the development of a society's intellectual and manifold forms of expression. A process began that lasted all of twenty years and culminated in a remark made to general surprise by Culture Minister Rashidov in 2012: "If I had to complete my works in Bulgaria I would have stopped creating art a long time ago."[3]

---

2 Boubnova, I., 2000. *From defects to effect. Self-colonization as an alternative concept to isolationism* [online]. [viewed 28.10.2015]. Available from: http://eipcp.net/transversal/1100/boubnova/en

3 Georgieva, A. and Rashidov, V. Talantat e siguren v sebe si a posredstvenostta vdiga samo shum. (Talents are self-assured and the mediocre merely noisy). [online]. *Novinar* online daily newspaper, p. 2. Available from: http://mc.government.bg/files/1634_892_Novinar-20.10.10.pdf, p. 2 [03.02.2014]

The devaluing of sectors that cannot be commodified also took place in Austria, when, in 2001, the concept of "orchid studies" was coined, which implies that the political elite regards culture and education as luxuries that can be seen as dispensable in times of economic hardship. The challenge facing a common economic region must also be the consideration that humans are intellectual beings with an intellectual hunger that must be satisfied. The United Nations Universal Declaration of Human Rights states in Article 27 that "Everyone has the right freely to participate in the cultural life of the community, to enjoy the arts and to share in scientific advancement and its benefits".[4] However, social reality looked different, proof of which could be had by going to a theatre, for instance. Especially the heavily subsidized cultural institutions reached, then as now, a relatively small section of the population, because people with fewer education opportunities, with a lower income and a migrant background are particularly underrepresented in the audience – and not just in Bulgaria. The result of this policy was the emigration of a large number of Bulgarian artists. The absence of new critical subject matter in keeping with the times exacerbated the intellectual crisis in the country. Because of geographically differing migration patterns, global distribution of the arts and culture is uneven. Bulgaria is one of the countries that have lost out owing to this phenomenon, while Germany and England have benefited from intellectual concentrations. Is the topic of migration really only a passing phase, as the media claim, or is it a migration of identity we are yet to become aware of, and a deconstruction or appropriation of cultural goods? It is not just political, social or economic hardship that causes people to move the focal point of their lives; sometimes it is curiosity, adventurousness or a deep-seated need for self-fulfilment. This leads to a change in the monocultural concept of home(land) that has hitherto prevailed.

Whereas state-subsidized "institutions of high culture" are only now beginning to open up, interculturality has long been a subject dealt with by the free theatre scenes throughout Europe in their work. The *Tanz der Toleranz* (Dance of Tolerance) project organized by Caritas in Vienna and the activities of the "Brunnenmarkt Passage" there clearly demonstrate how social policy can combine with art and make the practice of art accessible to everyone. Seen in that light, cultural institutions that shy away from embracing interculturality are increasingly at risk of marginalizing themselves in future. In order to be able to create a successful concept for cultural policy, those occupying the relevant offices in Bulgaria should familiarize themselves with the subject of cultural migration. Especially so that they can answer the question of how the emigration and immigration of artists influenced the form and content of art throughout Europe in the twentieth

4 Resolution of the General Assembly, 217 A (III). Universal Declaration of Human Rights, Preamble. [online]. Available from: http://www.un.org/en/documents/udhr/, 10.12.1948.

and twenty-first centuries. This area of research is still relatively young and not a topic of discussion in Bulgaria. The social circumstances of artists has worsened dramatically since the 1990s, and this calls for a high degree of mental flexibility, an intensive search for new business models and forms of production and a new relationship with audiences. The new economic reorganization of Bulgarian society accelerated the emigration of many artists, whose hopes had been based not only on the aspect of self-fulfilment, but also on the prospect of higher earnings. But what was the reality for those who had emigrated to Austria, for example?

In 2008, the Austrian Federal Ministry for Arts, Education and Culture commissioned the Vienna research institute L&R Sozialforschung, in cooperation with Dr. Gerhard Wohlfahrt of Graz University, with a survey to obtain current information on the social circumstances of people engaged in every sector of the arts. The findings were sobering, and as follows: the total personal income of people engaged in artistic activities (also when income from non-artistic activities is added) is significantly lower than that of other occupational groups. On average, the annual net income from artistic activities in the year under review was EUR 4,500; those engaged in the film business and performing artists could generally earn slightly higher incomes.[5] The living and employment situation of creators from Bulgaria is currently only partially known, but it seems reasonable to assume that their situation does not greatly differ. A small minority has succeeded in reaching the top, both professionally and socially; one that may be mentioned is the first woman to be admitted to the Vienna Philharmonic, a Bulgarian. Then there are the successful musicians at European state opera houses. The fact remains that artists with a migrant background are influenced by their socialization in the country they have moved to just as much as by the culture of their country of origin. This mingling of cultures inevitably leads to changes in society that find expression not just in national cultures, but also transnationally in shared values.

In the course of the opening up of the East to Western Europe, artistic statements were heard that attracted a great deal of attention and appreciation. Seen from their perspective, many works gain in depth and forcefulness – for example, the soldiers marching naked in the video by the Polish artist Artur Zmijewski. A prime example is the ninety-part work *Red–Pink* (1973–1981) by Zagreb-based Mladen Stilinovic who worked with the ideological themes and the political and sexual connotations underlying the messages conveyed by these two colours.

The opening of the borders also gave many Bulgarian artists of the new generation the hope that they may be appreciated outside Bulgaria and that recognition would not depend on membership of a political party. It soon became clear that

5 Lechner, Reiter und Riesenfelder Sozialforschung OEG, *Zur sozialen Lage der Künstler und Künstlerinnen in Österreich* – summary of the findings. [online]. L&R Sozialforschung. [viewed 17.03.2013]. Available from: http://www.lrsocialresearch.at/files/KURZFASSUNG_studie_soziale_lage_kunstschaffende.pdf , p. 2.

they are not part of the new shared values; instead they are exotics in a scenario within the controlled norms of a minimal cultural exchange, with geopolitical overtones. The reason often given for the lack of "cooperation" with Bulgarian artists was the insufficient infrastructure in the country itself and the failure of public support. This process in modern Bulgarian art led to thought-provoking artistic statements in many works and a new process of self-discovery on the part of Bulgarian artists. The unique sensitivity aroused by the feeling of being misunderstood formed the basis of a new artistic reflection with regard to the problems of globalization, the environment etc. One of the central principles of integration, mobility, is replaced by a migration of ideas. This leads to a new terminology, such as self-colonization, a term coined by the Bulgarian sociologist Alexandar Kyosev. This term was derived from the concept of self-exploitation. That contemporary art was capable of contributing to a modern image was something even the Ministry of Culture in Bulgaria failed to recognize for a long time. These objectives come nowhere near meeting the needs of the local art scene. Does modern Bulgarian art still require a visa? Sadly, yes! It is now of a material nature and building a big wall.

This also affects artists from Western Europe. In order to circumvent this wall, artists in Europe have found their own way and established NGOs in which they formulate and communicate what it is they need. Without these institutions as the basis it would be impossible to define this content and these events in a world beyond the real hierarchies and canons of the failing cultural political models and to communicate them internationally without restrictions.[6] In Bulgaria, this process took longer because the Ministry of Culture has regained control over the independent arts centres in the various sectors. The exchange between artists took place at European level; this happened in a parallel environment due to the shift to independent forms of integration. For Bulgaria, examples of these are Artprojectdepot, ICA Sofia, the Red House, Cee-art, Biotope Installation etc.

Works by modern artists nowadays only reflect the context. That means they do not consider the marketing. This often happens without support of any kind from an institution. Not just in Bulgaria, but all over Europe artists are single-mindedly pursuing their ideas. However, it is difficult for them to survive without between linked to one another. Consequently, they turn themselves into a "secret society" with its own language and produce projects such as "Talks", launched by the "bg- art project Depo" organization. Such projects provide a global platform for active artists and allow them to exchange ideas about content, works, exhibitions etc.

6 Hasebach, D., Klein, A. et al. *Der Kulturinfarkt: Von Allem zu viel und überall das Gleiche. Eine Polemik über Kulturpolitik, Kulturstaat, Kultursubvention.* 2nd edition. Munich: Albrecht Knaus Verlag, 2012, p. 56.

All this is strongly reminiscent of the birth of "underground culture" in the last century. The difference is that artists join a larger "family" of art networks which, as in the last century, are regarded as a true sign of pluralistic democracy in action. The dynamics of all these processes of workmanlike creation by Bulgarian artists in recent years represent an alternative to the missing institutional concept "Quo vadis, Bulgarian art and culture?" and themselves write a new chapter in the history of art in Bulgaria that can be described as especially arresting.

Bulgaria is among the leading countries in the world for the number and diversity of cultural and historical monuments on its territory. In the regions bordering Bulgaria and in the country itself the remains of over 7,000 years of history and seven civilizations such as the prehistoric, Ancient Greek, Roman, Thracian, Byzantine, Muslim and Bulgarian are to be found. The non-movable cultural heritage alone includes over 40,000 documented monuments of global significance (seven of which are listed as UNESCO World Heritage Sites), while the oldest gold ever found is also part of Bulgarian history. The state museums contain over five million movable cultural monuments. It is particularly smaller countries like Bulgaria that find possibilities in the EU through cooperation and synergies that enable them to maintain active cultural autonomy with no loss of quality and to present their own specific national contribution. The EU offers itself as a platform of singularities to show the cultural diversity and its independence as a specific strength of this community. Although common measures in cultural policy have been laid down in the EU as a result of various committees and cooperation agreements, many questions remain unanswered: Is there an agreement on the form that a harmonized cultural policy might take and the shares of funds to be allotted to it? How will the principle of subsidiarity be upheld in order to preserve every single unique characteristic of each country? Is it even possible to speak of harmonized European aims, and which subjects are classified as European and which as national? (Communication 2007). More questions can be added to this list. Above all, the questions concern those topics recognized as nationally important and how to achieve a balance between large countries and small ones. Last but not least, it must be asked which cultural politicians will be responsible for implementing the directives agreed upon and which tools can be used to gauge the extent of consideration paid to national cultural singularities.[7] Every one of these questions is of a fundamental nature and requires a suitably dynamic discussion in which the smaller EU members such as Bulgaria must also take part. This necessitates not only the active involvement of the EU authorities, but also means that Bulgaria itself must assume an active leading role through its cultural institutions. Regrettably, it is apparent that many opportunities have been missed in both areas, not

7 Fisher, R. *A Cultural Dimension of the EU's External Policies – from Policy Statements to Practice and Potential*. Amsterdam: Bookmanstudies, 2007.

least because the Bulgarian Ministry of Culture acted as nothing more than an appendix of the national cultural organism. Not the least important question is whether it makes sense, in these dynamic times of scarce resources, to support and create new bureaucratic structures or whether the time has come to do away with ponderous culture ministries. Instead, the establishment of decision-making bodies should be considered which are detached from politics and are used decentrally and therefore made democratic. In addition, the potential provided by a country's cultural infrastructure – such as networks of theatres or libraries – should be exploited more.

In an analysis of strengths and weaknesses, the Bulgarian state shows a pioneering route for cultural institutions on EU territory. The focus is again solely on funding, since the culture and arts sectors are dismissed as superfluous luxuries. At first sight this may seem perfectly understandable in times of economic crisis, but in the long term it is not really constructive, since a perspective of this kind removes a country's cultural identity from the line of vision and thereby contributes to an undermining of its intellectual foundations.

1.1 Formation of the concepts of culture and cultural policy

Following his departure from Russia after the revolution of 1917, the painter Wassiliy Kandinsky wrote, in his writings on art: "Every work of art is the child of its time, often it is the mother of our emotions. It follows that each period of culture produces an art of its own, which cannot be repeated. Efforts to revive the art principles of the past at best produce works of art that resemble a stillborn child …"[8]

The concept of culture with its complex facets and forms of communication takes concrete form in the cultural practices and cultural policy of each individual country. It is the task of cultural policy to create the basic conditions and consequently the structures necessary for making creative work possible. Edward Said says on this subject: "Culture is always historical, and it is social – particular people in a particular place. Culture always implies contention among different definitions, styles, rival world views and interests."[9]

Tasos Zembylas argues: "*Dialectic of Enlightenment* (1947) by Theodor W. Adorno and Max Horkheimer gave the concept of culture a new interpretation that is specific. The culture produced in the 20th century is not the culture itself but a 'triumph of the invested capital'."[10]

8 Kandinsky, W. *Concerning the Spiritual in Art*. New York City, 1946.

9 Said, E. *Kultur, Identität und Geschichte*, cited in Educult. *Kulturelle Bildung für bildungsferne Schichten*. Study for the Wiener Volksbildung society. Vienna, 2004, p. 29.

10 Zembylas, T. *Kulturbetriebslehre, Grundlagen einer Interdisziplin*. Vienna, 2004, p. 49.

1. INTRODUCTION

In the current debate on state funding, the argument is repeatedly put forward that the state needs the integrative power of culture and acts in its own interests when it promotes the autonomy and pluralism of culture. Other commentators raise the critical objection that a concept of culture that goes beyond art ultimately causes the very objective – which is to enable the population to assume responsibility and exploit the resulting cognitive potential in society – to use art for economic purposes. To regain autonomy, there have recently been calls to abandon the concept of culture that goes beyond art and revert to a pure art policy because only then can it be a field for political-social examination. This shift in interpretation is also influenced by the world's difficult financial situation, and criticism of a more comprehensive concept of culture is also coming from culture management. Criticism of a broad concept of art is also made on the basis of the equation that the broader a concept of culture, the more inevitable funding with subsidies becomes. The extended concept of culture prevalent in the 1970s that was orientated to social values, completely obliterated the parameters of the civil concept of culture and saw art as a means of communication led to an expansion of infrastructure. However, the extension of the notion resulting from the incorporation of these dimensions did not lead to any modification of structures, so that the traditional institutions remained and the costs rose to such a degree that they could no longer be paid in times of reduced public funding.

The current concept of culture, it is argued, leads to marginalization and supports the tendency towards political and commercial exploitation. As a consequence of this reconstruction, efforts must be made in future to close the widening gap between the worsening socio-economic conditions experienced by art and the problem-solving potential of a broad concept of culture. Accordingly, a concept of culture needs to be formulated that supplants the currently prevailing economism, includes, in consequence, historical, sociological, aesthetic and political components and leads to a paradigm shift in both the theory and politics.

With regard to the exploitation of the concept of culture, however, it is apparent that the various terms survive and the "narrow" is justified with reference to the "broad". It emerges that a broad concept of culture remains largely indeterminate and that suddenly it is culture in the narrower sense that is meant after all.

One trend in the current development of the concept of culture can be defined as an association of a social-scientific understanding with semiotic approaches. Semiotics, which according to Umberto Eco is to be understood as cultural theory that either investigates the signs of everyday life and their political implications or, as the cultural semiotics of Yuri Lotman's Moscow circle does, explains culture as a secondary system of reality with a modelling function, replaces the structures with a theory of culture as a system of signs.

However, with the advent of post-structuralism the concept of signs also changed: signification is now a moment of fleeting stability, and new possibilities of interpretation are constantly emerging. It can therefore no longer be a question of identifying an underlying grammar; instead, the process of producing meaning must be analysed.

Clifford Geertz made two proposals regarding the concept of culture and the concept of man:

> "The first of these is that culture is best seen not as complexes of concrete behavior patterns—customs, usages, traditions, habit clusters—as has, by and large, been the case up to now, but as a set of control mechanisms—plans, recipes, rules, instructions (what computer engineers call 'programs')—for the governing of behavior. The second idea is that man is precisely the animal most desperately dependent upon such extragenetic, outside-the-skin control mechanisms, such cultural programs, for ordering his behavior."[11]

For this reason, everything a person does is cultural, including pragmatic and merely extrinsic behaviour that is also enclosed in the world of symbolic meanings in which humankind lives. Human beings are not just creators and creatures of social institutions and regulations, but are equally producers and products of intellectual and ethical meanings with which they are in the habit of even violating and modifying the social institutions and rules.

> "Marxism proposed the concept of class and the concept of class struggle to explain cultural formations. Structuralism and post-structuralism, on the other hand, identified an omnipresent and all-pervading 'symbolic order' or an anonymous personal pronoun 'it' as the vehicle of culture. Systems theory, on the other hand, speaks of the generative innate dynamics of social systems which produce culture autopoietically, i.e. without external impulsion and without a vehicle. In all these models, the notion of a medium in the shape of an individual has irrevocably disappeared."[12]

Culture takes concrete form in society because humans are cultural beings. Accordingly, social interaction must always become culture which means it develops meanings for individual and social action. Culture then stands for the characteristic patterns of meaning of an entire society, for the sum of the "believed realities", for its overall culture in the implicitness of social tradition. By this, not only the ideas behind each culture is meant, but also the social forms of its cultic and ritual preservation and its formal basis in institutions as well as the whole area of its aesthetic materialization. Culture spreads in every society – within different social groups and in different forms. Representative culture, folk culture, high culture and everyday culture are only one expression of this. Documenting and describing the spread of culture in a particular society is always an empirical un-

[11] Geertz, C. The Impact of the Concept of Culture on the Concept of Man. In: J. Platt, ed. *New Views of the Nature of Man.* Chicago: University of Chicago Press, 1965, pp. 93–118.

[12] Zembylas, T. *Kulturbetriebslehre, Grundlagen einer Interdisziplin.* Vienna, 2004, pp. 45-46.

dertaking. Culture is dynamic; it is not an object but a relation and is therefore in constant flux.

On this subject, Charles Landry says with regard to Bulgaria:

> "The first step of a policy, in our view, will be taken when the political debate begins which in turn leads to the definition of further goals within the bounds of what is possible, followed by the elaboration of the strategy which determines the limits of action in the particular context and which clearly defines the priorities that emerge through structures, methods, procedures. A balance is drawn of the results of this process, they are assessed and, if necessary, corrected."[13]

1.2 Studies on cultural policy in Bulgaria

During the transformation process, Bulgaria has made great progress and has been a member of the European Union since 2007.[14] However, there is still a lack of transparency in the administration of cultural institutions and their financing, and this constitutes a challenge in the context of cultural policy in the EU as a whole. In all, there are only four studies that provide an analysis of the state of Bulgarian cultural policy. Two of them date from before 1995, the third from 2001 and the fourth from 2009.[15] For anyone interested in finding out about Bulgarian cultural policy and unfamiliar with the processes in the country, the entire period from 1995 to 2008 remains utterly inaccessible.[16] While certain processes have been documented individually and in detail, a more wide-ranging summary of national developments in culture – also with regard to political changes made by decision-makers – is absent. The lack of information hampers the aims that the EU is pursuing: it makes it more difficult to develop concepts for cooperation.

This research project aims to make fundamental and decisive procedures of cultural policy in Bulgaria accessible, shed light on the budgeting of existing cultural institutions and show the developments in the country. One of this study's primary objectives is to illustrate the rapid development of electronic media in recent years (in 1995 there were three television stations; by 2008 the number had already grown to over 120) and to analyse the development of the previously centralized theatres after the theatre reform and the changes that have taken place in the cinema and literature sectors.

---

13 Landry, C. *Bulgaria's Cultural Policy in Transition: From the Art of the State to the State of the Art.* London, 1997, p. 20.

14 Accession to the EU on 01.01.2007.

15 Koprinarov, L. *Balgarskata kulturna politika 1990–1995 (Bulgarian Cultural Policy, 1990–1995).* Sofia: In stitute of Culturology, 1996.

16 Dimitrov, G. *Kultur im Transformationsprozess Osteuropas. Zum Wandel kultureller Institutionen am Beispiel Bulgariens nach 1989.* Munich, 2009.

This study is intended as a contribution to the cultural policy discourse, both in general and in the country itself. It is intended to be the starting point for an evaluation and analysis by means of which Bulgaria defines its position within the European Union.

The development of cultural policy in Bulgaria cannot be seen in isolation, but must be examined in the context of the political transformations and economic cataclysms. The question is how culture managed to survive at all in the face of hyperinflation of 330% (1995).[17] This study should be understood as both an investigation into the cultural history of Bulgaria from the collapse of communism to the present day, as well as an attempt to look ahead at the possibilities for guiding the country that may arise in the future. This raises the question of social responsibility. After the fall of the communist regime, a process of decentralization of culture gradually started. Bulgaria's new constitution of 1991 creates the legal basis of a pluralist democracy and its objectives, and refers to the state's obligations towards culture which are defined as follows in Section 23:

> "The State creates the conditions necessary for the free development of the sciences, education and art and supports it. Further, it ensures the preservation of the national historic cultural heritage."

Section 39, Paragraph 1:

> "Every citizen has the right to express his or her opinion freely, in writing or orally, acoustically, visually or in any other form."

Section 40, Paragraph 1 runs:

> "The printed media and other means of mass information are free and are not subject to censorship."[18]

Bulgaria now had the task of solving a fundamental problem: the transition from the centralized planned economy to private enterprise, liberation from an administration dominated by ideology, decentralization of cultural institutions and drafting a concept for systematic funding on the basis of an agreement to be reached with each creator. The budgeting model that had been used up to then was found to be plainly unsuitable because the existing and effective structures had either been destroyed or taken out of the hands of the professions. At the same time, it

---

[17] Bulgarian National Bank, statistics. Inflation in Bulgaria. Exchange rate of USD to BGN from 1995 to 2006.

[18] Konstitutsiya na Republika Balgariya (Constitution of the Republic of Bulgaria), Darzhaven vestnik (State Gazette) no. 56, 12 Jul 1991 (author's translation). Publ. 13 Jul 1991, effective from 13 Jul 1991, amend. No. 85, 26 Sep 2003, amend. No. 18, 25 Feb 2005. No. 27, 31 Mar 2006. No. 78, 26 Sep 2006. Ruling no. 7 of the Constitutional Court, 2006. No. 12, 6 Feb 2007 Available from: http://www.parliament.bg/bg/const (status 06.06.2008). cf. Constitution of the Republic of Bulgaria. [online]. [viewed 21.02.2012]. Available from: http://www.verfassungen.eu/bg/verf91.htm (status 05.11.2010).

was expected that the culturally knowledgeable citizens of the country abide by the constitution.

However, in times of crisis culture is always pushed down the list of priorities. Stabilizing the economy takes precedence over reforms in the culture sector. In Bulgaria, too, this led to considerable losses, although the economic situation has improved markedly since the year 2000. A specific indicator of a country's cultural policy is the per capita spending on culture.

In this context the question must be asked of how the state behaves towards artists and others engaged in the arts, the strategy it employs in this regard and what official measures and legal parameters are created to make culture possible. This question is of great importance for future development in the context of the European dialogue on culture. There is the widely held view that also in a market economy cultural activity takes the market as its sole reference point. The situation of the economy as a whole should be the yardstick by which the level of subsidies is measured that the state can afford for the preservation and continued development of cultural institutions. Other aspects are the consumption of culture and the possibility of paying members of the public for "consuming" culture, so to speak. In this way, the state guarantees the range of competing art by law. The following factors play a decisive role in this:

- free market for grants
- financial support of projects
- sponsorship (tax reductions for companies and individuals who support culture)
- appropriate legislation to regulate this market

Seen as separate action fields, the culture sector and cultural industry are, from the perspective of cultural institutions studies, independent sectors in society with their own logic, rationale and dynamics. Consequently, from the same perspective, the cultural industry and cultural activity must not be seen as a residual of the nation. Of course, the level of funding possible in the culture sector is closely linked to the dynamics of the economy (stagnation-growth), but in the discourse on principles it does not base the justification of its existence on "the situation of the economy as a whole". If society's relationship with culture were understood as inseparably linked to the economic situation, considerable losses for cultural networks would result in times of stagnation. This was the case in Bulgaria.

Seen in this light, the following analysis is based on a correct premise:

> "As the necessary process of mediation, culture is implicated in a logic of lack. Culture is the medium of information, the supplement, which substitutes in human life for the fact of inadequate genetic coding, instinctual wiring, sensory relations, the real, or what have you. Culture is the medium/agency by which the chaos of reality is transformed into an ordered—read "manageable"—sense of human reality. As such culture is not just descriptive but is embedded within a project for (future) action."[19]

According to UNESCO, culture also defines itself as "the flourishing of human existence in all its forms and as a whole".[20]

In the light of the aforementioned definition of culture, the concept of culture propounded in this publication is not to be understand in an anthropological sense in which the life of Bulgaria's population in all its aspects is portrayed; rather, it is intended that music, dance, folklore, literature, painting, visual arts cinema etc. stand for themselves.[21]

1.3 Scientific questions and methodology

The areas chosen for examination in this publication aim on the one hand to present the qualitative aspect and, on the other, the economic aspect in order to show the influence of each.

The questions asked by the present work are:

- Do the aims of politics and cultural institutions correspond to the results?
- If the aim of private enterprise is to achieve maximum profits, why do cultural institutions in Bulgaria often take a different viewpoint?
- What is the yardstick for measuring productivity in a cultural enterprise?
- No comprehensive study of Bulgarian cultural policy exists for the period from 1995 to 2008.
- The National Statistics Institute only began to apply new methods to document developments in Bulgaria's culture sector in the year 2000.
- Although the political parties have cultural programmes, they are unknown to the general public.
- There is no broad consensus on cultural legislation in the country itself.
- Laws already passed by parliament have still not been put into effect.
- From 1988 to 2006, not a single Minister of Culture ever wrote a report on his work that could have been presented and discussed in public.
- Before 2006 there was no national cultural programme. The budget of the Ministry of Culture for 2008 provides solely for subsidies for the maintenance of buildings.
- The manifestos of the political parties for the entire period from 1995 to 2012 deal with no more than fifteen points. However, no concepts for the implementation of these points were ever put forward.

---

19 Grossberg, L. The Victory of Culture, Part 1: Against the Logic of Mediation. In: Angelaki. *Journal of the Theoretical Humanities* 3 (3), pp. 3–29.

20 UNESCO. *Our Creative Diversity. Report of the World Commission on Culture and Development*. France, 1995, p. 24.

21 Hofecker, F. O. Zur Definition des Kulturbudgets in Österreich nach LIKUS. In: F. O. Hofecker and P. Tschmuck, eds. *Kulturpolitk, Kulturforschung und Kulturstatistik: Zur Abklärung einer spannungsreichen Textur*. Innsbruck, 2003.

- The Culture Ministry's priorities are not clearly defined for the general public.
- There is no database of press publications on the cultural policy debate.
- In the period under review, 1995 to 2012, no culture budgets of municipalities were published or investigated, and neither were their activities in the culture sector during that time.

There were no ulterior motives behind the selection of the five municipalities mentioned in this publication. Sofia and Varna are the biggest cities in the country and the three other municipalities are intended to serve as selected examples of cultural policy in Bulgaria.

The sources of this work are firstly the current legal provisions and bye-laws. It has proved very difficult to consult these sources for information because the period of time is too long to obtain and present a consistent view. The sources include the reports of the National Statistics Institute, the ministry responsible for culture and the annual reports of the Ministry of Finance.

Thirdly, published parliamentary records, selected question and answer sessions in parliament, the accounts of several cultural institutions, audits carried out by the Audit Office, press articles etc. also serve as sources. A fundamental difficulty encountered by this study arises from the absence of observations and the lack of attention paid by the country's politicians to critical deliberations. A further problem is the absence of any archives where articles dealing solely with cultural policy could be collected.

It should also be mentioned that the Institute of Cultural Studies has since been closed down due to a shortage of funds. Under these circumstances, the methods adopted focus on analysing the figures using triangulation of a combination of data from various sources or collated at different times and/or in different places by different people. Using these different data sources made it possible not only to reduce the number of potential gaps to a minimum, but also to avoid any errors that may have occurred. Often, the facts seem so obvious that they are taken for granted. Questioning them, however, reveals paradoxes, which is perhaps not surprising in an area as unexplored as Bulgarian cultural policy has been in recent years.

The study also sets itself the task of presenting the information gathered from 1995 to 2012 (as far as it was accessible) to make sure that it is not lost in the future. It can therefore justifiably also be regarded as a survey of cultural history.

Following on from that, the present study uses hermeneutics for the processing and interpretation of the data.

Cultural policy in the country following the fall of communism has experienced several transformations. One of the most important of these is that initially the conviction arose that those elements unable to survive in the new market situation had no important contribution to make to society. Accordingly, culture acquired its own survival strategy which gained a dimension and significance of its own that went beyond the individual in the social and national group. The main problem was and remains that the social-political component of culture has yet to be recognized. That makes the analysis of cultural policy in Bulgaria in the years 1995 to 1999 particularly difficult and absorbing because these years are marked by the major economic and political crises in the country and the number of published records of Bulgarian cultural life is extremely meagre.

Although the question of the status of culture in the country was often asked, no answer was forthcoming. This meant that it was not possible to foresee and prevent the impending collapse. It also became apparent how important forward-looking cultural policy is in order to answer the question of identity, coalescence and interaction among people.

1.4 Cultural statistics in Bulgaria: Problems and Perspectives

In Bulgaria there is no central contact centre for cultural statistics and no research institute dealing with this topic. Following closure of the Institute of Cultural Studies, only one publication relevant to the subject has appeared: the book *Bulgarian Cultural Policy 1990–1995* by L. Koprinarov and his team (1996). The gaps that remain unexplored in the cultural landscape are consequently fairly large. However, for several years the Council of Europe's CultureWatchEurope Initiative has been continuously publishing analyses that are also made available to the general public by the Open Society foundations. Another source of cultural statistics for Bulgaria is the Compendium of Cultural Policies and Trends in Europe.[22] The Ministry of Culture did not deem it necessary to publish a final report on its activities until June 2009. The National Statistics Institute provides information on cultural institutes and publications, but no analysis of their problems and prospects.

"The main sources of data are the investigating bodies of each cultural institution. The data is collected by the National Statistics Institute (the central office of statistics) via the regional statistics offices. Data on periodicals and irregularly issued magazines is gathered by the St. St. Cyril and Methodius National Library."[23]

[22] Council of Europe/ERICarts. *Compendium of Cultural Policies and Trends in Europe*. [online]. [viewed 18.02.2012]. Available from: http://www.culturalpolicies.net/web/index.php Open Society Institute (Soros Foundation), Sofia. [viewed 27.11.2011]. Available from: http://www.osf.bg/?cy=99 Observatory of Cultural Economics, Sofia. [viewed 27.11.2011]. Available from: http://www.culturaleconomics.bg/

[23] Natsionalen statisticheski institut (National Statistics Institute). *Statisticheski godishnik na Narodna Repub- lika Balgariya* (*Statistical Yearbook 2005*). Sofia, 2006, p. 445.

Another problem is visitor numbers. The report of the Audit Office for 2007 contains the following remark about the National History Museum: "No records exist of the number of tickets sold at inflated prices."[24]

This means that the price adjustments were not communicated to the National Statistics Institute. As a result, the information on museum revenue is statistically incomplete. And if one knows that the state failed to exercise any control whatsoever over the National Palace of Culture (NDK) through all the years following the end of communism (and that the Palace therefore represented an autonomous structure that operated like an individual enterprise) it will become clear that all these figures (e.g. in the categories of dance, theatre etc.) in the individual reports must be considered highly dubious on the basis of their scope and the diversity of the programme alone. This is probably a consequence of the censorship that was in place prior to 1989 and the subsequent gradual process of decentralization. The period investigated, 1995 to 2012, reveals a wildly proliferating cultural jungle with numerous outdated branches. Projections are made from the data from the National Statistics Institute using the "mathematical procedure". But a look at the municipalities examined shows a huge variety of definitions in the cultural items, which is why they were categorized and recorded differently by the National Statistics Institute:

> "Since 2002, not even statistics of the National Statistics Institute have been collected in their entirety for the libraries as a consequence of a decision made by the management of the Statistics Institute and the negligence of the Culture Ministry."[25]

Of the visual arts, the country only registers film production. The development of the applied arts was not monitored by national statistics. In addition, state funding proved to be enormously difficult. These funds are necessary, however, to make sure that they can survive in the art market despite their limited competitiveness and can realize their great potential.[26]

---

24 Smetna Palata (Audit Office). *Doklad za rezultatite ot izvarsheniya odit na finansovoto upravlenie na byu- dzheta na natsionalniya istoricheski muzei* (*Report on the findings of the inspection of the financial manage ment of the budget of the National History Museum*) 01.01.2007–31.12.2007, report no. 0700000208, no. 286. Sofia, 06.11.2008, pp. 1–2. See also: Institut za pazarna ikonomika (Institut of Market Economy). *Uspekhite i provalite na balgarskite pravitelstva 1998–2007. Pregled na oditnite dokladi na Smetnata Palata* (*The successes and failures of the Bulgarian governments 1997–2007. Examination of the economic reports of the Audit Office*). [online]. Trust for Civil Society in Central and Eastern Europe, 2008. [viewed 19.02.2012]. Available from: http://ime.bg/uploads/b205d6_FullReport.pdf

25 Sayuz na biblioteknite i informatsionnite rabotnitsi (Association of Employees of Libraries and Information Services), 2004. *Za neobchodimostta ot neotlozhni merki za reshavane na osnovnite problemi na bibliotekite v Balgariya* (*On the necessity of solving the problems of libraries in Bulgaria*). [online]. [viewed 21.02.2012]. Available from: http://www.lib.bg/za_neob.htm (status 21.04.2004).

26 Agentsiya za ikonomicheski analizi i prognozi (Agency for Economic Analysis and Forecasts).

The culture budgets in Bulgaria vary from municipality to municipality. Accordingly, it is the task of cultural politicians to question these various lump sums. In the capital Sofia, for instance, the costs of the zoological gardens are included in expenditure on culture, as are the costs of repairing the Vrana palace.[27]

That several countries are currently faced with this phenomenon is shown by the following quote by Franz-Otto Hofecker speaking about Austria: "The call heard from various quarters to provide reliable figures in the field of culture has recently been coming with ever greater frequency from a discourse on cultural policy within the cultural sciences which is becoming increasingly visible."[28]

1.5 Selected Development Indicators since 1989

In 1989, Bulgaria still had a population of 8.9 million. By 2012, this had dropped to 7.6 million. Population density was 70 people per km. The population fell with increasing speed as the years passed. According to the World Health Organization (WHO), life expectancy was 69 years for men and 76 years for women.

Table 1: Selected development indicators, 1995–2008[29]

Indicators	1995	1997	1999	2001	2003	2005	2008
Population, million	8.4	8.3	8.2	7.9	7.8	7.7	7.4
Ages 0–14	1.7	1.7	1.6	1.5	1.4	1.3	1
Ages 15–64	6.6	6.7	6.78	6.8	6.8	6.9	5.3
Age 65+	1.5	1.5	1.6	1.6	1.6	1.6	2.5
Population, female	5.1	5.1	5.1	5.1	5.1	5.1	
Population density (people per km2)	75.93	75.13	74.19	71.20	70.71	70.00	
Birth rate (per 1,000 people)	8.60	7.70	8.90	8.60	8.60	9.00	
Mortality rate (per 1,000 people)	13.60	14.60	13.60	14.20	14.30	14.20	
Population growth (annual %)	-0.43	-0.53	-0.60	-1.88	-0.59	-0.30	
Urban population	6.7	6.8	6.8	6.9	6.9	7	5.4
Rural population	3.2	3.1	3.1	3	3	3	2.2

Natsionalen plan za razvitie na Republika Balgariya za perioda 2007-2013 (National Development Plan of the Republic of Bulgaria for the Period 2009–2013). Sofia, 2005, p. 112.

27 Budget of The municipality of Sofia, 1999.

28 Hofecker, F. O. Introduction. Quo vadis Kulturstatistik? Einige Anmerkungen zum Verhältnis von Kultursta tistik, Kulturwissenschaft und Kulturpolitik. In: F. O. Hofecker and P. Tschmuck, eds. *Kulturpolitk, Kultur forschung und Kulturstatistik: Zur Abklärung einer spannungsreichen Textur*. Innsbruck, 2003, p. 10.

29 World Bank. World Development Indicators database, 2009. [online]. Available from: http://www.euro.who.int/Document/E90023.pdf. National Statistics Institute. Sofia.

In 2008, the unemployment rate was 5.9% and the average wage BGN 538. Government-backed bonds reached BGN 10.9 thousand million equating to 16.5% of GDP. Gross external debt amounted to BGN 36.4 thousand million, or 107.1% of GDP. The international reserves at the Bulgarian National Bank (including coverage of the currency board and the obligatory reserves of the commercial banks) totalled over BGN 28 thousand million. The market analysis for 2009 ran as follows:

"The demand for banking services has grown as confidence in the sector has gradually returned and incomes increased since 1997. Total assets of the commercial banks rose by 45% in local-currency terms in 2005 and are estimated to have grown by around 23% in 2006. Banks have increased their lending, particularly to households, and have shifted away from their previous pattern of holding large deposits overseas. With the government running a budget surplus since 2003, lending to the private sector has been growing more quickly than total lending. After these increases, loans to the non-financial sector accounted for 66% of deposits in September 2006. The Bulgarian economy is still mainly cash-oriented, but the use of debit cards is increasing. Bulgaria is one of the fastest growing countries in Eastern Europe by assets, loans, deposits and profitability of the sector. The credit card market in Bulgaria is all set to take off in a big way as it has a significant potential for expansion because only 3% of payment transactions are made by credit card."[30]

On average, 85% of the female working population and 89% of the male working population earned income liable for insurance contributions. Average pensions for women were 26%–30% lower than those of men. According to a report by the World Bank, cash transfers from abroad amounted to almost USD 2 thousand million, or 5% of GDP, in 2007.[31] These transfers were not investment, but money sent by Bulgarians living abroad. In 2008, the financial crisis reached Bulgaria. Following the growth of 7.1% in the first half of 2008, to which every sector contributed, industrial production sank by 5% in November 2008, the construction industry shrank by 14.9%, wholesale trade by 6.6% and the retail trade by 1.2%. In 2009 and 2010 there was no growth of GDP. EU subsidies for infrastructure projects in the transportation and environment sectors brought an important boost, as did corporate investment in modernization and staff training. In 2009, the informal economy in the various sectors in Bulgaria accounted for between 20% and 35%, according to a study carried out by the Centre for Democratic Research. These figures are contained in the so-called hidden economy index. Among the principal components of this index are levels of taxation, corporate turnover and employers' contributions to health insurance and retirement pensions for employ-

[30] Bulgarian Banking Sector Analysis, indicators for 2008. [online]. [viewed 20.02.2012.] Available from: http://www.rncos.com/Report/IM587.htm.

[31] Sabev, D. *Sreshtu deflatsiyata valutniyat bord v Balgariya e bezsilen* (*There is no recourse against the defla- tion of the currency board in Bulgaria*). [online]. [viewed 19.02.2012]. Available from: http://money.ibox.bg/comment/id_570998032

ees. According to the study, the largest share of the informal economy is found in the construction and real estate sectors. The unwillingness of employees and employers to pay the full tax rate due on their earnings is a result of the high insurance premiums.

Despite the low flat tax rate, most people did not complete their income tax returns because of the high social insurance contributions. It was precisely the existence of minimal insurance rates and, accordingly, a minimum wage, that encouraged tax evasion. CEOs of companies know that the state accepts the declaration of low incomes, and this too facilitates tax evasion.

A large percentage of employees did indeed receive considerably higher wages. Paradoxically, higher minimum wages would have disastrous consequences, such as a sharp rise in unemployment and a spread of the black economy.[32] The lower tax and social insurance rates that were introduced, improved controls on the part of the Bulgarian government and economic growth were all based on loans issued domestically and direct investment from abroad. They led to a reduction of the informal economy of 30%. The impact of these measures on the black economy was limited because law enforcement measures were not tightened.[33]

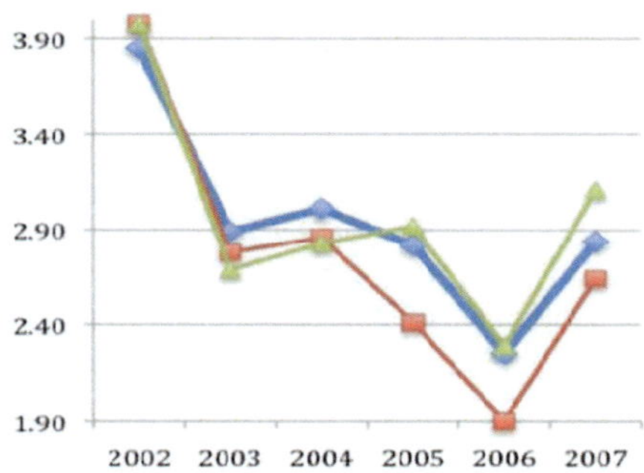

Figure 1: Dynamics of the black economy in Bulgaria 2002–2007: Secret economy index[34]

Legend:
Blue: Black economy
Red: Undeclared employment
Green: Undeclared turnover, hidden turnover

[32] Ganev, P. Minimalnite pragove i sivata ikonomika (Minimum values and the informal economy). [online]. In: *Dnevnik*, 22.09.2008. [viewed 19.02.2012]. Available from: http://www.dnevnik.bg/show/?storyid=553161

[33] Tsentar za izledvane na demokratsiyata (Centre for Democratic Research). Policy paper. *Za ednakvi pravila i pochtena konkurentsiya politiki za protivodeistvie na sivata ikonomika i koruptsiyata v Balgariya* (*For the same rules and fair competition, strategies for fighting the black economy and corruption in Bulgaria*). [online]. Sofia, May 2008. [viewed 22.02.2012]. Available from: http://www.econ.bg/content/fileSrc.pdf

[34] Vitosha Research: Tsentar za izledvane na demokratsiyata (Centre for Democratic Research).

The secret earnings in Bulgaria turned into a source of corrupt payments for all kinds of ends, from protection money to exerting influence on the government. At the core of the black economy are syndicates of politically allied companies that aimed to promote their own interests to the detriment of their competitors by means of connections with local and central authorities. Companies of this kind exploited the profits they made from the politically shielded secret monopolies to take control of the state and so preserve the preferential treatment they receive and to found chains of licit companies. These were intended to act as screens in the event that difficulties arose from more stringent inspections by the authorities. Similar strategies were used in those sectors of the economy particularly subject to excise duties such as the production of cigarettes and alcohol, duty free trade and the sale of fuel, as well as in state monopolies and sectors dependent to a large degree on public contracts such as energy supply, the health service etc.[35]

Table 2: Gross Domestic Product 2003–2008[36]

Year, gross domestic product (GDP) in thousand millions		Difference
2003	50.6	
2004	57.1	12.91%
2005	61.6	7.88%
2006	71.6	16.29%
2007	78.6	9.78%
2008	86.7	10.23%

Year, gross domestic product (GDP) per capita, USD T		Difference
2003	6,000	
2004	7,600	15.15%
2005	8,200	7.89%
2006	9,600	17.07%
2007	10,700	11.46%
2008	11,800	10.28%

The reduction of the tax on profits from 15% to 10% in 2007 can be seen as a feather in the cap of the Bulgarian government. The same applies to the introduction of the 10% flat-rate income tax in 2008.

The decision to reduce the tax burden had a positive impact on the national budget and on the real sector especially with regard to levels of employment in the country. In a joint statement made to the President, the Chairman of the National Assembly, the Prime Minister and the Minister of Culture, the associations of creators expressed their reservations about the introduction of the flat tax. The declaration was signed by the associations of film industry professionals, visual artists, writers, painters, composers, translators and architects. The associations were concerned about the government's decision to introduce the flat tax because it would mean the end of favourable taxation, namely the eligible costs of the liberal professions, and a drastic cut in the earnings of those engaged in creative activities. The majority of artists lived on fees, but this change in taxation condemned them to even greater poverty.

[35] Vitosha Research: Tsentar za izledvane na demokratsiyata (Centre for Democratic Research).

[36] CIA World Factbook. Version 16. Bulgaria, 2008.

The Austrian trade commissioner in Sofia highlighted the fact that Austria was the biggest investor in Bulgaria; the country's investments were higher than second-ranked Germany's and third-ranked Italy's combined.[37]

Strazimir Angelski analysed the developments in 2009 in the following terms:

"After 1998 Bulgaria achieved a significant growth in GDP. In 2005 it was 5.5%. During the second half of the same year the growth path was disturbed by the floods in the country, which hardly [*sic*] hit the agriculture sector. For the second quarter of 2006 the country accumulated the highest growth of 6.6% since the beginning of the changes. But despite of this positive development the income gap, in comparison to the EU countries is still large. In 2004 GDP per capita was $3.123, which accounts for 31% of the average level in EU-25. In order to close this gap it is recommended by the World Bank, The International Monetary Fund and the EU mainly an improvement of the productivity (the output growth is below its potential), increasing the employment rate to 70% until 2010, and continuing of the structure reforms."[38]

According to the Index of Economic Freedom:

"Bulgaria's economic freedom score is 64.6, making its economy the 56th freest in the 2009 *Index*. Its overall score is 0.9 point [*sic*] higher than last year, primarily as a result of improved business and fiscal freedom. Bulgaria is ranked 26th freest among the 43 countries in the Europe region, and its overall score is well above the world average. Overcoming initial delays in the transition to a market-oriented economy, Bulgaria has pursued comprehensive economic reform and trade liberalization. Six of Bulgaria's economic freedoms are well above the global average. The country's private sector, which accounts for about 75 percent of the economy, benefits from low taxation and a sensible regulatory environment. Bulgaria's fiscal freedom has been further enhanced by the implementation of a flat income tax rate of 10 percent, which is one of the lowest rates in the world."[39]

Table 3: Gross domestic product 1989–2005[40].

	1989	1990	1991	1992	1993	1994	1995	1996	1997	1998	1999
Actual GDP	-3.5	-9.1	-8.4	-7.3	-1.5	1.8	2.9	-9.4	-5.6	4.0	2.3
Inflation		64.0	419.0	91.3	72.8	96.0	62.1	121.6	1058.4	18.7	2.6
Foreign direct investment	n/a	0.0	0.7	0.5	0.4	1.1	0.8	1.4	4.9	4.2	6.2
Current balance of accounts	-3.7		-1.0	-4.2	-10.1	-0.3	-1.5	1.7	10.1	-0.5	-5.0

37 Austrian Economic Chamber. News. UBI Union Bankindustrie, 2005.

38 Angelski S. *Bulgaria – an Economic Overview (Univ. of Economics Bratislava, Price Decision Making, Working Paper)*, Bratislava, 2009, p. 7.

39 Index of economic freedom, Heritage Foundation and *Wall Street Journal*. [online] Available from: www.heritage.org/index/Country/Bulgaria (status 14.01.2009).

	2000	2001	2002	2003	2004	2005
Actual GDP	5.4	4.1	4.9	4.5	5.6	5.5
Inflation	10.3	7.4	5.8	2.3	6.1	5
Foreign direct investment	7.9	5.9	5.6	10.4	8.4	10.8
Current balance of accounts	-5.6	-7.2	-5.3	-9.3	-7.5	-11.8

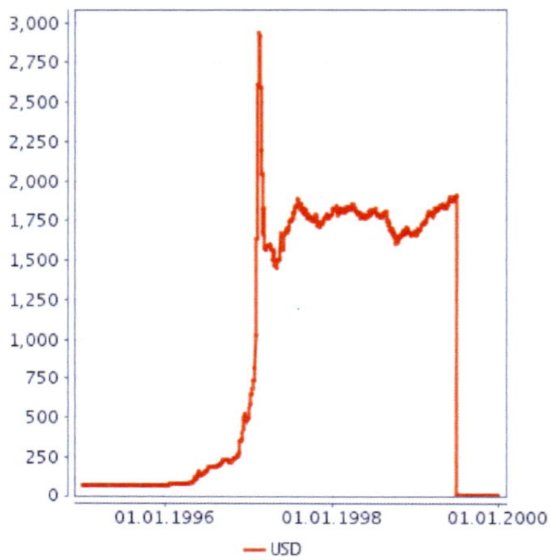

Figure 2: Exchange rate BGN / US dollar, 1996–2000[41]

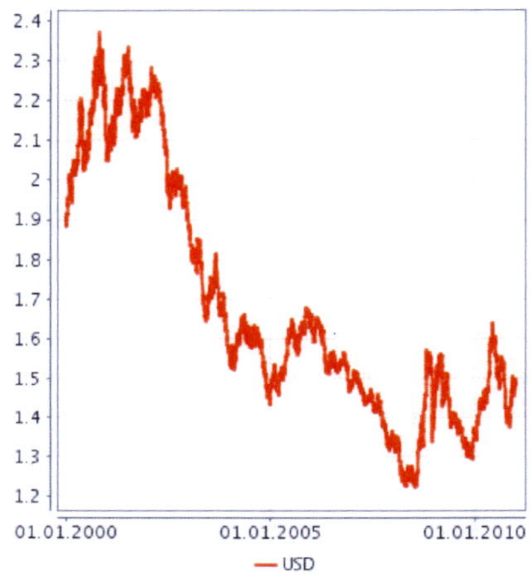

Figures 3: Exchange rate BGN to US dollar, 2000-2010

"During 2005 Bulgaria generated the highest current account deficit. The main drivers for the negative development of the curve were mainly external factors. Due to the country's dependency on energy resources and the increase in their prices in the world markets the country's current account deficit reached €2.427 billion. The increase of the market prices was a driver for inflation process in the country as well. The dynamic of financial account however was stable and it covered the deficit on the current account. Hence the overall balance was at small surplus and the negative trend in the current account did not have a negative impact on the general economic development."[42]

In 2008, the economy grew at an average rate of 6.27%. The average rate in rural areas was 17.86%. There were 141 municipalities with an unemployment rate of 35%.[43]

40 IMF, NSI, BNB

41 Bulgarian National Bank, statistics. [online]. Available from: www.bnb.bg/ (status 12.04.2011).

42 Angelski S. *Bulgaria – an Economic Overview (Univ. of Economics Bratislava, Price Decision Making, Working Paper)*. Bratislava, 2009, p. 13.

43 Agentsiya po zaetostta (National Employment Agency, Ministry of Labour and Social Policy). [online]. Available from: http://www.az.government.bg/eng/index_en.asp (status 12.07.2009).

2. THE BIRTH OF BULGARIA AS A CULTURAL NATION

Under the rule of Asparukh, the Bulgars united all the communities living on this territory in the year 679, establishing their supremacy and, having defeated the Byzantine Empire, founded a Bulgarian state. A treaty between the Bulgarian Khaganate and Byzantium was signed in 681.

The newly founded state was recognized by Byzantium and other powers and, from 681 to 1018, spread out over large parts of the Balkan Peninsula. The fact that it was not part of the Christian culture hampered its development, however. As a result, Tsar Boris I had himself and all his subjects baptized, and introduced Christianity into Bulgaria in its Byzantine form.

The Tsar also introduced the Cyrillic script, thus giving a considerable boost to the further development of Slavic literature. In addition, he exploited the conflicts between the two leading centres of Christianity, Rome and Byzantium (Constantinople) to obtain maximum autonomy for the young Bulgarian church.

Under Tsar Simeon I, Slavic literature and the Old Bulgarian language became the official means of communication of church and state. Following Simeon I's victory over the Byzantine army, the autonomous Bulgarian patriarchate was founded.

The Cyrillic alphabet originated with the brothers Cyril and Methodius who, in 863, were given the task by the Byzantine Emperor Michael III of converting the West Slavs to Christianity and organizing formal Christian worship in the language of the Slavs in Great Moravia. This they did at the request of the Great Moravian Prince Rastislav.

To this end, Cyril (also known in Bulgaria by his original name of Constantine-Cyril, the philosopher) created a new alphabet – the Glagolitic alphabet. This was used for religious texts, state documents and books. In 886 the alphabet was banned in Great Moravia and the pupils of Cyril and Methodius saw no other option than flight to Bulgaria, where they founded a university. Later on, the two brothers were obliged to travel to Rome to defend the script and the use of the Slavonic vernacular in the liturgy. In Bulgaria, the alphabet was used from the ninth century. Recognition by Patriarch Antonios ushered in a second cultural revolution in Bulgaria and aided the spread of Christianity and the Orthodox Church. The Glagolitic and Cyrillic scripts (the latter was devised in the late ninth century by Clement of Ohrid using Greek letters, but named after his teacher Cyril) was used by the Old Bulgarian scholars of the ninth, tenth and eleventh centuries in their writings.

2. THE BIRTH OF BULGARIA AS A CULTURAL NATION

From 1018 to 1186, Bulgaria was subjugated by Byzantium. In 1186, Bulgaria was able to restore its independence and maintain it for approximately two centuries. In 1393, Bulgaria was occupied by the Turks and remained part of the Ottoman Empire for five centuries.

Islam became the dominant religion, and the state and social structures, and legislation too, were governed by Muslim laws. The tragic end of the Second Bulgarian Empire in the late fourteenth century brought Bulgaria's cultural rise to a halt. Once the Ottoman Turks had conquered the country and seized power, the country's cultural development stagnated. The culture of the conquerors became the official culture of the Bulgarians, and the Orthodox Church was supplanted by Islam. This cultural shift caused conflicts with the traditional Christian cultural values of the Bulgarian people. With the destruction of the Bulgarian state, the prime mover of Bulgarian culture, the Bulgarian Church, was also destroyed. The majority of monasteries and churches were defenceless in the face of this destruction and were torn down. Some of the clergy succeeded in leaving the country in time. The legacy of this conflict can be found in the country's subsequent cultural development, in the resistance of the Bulgarian population and the enormous sacrifices it made to maintain its own identity in the face of enforced religious conversion. Despite this resistance, the language, over the course of centuries, adopted alien lexical and grammatical forms from the Ottomans.

In an age when the Renaissance was emerging in Italy and was being embraced by other European nations, Bulgaria, like every other Balkan nation, was excluded from this dynamic development. The Christian Bulgarians saw the destruction of their Christian culture and the traditions that had emerged from it as a test of their faith. This psychological level ensured the survival of their identity. In Bulgarian historiography there are two concepts that offer differing portrayals of the country's cultural development during Ottoman rule. For Marin Drinov, Ivan Shishmanov et al. these centuries are a "dark age". Other historians are of the opinion that they were part of a continuous process of cultural development.

With the elimination of the clergy and the nobility, the country lost its religious and intellectual elite, and without its support the potential for further advances in literature, painting, architecture and music shrank to a minimum. The culture of this time can no longer be described as an elite culture because it had transformed itself into a popular culture. It was of great importance to Bulgarian society and the preservation of the nation's identity.[1]

The function of the ruined structures, which were directly linked to the structures of the elite, was taken over by the family. The patriarchal model now served as a means to preserve values. This led to a reorganization of cultural life and the establishment of a new model that was adopted permanently by subsequent

---

1 Genchev, N. *Balgarsko Vazrazhdane* (*Bulgarian Revival*). Sofia, 1986, p. 1.

generations. The Christian Balkan peoples did not absorb the prevailing elitist Muslim culture completely. Tradition, faith and language are the only way of preserving and passing on Bulgarian culture. The emigration of Bulgarian scholars of the Tarnovo and Magnaura Schools to the Danube Monarchies, Wallachia and Moldova brought significant advances to Orthodox Christianity in those countries. Bulgarian remained the official language of the intellectual elite in Wallachia until the seventeenth century.

Many scholars fled either to Moscow or Kiev, among them the great cleric and metropolitan of Kiev, Gregory Tsamblak (1413–1420), and Cyprian, one of his predecessors (1390–1406) who was also metropolitan of Moscow and all Rus'. Among his most important works is *The Life of Peter*, written about his predecessor. Most of the Bulgarian intellectuals found refuge in the monastery on Mount Athos in modern-day Greece and saved important documents and written testimonies on Bulgaria from destruction by the Ottomans. Other scholars managed to find safety in Serbia, which at that time had not yet been occupied by the Ottomans, where they founded the famous Resava School in which scholars and scribes of all the Balkan nations lived and worked. Among them were Gregory Tsamblak and Constantine of Kostenets, who wrote the major philological work *A History On the Letters* and a biography of Stefan Lazarevic (1431).

The first step towards preserving the script and language was the reconstruction of the monasteries as centres of scholarly work and culture. This process began in the second half of the fifteenth century. Until the late seventeenth century, intellectual and religious life was based in western Bulgaria. Important centres were the monastery in Rila and the monasteries around Sofia, since the town had been spared Ottoman occupation until the mid-fifteenth century. In Rila Monastery, many manuscripts of the Tarnovo School were kept. Among the monastery's tasks was teaching and copying the Scriptures. This revived the model of a cultural centre. Geographically, the western parts of Bulgaria were near the important cultural centres that had not been conquered by the Ottomans, such as Ohrid and the monastery on Mount Athos, both of which possessed libraries containing a wealth of valuable documents.

In the second half of the fifteenth century, work at the monasteries of the Sofia Eparchy became particularly intensive. In these monasteries, the so-called Sofia Literary School was formed. One of the school's foremost representatives was the priest Peyo, who recorded the life of Georgi Novi Sofiiski and was burnt at the stake on 11 February 1515 by the Ottomans. His successor, Matei Gramatik, recorded the life of Nikola Novi Sofiiski and in 1555 suffered the same fate as his predecessor, dying at the hands of the conquerors. The name of Jakov Kraikov Gramatik, who was born near modern-day Kyustendil, is very closely linked with Sofia because he opened Bulgaria's first printer's shop. He bought a printing press in Venice which had Slavonic characters and printed four prayer books in Church

Slavonic, which were distributed by the bookseller Kara Trifol from Skopje in Bulgaria.[2] This initiative ended with Kraikov's death.[3]

It was nonetheless possible to preserve national traditions and the Christian religion over the centuries. The nature of the present-day Bulgarian nation has its origins in the process of emancipation of the Bulgarians from their cultural and political environment in the period from the mid-eighteenth century to independence in 1878, after which they constituted a principality as an ethnic community with historical traditions and political perspectives. The beginning is marked by the creation of numerous histories of the Bulgarian nation which were intended to familiarize eighteenth-century Bulgarians with their own past and consequently strengthen their belief in themselves. This process is described in history as the "Bulgarian National Revival". The Slavonic-Bulgarian history written by the monk Paisius of Hilendar in 1762 is regarded as the first, best known and most influential of these histories.[4] The book mythologizes the origin and grandeur of the Bulgarian nation and enables the people living here to see themselves as part of world culture. Paisius of Hilendar points out that the Bulgarians are part of the largest community of Christian nations. He concentrates on the essential aspects of Bulgarian history and describes the glorious years of the First and Second Bulgarian Empires that ended with conquest by the Ottoman Turks. In his book he explains how distinct the Bulgarian nation is thanks to its uniqueness and how it distinguishes itself from the surrounding regions with its language, religiosity and history. He reminds his readers that the Ottomans are not Christians and the Greeks are not Slavs. The monk explains the difference from the Serbs and other Slavic peoples by means of a list of national units created by Bulgarian dynasties of nobles that have already died out. The dream of independence that this book awakened in the people came true after liberation from Ottoman rule following the Russo-Turkish War of 1877/1878. Orthodox Christianity again became the state religion. The constitution of 1878 incorporated the values of European culture. Following liberation in 1878, the education system, culture and the sciences, industry and roads developed in Bulgaria. From 1887, the House of Saxe-Coburg and Gotha ruled in Bulgaria, staying nominally in power until 1946.

2 Atanasov, P. *Jakov Kraikov: knizhnovnik,iIzdatel, grafik XV v.* (*Jakov Kraikov, scholar, publisher, illustra tor, 15th century*). Sofia: Nauka i Izkustvo, 1980.

3 In February 2007, an exhibition was held in Vienna, *Bulgarian books printed in Vienna, 1845–1878*. The ex- hibition was a joint initiative of the Austrian National Library and the St. St. Cyril and Methodius National Library in Sofia and aimed to present a wide selection of books and periodicals printed in Vienna from the time of Bulgaria's Revival. Cf. Karmen Moissi, P. In Wien gedruckte Bulgarica des 19. Jahrhunderts im Bestand der Österreichischen Nationalbibliothek (ÖNB). In: *Wiener Slavistisches Jahrbuch*, Vol. 55/2009. Vienna: Austrian Academy of Sciences, 2009, pp. 67–94.

4 The book can be viewed online at: http://www.slovo.bg/showwork.php3?AuID=15&WorkID=94&Level=1

The idea of Bulgaria as a cultural nation that emerged in the years of the Bulgarian National Revival received a logical addition several years later with a concept of a bourgeoisie of Central European character. Whereas the various ethnic groups had previously distinguished themselves by dint of their specific cultural, religious and linguistic characteristics, they could now profess themselves as Bulgarian nationals. Domestic politics guaranteed the constitutional principle of equality among all citizens.[5] In every other sector of society, on the other hand, the idea of a Bulgarian cultural nation continued to prevail. This period is characterized by the growth of national pride and the foundation of numerous societies for the promotion of national culture and identity. It goes without saying that the Bulgarian nation is very plastic and multidimensional since many ethnic and national groups have become part of it. Generally, it can be asserted that it is tolerant towards minorities. In the past, various large groups of people have found refuge in Bulgaria; in the fifteenth century, for instance, Spanish Jews; in the seventeenth century Russian Cossacks, and later Armenians who were being persecuted in Turkey and Russian White Guardsmen after the Russian Revolution. It is important to emphasize that Bulgarian society has often spoken out to protect and defend persecuted ethnic groups, for example during the rescue of Bulgarian Jews during World War II – an event unique in Europe – and to mention that the integration of minorities did not happen through assimilation, but through recognition of rights. This is a central component of Bulgaria's national psychology: openness towards other cultures, and reflection.

On 9 September 1944, the Fatherland Front, an opposition movement, seized power with the aid of the Soviet army and established a communist regime which was modelled on the Soviet Union and was to rule until 10 November 1989. Culture was now centralized and state-run, and the Bulgarian Communist Party exercised an ideological monopoly. The seizure of power by the Communist Party in 1944 put an end to the people's perception of themselves as a nation, since the fundamental ideological principle of the communists included the flat denial of nationhood and violently stopped efforts motivated by the nation-state principle to identify Bulgarian society with its values. The nation's unity was destroyed by dictatorship and the hitherto prevailing system of values replaced by ideologies. A first attempt to revive the idea of ethnicity was made in the 1970s and succeeded with the celebrations "1300 Years of Bulgaria" which were prepared with great scrupulousness over a ten-year period.

Another unifying celebration came about when, in 1980, Pope John Paul II proclaimed the brothers Cyril and Methodius, creators of the Slavonic script, patron saints of Europe. Bulgaria celebrates this day of the Slavonic script on 24

[5] Constitution of the Principality of Bulgaria. [online]. [viewed 12.06.2013.] Available from: http://www.verfassungen.eu/bg/verf79-i.htm

May, which is one of the country's most popular holidays with a tradition stretching back over centuries. The promotion of the Bulgarian language as a vehicle for Bulgarian culture and tradition must be seen and understood as an essential element of modern cultural diplomacy. Apart from Bulgaria, the Cyrillic script is currently used in Belarus, Kazakhstan, Macedonia, Mongolia, Russia, Serbia, Tajikistan, Uzbekistan and Ukraine.

Bulgaria's transition into a democracy in 1989 was far more peaceful than it was in Romania. The revolution also entailed the famous economic regrouping of society which led to 1% of the population amassing immeasurable wealth at the expense of the rest of the population, which led to social polarization. The early 1990s saw the arrival of another new phenomenon, known as the "Bulgarian ethnic model". This originated owing to people's fears for their livelihoods, the enforced expulsion of Bulgarian Turks and the Balkan War with its ethnic cleansing in former Yugoslavia.

Bulgaria's full membership of the Council of Europe (1992) and its status as an associate member of the European Union can be seen as recognition of the country's peace-making role. There follows a list of significant events for the state of Bulgaria and the restructuring of its institutions and organs:

- January 1990: Amendments to the communist constitution
- 1991: Adoption of the new democratic constitution
- 1992: Accession to the Council of Europe
- 1993: Association Agreement between Bulgaria and the EU
- 1994: Signing of the European Charter
- 1994: Associate Member of the WEU (Western European Union)
- 1998: IMF grants Bulgaria a loan of USD 1.8 thousand million
- 1999: Start of EU membership negotiations
- 2004: Accession to NATO
- 2007: Accession to the EU

Since Bulgaria's accession on 1 January 2007, Bulgarian has been one of the official languages of the European Union. This means that all documents are also written in Bulgarian. The Cyrillic script follows the Greek and Latin alphabets as the third officially recognized alphabet in Europe. Bulgaria is the first member of the European Union that uses the Cyrillic alphabet, which is recognized as part of Europe's cultural diversity and identity.

2.1 Aspects of Social Cohesion in Bulgaria

Multiculturalism, a distinguishing feature of the globalized world, transformed the fundamental principle that had previously prevailed with regard to the formation of a nation and replaces it with the principle of the rights of groups and minorities. This means that the question of cultural integration could become increasingly complex over time, since it could be challenged by one group or another within society. The absence of a standard definition of nationhood makes an intersection of ideas and new hypotheses possible. For the countries of Central and Eastern Europe, many social facilities and ideas still appear utopian. For instance, no comprehensive studies have so far been conducted into the relationships between culture and social context. The customary term used here, social cohesion, is primarily defined using keywords and expressions such as shared values, tolerance, dialogue between minorities and hope for the future. A declaration of the second summit of the Council of Europe states: "Social cohesion is one of the foremost needs of the wider Europe and should be pursued as an essential complement to the promotion of human rights and dignity..."[6]

The focus of social cohesion in Bulgaria can be explored in three main areas: national cohesion, reconciliation between ethnic groups and minorities, and the economic stratification. A good example of national cohesion is cultural life within communities, for instance the *chitalishta* mentioned below which are culturally unique, function as community centres, libraries and/or theatres, and were established during the National Revival.

A distinguishing feature of Bulgaria has always been the peaceful coexistence of disparate religious and ethnic groups.

So what has really changed with respect to minorities since the revolution in 1989? Two points in particular need to be mentioned that indicate a shift of mentality. The first of these is the term "minority" itself, which in the past was almost completely missing from political lexicons when subgroups were at issue whose feeling of identity was different from that of the predominant nation. Today, minorities are spoken of everywhere in Bulgaria, although the term is also prefixed by a definite article (*the* minority) as a synonym for Roma. This is a qualitative change, and it arrived after many protracted discussions about how to refer to "gypsies" in the news and in public discourse. Whereas in the past, when reporting a crime involving a member of this ethnic group the mass media would scarcely fail to mention his or her origin, the ethnic background of offenders is nowadays not mentioned at all. Of course, this does nothing to reduce the crime rate, but it does prevent the vilification of a segment of society which, owing to the comparatively low education standard and social standing of its members, and owing to common elements of its traditional culture, is more prone to ignoring norms and laws, as V. Stoyanov said in one of his lectures.[7] The attempts under-

[6] Council of Europe/Committee of Ministers. Second Summit of Heads of State and Government, Final De claration and Action Plan. [online]. Strasbourg, 10–11 October 1997. [viewed 19.06.2014]. Available from: https://wcd.coe.int/ViewDoc.jsp?id=593437&Site=CM

[7] Stoyanov V., 2009. *Minderheiten in Bulgarien aus historischer Sicht und in der Gegenwart* (*Minorities in Bulgaria from a historical perspective and in the present*). [online]. Lecture for the Dept. of Political Science at Klagenfurt University. Sofia, 1 September 2009. [viewed

taken for many years to create an ethnically homogeneous and unified Bulgarian nation were abandoned once and for all. The inexorable restoration of revoked or curtailed rights and freedoms of minorities began, especially those of the Muslim population. This calmed the situation in ethnocultural terms and consequently aided the preservation of peace.

Bulgaria has committed to respecting the international agreements relating to human rights and the protection of minorities.[8] This was not always easy and still encounters fierce resistance in particular sections of society today. However, the competent authorities found a solution by solving disputes on "formal grounds". All this has benefited the activities of numerous associations of minorities in the social or cultural sector that were revived or established after 1990, as well as the work of many NGOs and the Bulgarian branches of international legal protection organizations that deal with the situation of minorities. In this way, the ethnic and religious minorities in Bulgaria experienced a palpable renaissance that took place in accordance with the legal stipulations accepted within the EU.

It was not just particular subgroups that benefited from this, but ultimately the entire nation because it reduced the potential for conflict among the minorities as a possible disruptive factor. They all now have their own cultural societies, and these contribute to strengthening and developing their ethnic identity. The Turks now have a political party with permanent representatives in parliament for the first time. Native languages are being taught at school again; there are no more constraints on the practice of religion. The coexistence of Muslims and Christians in mixed districts is not strained. The majority of both religious communities makes a similar contribution to coping with the responsibilities of the transition.

The trend towards a drop in the ethnic Bulgarian population continues, either because of the aforementioned higher mortality rate or the emigration of people in the employable and family-rearing age group. Figures from the National Statistics Institute show that the permanently resident population had dropped to 7,606,551 at the end of 2008, which is 322,350 fewer than in the last census, or 33,700 (0.4%) fewer than the previous year, 2007. From 1989 to 2012, the population of Bulgaria fell by over half a million. That is 6%. The number of lost ethnic Bulgarians and Christians fluctuates between 2.1% and 2.8%. The number of Turks also fell, although their percentage in the overall population rose slightly, by 0.05% (from 9.4% to 9.45%). The number of Roma, on the other hand, increased from 3.7% in 1992 to 4.67% in 2001, a rise of 0.97%.[9] The other ethnic groups have

---

09.06.2014]. Available from: http://www.ihist.bas.bg/sekcii/CV/_private/Valery_Stoyanov/VS_Minderheiten.htm

8 Law on the ratification of the Framework Convention for the Protection of National Minorities, published in Darzhaven vestnik no. 18, 26 February1999.

9 Law on the ratification of the Framework Convention for the Protection of National Minorities, published in Darzhaven vestnik no. 18, 26 February1999.

also grown. Their share of the total population has risen by 1.1% to 1.97%. That means that the ethnic minorities in the country have made slight gains in their member numbers compared to the constituent people. Whereas in 1992, Bulgarians accounted for 85.7% of the total population, their number has now dropped to 83.9%. Whereas other ethnic groups accounted for 14.3%, in 2001 this figure had risen to 16.1% of the total population. However this development is to be interpreted, one thing is clear: the Bulgarians find the burdens imposed by the transformation harder to cope with and the ethnic minorities are now in a far better position than before. Experts feel confident enough to predict that owing to the unfavourable social-economic processes in Bulgaria the country's population will have reached approximately 5,166,000 by the year 2060 – which is lower than the figure of 5,478,741 recorded in 1926. This problem is not due to a fall in the total number of Bulgarian citizens, but in the falling educational and cultural standards of those who will produce the gross domestic product. Even today, 30% of all children (not including Roma) fail to reach the highest grade, grade 6, at elementary school. However, this percentage has been reduced following numerous initiatives starting in 2011.[10] This means, however, that these children will have to be satisfied with employment in branches where no qualifications are required, or face being excluded from the labour market altogether. The situation is exacerbated by the phenomenon of an ageing population; in 2010 the percentage of the employable population was approximately 63%, but in 2060 the figure is likely to be around 50% while the percentage of senior citizens is expected to rise from 23% to 37% in the same period. Admittedly, this is not an exclusively Bulgarian phenomenon, but a general European trend which is being offset partly by taking in immigrants from the Arab-Muslim world. But in our case, assuming the present trend continues unchanged, the majority of the employable Bulgarians in 2060 will be under-qualified, and this will have an impact of the quality of life of those who have reached retirement age.

Despite budgetary constraints, the Ministry of Culture offered financial support of projects for minorities. The projects include the Information and Cultural Centre for Roma in Bulgaria, the Roma Music Theatre, festivals and individual art projects. Within the Ministry of Culture, a public council for cultural diversification was created. NGOs such as Open Society, international activities such

---

10 Dimitrov, D., Grigorova, V. and Decheva, J. Grazhdanski doklad za izpalnenieto na natsionalnata strategiya za integratsiya na romite i plana za izpalnenie na desetiletie na romskoto vklyuchvane v Balgariya 2012 (Citizens' report, implementation of the national integration strategy for Roma and implementation plan for the decade of integration of Roma in Bulgaria, 2012). Open Society Institute, Sofia, indie Roma97 social foundation, Roma Health foundation, Roma Academy of the Arts, Education and Culture, Inegro association, Amalipe Centre for Interethnic Dialogue and Tolerance, World Without Borders. Sofia, 2012, p. 37. See also: National Council for Cooperation on Ethnic and Integration Issues. [online]. [viewed: 12.01.2013]. Available from: http://www.nccedi.government.bg/index.php

as SEGA, media events and so on also support these projects. This support has as its basis sociological investigations that show that minorities are communities that consume more culture than they produce. They are communities that engage in an exchange of so-called subcultures. That is also one reason for the foundation in 2003 of two large cultural institutes in regions with a comparatively large percentage of Turkish speakers (Kargali, Razgrad). These institutes had the task of founding drama groups and music groups, on the one hand to preserve the distinctive nature of the minority, on the other to further strengthen the national dialogues.

The NKEF (National Committee for Ethnic and Demographic Issues) was founded in 1997 following a resolution issued by the Ministry of Culture, and in 2004 it became the National Council for Interethnic Interaction (NRI). The Council has a purely consulting function. In 1999 a government scheme was launched for the integration of Roma in Bulgaria, and this also serves as protection against discrimination. The main thrusts of the scheme are the extension of existing legislation on sport, education and health care, and it also contains articles against discrimination. In 2004, the budget for the Society for the Integration of Minorities in Bulgaria was drawn up.

Recently it has become increasingly clear that many Bulgarians associate the transition with the loss of traditional values while at the same time demanding as necessary a renaissance of Bulgarian culture based on the values of the Bulgarian National Revival. Both the will and the ambition exist; these are important preconditions of the preservation and definition of the country as a cultural nation in the future. Currently Bulgaria is once again searching for continuity between the generations, which has been disrupted and has reached a point at which the deintellectualization must be stopped. The solution to Bulgaria's manifold problems lies in the development of society itself in which culture and education should once again play the leading role in the public political discourse. For Bulgaria as a nation, the answer to the question of what vision the country has for the future is of vital importance. The interpretation of the difficult economic and political changes in the recent past is one aspect of the search for the language to be used in the dialogue on domestic policy.

2.2 Debates on Cultural Policy

In the years following the fall of communism, the debates on cultural policy in the country focused on topics such as decentralization, funding and the legal basis that should safeguard the functions of the cultural institutions.

Decentralization was at the heart of many of the reforms carried out in Bulgaria. The transfer of political, financial and administrative responsibilities from central government to the municipalities has been one of the principal tasks in

Bulgarian politics since the early 1990s.[11] The most pressing problems relating to culture were discussed in three round-table sessions in 2001 and 2002. [12]

National Round Table on 15.12.2001 in Svishtov

The first event, titled "Access to culture for all citizens in towns, small towns, town centres and villages. Interaction between professionals and amateur artists" was aimed at municipal level 13. The views expressed during the round-table discussion ranged from the opinion of the taxpayer to the development of a national cultural policy and support for the development of local-cultural activities such as the foundation of a new fund for amateur artists. This proposal was based on the fact that amateur art plays an important social role in Svishtov. Well-developed forms of local amateur art existed there thanks to social awareness, a feeling of responsibility and the goodwill of many local stakeholders who often made vital contributions to donations and grants. The model of cultural development in Svishtov would be a worthwhile subject for a separate case study, presenting as it does a positive exception to the prevailing picture of cultural activity in urban settings.

National Round Table on 26.01.2002 in Plovdiv

The snapshots of the cultural problems in these towns have proved that the cultural requirements identified there have more to do with current developments in other regions and the general cultural context of post-socialist Bulgaria than with those in Plovdiv.

National Round Table on 16.02.2002 in Varna

The main focus of this round table was decentralization of cultural life and access to culture in various community centres belonging to the region of Varna. These problems were either solved or changed by means of a topological diagnosis of the situation – in large districts of the town, in small towns near Varna, in relatively distant small towns and in villages with cultural community centres. The national discussion, which was at the same time the concluding event of the National Round Table project, was held in Svishtov owing to the positive experiences gained at the first meeting. Among the main objectives of the national discussion for central and local authorities was agreement on the principles and priorities of a joint political programme. The aim of this programme should be to resuscitate cultural life in Bulgaria. However, many of the political representatives invited to

[11] Natsionalno sdruzhenie na obshtinite v Balgariya (NAMRB) (National Association of Towns and Munici- palities in the Republic of Bulgaria). [online]:[viewed 19.02.2012]. http://www.namrb.org/?act=cms&id=175

[12] Deleva, M. *Technological Culture Park (Policies for Culture)*. Sofia, 2004, pp. 25–27. Tomova, B. *Finansirane na izkustvata i kulturata v Balgariya – mezhdu darzhavata i pazara* (*Financing the arts and culture in Bulgaria – between the city and the market*). [online]. Ikonomicheski doklad po proekt "Technologicen Park Kultura" po programata "Politiki za kultura" (Economics essay on the "Technological Culture Park"). Sofia, 2001. Available from: http://www.tpc.cult.bg/doc/TPK1Finansiranenaizkustvata.doc (status 24.02.2005).

the meeting were unable to attend. Representation of the Ministry of Culture and of various parliamentary organs was insufficient. This hampered the attainment of a joint objective.[13]

In Brussels, a round table on the topic "How the state builds its image in front of the world" was organized as part of the festival "Europalia Bulgaria 2002 – The Red House, Centre of Culture and Debate". The following points were discussed: The legislative framework, the form of funding and the state policy with regard to presenting Bulgarian culture in the world, the image of Bulgaria in the EU, the stereotypes and possibilities for change, and partnerships between the institutions to promote Bulgarian culture abroad.[14]

2.3 Cultural Policy in Government Programmes 2001–2005

The first session of the thirty-ninth National Assembly took place on 5 July 2001. The programme of the government under Simeon Sachsen-Coburg-Gotha relating to changes and objectives in cultural policy was very promising. It was clearly worded, detailed and promised numerous changes that were necessary in the entire culture sector.

Some of the programme's objectives were defined as follows:

- To link national cultural policy with regional cultural policy by ascertaining and supporting the potential at local level and by transforming regions and most especially the municipalities into active agents of cultural policy development
- To implement a permanent partnership between the state and NGOs and civil society for coordination and mutual support in the culture sector
- To focus efforts in cultural policy on supporting and promoting the accessibility of cultural education to adolescents and children with the aim of teaching national and universal cultural values and fostering their more active participation in cultural processes
- To create conditions for the development of cultural tourism and the creative sector
- A new media policy to support the priorities of national cultural policy.[15]

But instead of decentralization, a process of extensive centralization of the administrative structures began under this government on which the cultural institutions and the funding of culture were dependent. The arts centres, conceived as autonomous institutions, were gradually closed to artists so that they no longer had

[13] Deleva, M. *Technological Culture Park (Policies for Culture)*. Sofia, 2004, p. 26.

[14] *Chervenata kashta* (*The Red House*), 2002. [online]. Europalia Bulgaria. Available from: http://www.redhouse-sofia.org/index_b.htm (status 06.03.2005).

[15] Natsionalno Dvizhenie Simeon Vtori (Simeon the Second National Movement). Pravitelstvena programa (government programme). Sofia, 2001, p. 50.

access to information about their activities and the criteria for obtaining funding for the projects they put forward.

The national centres for the arts, such as the National Centre for the Theatre, the National Centre for Museums, Galleries and Performing Arts, the National Film Centre, the National Book Centre and the National Centre for Music and Dance were all founded by the Ministry of Culture following a lively public debate in 1991.

An important step in modifying the policy of funding the arts is a new structure contained in the Culture Ministry's organization chart that was devised in 1992 and named Centre of the Arts. The introduction of this structure within the Ministry of Culture soon raised the question of the importance of the individual cultural institutions as assessed on the basis of their activities and their economic results. Consideration of economic results was something entirely new. This Centre was the first step towards decentralizing the arts in Bulgaria. Everyone was entitled to submit a project which would then be rejected or approved for funding by a panel of experts. Development of the Centre continued until 1993.

In 1995, the Socialist Party returned to power. Once again, the question of redistributing the funds for culture from a central authority was raised, and centralization was a *fait accompli*. Following Resolution 23 of 1991, the centres were registered as non-profit organizations and funded from the budget for non-profit organizations in the culture sector. They were conceived and described as "organs", enabling the state to exercise its authority in the various branches of the arts sector. They did not at first have the status of legal entities, but the aim was to create conditions for decentralizing arts administration.

In 1993, one of the objectives was autonomous operation with the state having the task of securing the funds required for the activities, supporting sectors of the arts, and guaranteeing a stable environment for their development and unhindered operation independent of political vicissitudes. The operating principle was conceived by the Ministry of Culture in such a way that the Ministry itself did not produce culture, but instead merely fostered it as an autonomous field.

In 1993, the arts centres within the Ministry of Culture gained the legal status of non-profit entities. The corresponding resolution stated: "The National Arts Centres are specialized non-profit national budgets, units of the culture sector with the status of legal entities. They are administrators of budgetary loans in the execution of the budget."[16]

With this status, the arts centres become an instrument for the implementation of national cultural policy. The object of their activities is defined as the development and dissemination of various arts, the funding of projects in the arts, the

[16] Darzhaven vestnik no. 66 (1993). Resolution no. 139 of the Council of Ministers.

dissemination of information, the organization of events, festivals, conferences and symposia.

The centres and their activities are financed chiefly from the national budget, but also from the available funds, donations, bequests, grants etc. The establishment of other centres for the promotion of culture was also planned which, however, were not to be founded until nearly ten years later. When the national arts centres were founded, regulations were drawn up to govern their operation, and the centres were conceived as modern institutions corresponding to European and American organizations that would meet the requirements of the market and competition. They enabled the establishment and development of various types of organization in the arts sector as well as numerous sources and methods of funding these organizations. A new model of state subsidies for the arts, called project subsidizing, was introduced. This kind of model has long been known in many other democracies and can be regarded as a sign of the shifting political attitude in Bulgaria. As a result of government resolution no. 196 of 1996, the legal autonomy of the arts centres and their function as administrators of budgetary loans in the execution of the budget were rescinded. This meant the revocation of the principle of autonomy and a new centralization of all state tasks in the field of arts with the state itself; the Ministry of Culture once again became the sole producer of art.

The formal argument for what was evidently a backward step was that the centres, as administrators of budgetary loans for state organizations, had become too dependent on the direct preparation and execution of the budget. The centres within the Ministry of Culture were originally conceived as independent links between the corresponding arts sectors. They were intended as the organs of cultural policy with responsibility for implementing the objectives of cultural policy. Another argument put forward was the lack of experience that the institutes working in the arts had of administrating with their own budgets. Here, autonomy was emphasized as one of the centres' main problems, because the cancellation of subsidies meant that they lost their relative financial freedom. The split of responsibilities between the Ministry of Culture, which was responsible for creating the basic conditions for the country's cultural policy, and the arts centres as executive agents of this policy, was revoked. Although beset by difficulties and problems, this step was generally regarded as one of the most promising initiatives ever undertaken by the state and was therefore continued. In addition, the centres were still described as independent, but their autonomy could rarely be put into practice, especially because their freedom was all but non-existent.

The national arts centres were regarded as instruments of cultural policy in the country, and in 1997 their legal and financial autonomy was restored and remained in force until 2006 when they were reorganized in directorates of the Ministry.[17] The closure of these arts centres would not itself have been a problem if the Ministry had had a plan for making them more efficient. It would have been possible to present such a plan to the NGO sector and support it with arguments. The only centre to retain its function and autonomy was the National Film Centre because it was protected by its status as a state agency. It is to be feared that the autonomy of the centres of arts and culture will be revoked and a centralization implemented should the socialists come to power.

Because there was no specific strategy under the Simeon II government, preparations were made for this transition. His period in office will be remembered for the appointments of directors of the National Theatre and the National Opera, a move that undermined democratic competition for state cultural institutions.

During this period, state subsidies were granted with no clear criteria. The Ministry contrived to make management processes more obscure because there was no public accountability and the objectives in the programme were not implemented during the government's time in office, despite the good intentions. It was not until 2008 that they were at least partly implemented under the next administration. The Culture Minister's plans to open the National Gallery to foreign art and convert the Botanical Gardens in Balchik into a hotel will long be remembered. In 2010, a legal dispute broke out between the Ministry of Culture and the University of Sofia about ownership of the Botanical Gardens.

The agreement concluded between the Ministry of Culture and over forty non-government organizations in 2001 has proved to be of little value since the forms of public administration of the cultural process were marginalized, rendering its provisions nothing more than good intentions. The bill relating to cultural monuments and museums was introduced in parliament without consultation with NGOs.

The Culture Minister was repeatedly called upon to resign, but the government was not willing to implement its own cultural programme or to appoint a new minister who would have had the trust of the general public and been able to carry out the measures necessary to stabilize the culture sector.

An artist's rights, material equivalents, the criteria according to which an artist is appreciated and (freelance) artists' social security are all areas that posed ques-

[17] Postanovlenie na Ministerski Savet Nr. 149, za priemane na ustroistven pravilnik na ministerstvoto na kulturata i za zakrivane na natsionalnite tsentrove po izkustvata i kulturnite deinosti kam ministara na kulturata (Resolution no. 149 of the Council of Ministers pertaining to the closure of arts centres within the Ministry of Culture), 19.06.2006, Sofia. Preobrasuvat natsionalnite tsentrove po izkustvata v direktsii (The national arts centres will be converted into directorates). [online]. [viewed 19.02.2012]. Available from: http://www.vesti.bg/index.phtml?tid=40&oid=874589 (status 17.04.2006).

tions that ultimately remained unanswered in the period from 1989 to 2008. The absence of specific programmes for the protection of high and non-commercial art was a feature of all governments during that time.

Instead of the gradual withdrawal of the state from the administration of culture and the strengthening of the municipalities' financial independence, a centralization of cultural processes could be observed from 2001 to 2008. Because no party had won enough votes for a single-party government, a grand coalition was formed consisting of the Social Democratic Party, the Movement for Rights and Freedoms and the National Movement under Simeon II. The resultant government called itself a "Government of European Integration, Economical [*sic*] Growth and Social Responsibility". The vision presented by the nationalist party Ataka (Attack) for developing the arts in the country is of interest. Here are some excerpts of the demands formulated in great detail on page 47 of the party manifesto:

- Special fund for the publication of information on and the protection of the cultural heritage in the Bulgarian countries and a special budget for the worldwide popularization of Bulgaria
- A fund and scholarships for talented Bulgarian children and adolescents
- A fund and scholarships for the protection of Bulgarian folk music and its promotion in the world, and a law to protect the Bulgarian language.[18]

This description of the organization's future activities bears similarities to the manifesto of the Communist Party that ruled the country until 1989. The issue is scarcely the creation of new funds, more the replenishment of existing ones. Like the Communist Party before it, Ataka sees culture only in folklore. Perhaps the demand for support for folklore was a deliberate ploy to avoid the political discourse that sees art as something to be understood as an essential component of the ideology and the organization.

The new hope for creators was the new Minister of Culture from the Social Democratic Party who, as an actor, knew the problems facing cultural institutions very well. He expressed the view that no government in the twelve years from 1989 to 2002 had presented a long-term and sustainable programme for this kind of development. After the foundation of the three-party coalition, the governments presented its programme. The purport of its objectives in the field of culture was as follows:

The Ministry of Culture sets itself the aim of protecting the country's cultural traditions, encouraging private investment and maintaining and improving cultural infrastructure. To this end, tax incentives are to be created for investors in the fields of arts, culture and related research, for example sponsorship. One key element

[18] Ataka. *Ustroystvo i printsipi na organizatsiyata Ataka* (*Rules and principles of the Ataka organization*). Party manifesto. Sofia, 2005, p. 47.

of the planned amendment to legislation will be the removal of all regulation of art and culture institutions, and of artists themselves, so that they can operate in the market-place unhindered. Another objective of the Ministry of Culture is the decentralization of administration and involvement of NGOs in political decision-making processes. Furthermore, preservation of cultural heritage and its linkage to cultural policy will be pursued. As a result of its policy, the government will make the cultural diversity of society the basis of dialogue.[19]

In its programme, the government specifically set out its strategies for consolidation with the NGO sector and the promotion of NGOs. However, it neglected to explain precisely how this sector was defined. It was not clear from the programme whether the government itself would determine the priorities, which were subsequently to be supported presumably by private enterprise and non-government organizations.

What was new about the programme was the investment in cultural institutions and their definition, with special attention being paid to private funding. On the one hand, the government made it clear that it understood its own financial possibilities and limits in the culture sector, but on the other, it also expressed its target of greater flexibility and a new legal basis to regulate investment. However, it was not clear from this whether greater freedom of action for state cultural institutions would also mean the right to operate on a commercial footing. Furthermore, the government had not yet defined the preferences of its own investment policy, and the programme made it very clear that the process would be a long one.[20]

The development of culture creates the potential for faster economic growth thanks to the promotion of creative activities which emerged overall as the fourth sector to show dynamic development. The role of cultural resources (cultural monuments, museums, festivals, ethnographic complexes) was increasingly regarded as a priority for the Bulgarian economy, particularly for tourism. In addition, culture provided unique opportunities for the integration of minorities and disadvantaged groups in Bulgarian society. By stimulating creative activity, economic growth could be expected. The topic of culture was now included in the programme as a priority sector for the government, and cultural tourism was another new concept.

By not expressly naming the cultural industries in Bulgaria (for example publishing and film production) the government specified which branches of culture were a priority, would be developed and would receive additional funding. Cul-

[19] Pravitelstvo na evropeiskata integratsiya (Government of European Integration). Programa na pravitelstvoto na evropeiskata integratsiya ikonomiceskiya rastezh i socialnata otgovornost (Programme of the Government of European Integration, Economical Growth and Social Responsibility). [online]. Sofia, 2005, p. 20. Avail- able from: http://www.europe.bg/upload/docs/GovernmentalProgramme-final-bg.pdf (status 02.05.2006).

[20] Ibid, p. 40.

ture is regarded as one means of integrating minorities into a society. However, the programme did not cite any clear strategy for implementing this intention. There were many non-government organizations active in this sector. This raised the question of how cooperation between the state and these organizations could be coordinated. Many of these non-government organizations already had their own histories and were often partners in various discussions relating to the integration of minorities. The Ministry of Culture therefore planned to work on improving administration of the cultural heritage and to protect cultural monuments by reorganizing the network of national museums and modernizing the registration system. The participation of Bulgarian culture in European cultural initiatives and programmes for promoting and popularizing it in the European Union raised the question of investment in culture.

The creation of a national strategy for cultural development in Bulgaria accompanied by new legislation in the culture sector was a priority for the Ministry of Culture.[21] Appropriate normative support was to be lent to improving the network of cultural institutions. In addition, they were to contribute to propagating the domestic cultural market, which was regarded as part of regional cooperation, and have as their target the decentralization of their administration. Domestic regional cultural policy was undergoing a process of redefinition. To this end, the Ministry carried out a major reorganization of cultural activities at regional level. The growth of the domestic cultural market was set out in expansive terms, making it impossible to understand exactly what the intended objective was meant to be. Municipal expenditure on culture should have been increased considerably to guarantee wider consumption of cultural goods and an improvement in their quality. In Bulgaria, a mixed form of state and municipal funding has become widespread in recent decades. The Finance Act and the Protection and Development of Culture Act contain definitions relating precisely to the transfer of parts of the funding to the municipalities. By concluding specific agreements, the Ministry of Culture contributed 70% of the funds required for salaries, the municipalities 30%. The mayors undertook to sign contracts with the Ministry of Culture to ensure the best possible division of responsibilities in the funding process. However, when it came to actually carrying out the joint funding, the attitude of some municipalities towards their own culture became clear, as did the level of awareness among the public of the need for culture and the population's willingness to make cultural life a priority. The government programme ended with the sentence: "The coalition Government plans a gradual increase of the funds allocated to culture till the level of the European standards is reached."[22]

21 Zakon za zakrila i razvitie na kulturata (Protection and Development of Culture Act), Section 2, 2006. Darz- haven vestnik no. 106.

22 Programa na pravitelstvoto na evropeiskata integratsiya ikonomicheskiya rastezh i sotsialnata otgovornost (Programme of the Government of European Integration, Economical Growth and

At the end of the coalition's period in office, the promise to increase the funds earmarked for culture, which were provided for separately from GDP, remained unfulfilled. Comparison of the management programmes of the last three governments and the points they contain relating to cultural diplomacy allows several conclusions. The programmes placed most importance on integration in view of Bulgaria's impending accession to the EU – by bringing the legal basis into line and by participating in EU programmes and CE. Attention was also given to co-operation with international organizations and NGOs. Creation of a strategy for presenting Bulgarian culture abroad, considered a particularly important measure in the first programme, received no mention at all in the two subsequent government programmes, which raises the question of whether the state deemed such a strategy necessary in the first place and to what extent it would be continued following a change of government. The first two government programmes regarded Bulgarian cultural institutes as important mediators in the country's promotion abroad, although mention is made of the need for them to amend their activities.

"Bulgarian culture is our greatest argument when we speak of our EU membership."[23]

In his dissertation, Georgi P. Dimitrov analyses the situation and confirms the president's statement in his conclusion:

"If the transformation is also considered as a process of reorganization of the state structure, then both continuity and change are apparent with respect to cultural policy. Many cultural institutions – such as theatres, operas and orchestras – had to be reformed, but nevertheless remain fundamentally state-run (...) The change became evident most recently with the succession of the new generation."[24]

Bulgarian art, which sees itself as autonomous, and the artists' talent were among the main arguments, but politics was unable to guide this development. Bulgaria had an enormously rich cultural heritage, and if the artists in the country constantly created new and interesting works throughout this whole period, it was due only to their intrinsic motivation.

On 27 April 2005, for instance, the avant-garde artist Ivan Moudov invited businesspeople, diplomats, artists, gallery owners and others with an interest in art to his performance Action MUSIZ (Museum of Modern Art) at Podujane railway

Social Responsibility), 2005.

23 Parvanov, G. *Kulturata e nai-golemiyat ni argument za chlenstvo v Evropeyskiya Sayuz* (*Culture is our great est argument for EU membership*). [online]: [viewed 19.02.2012]. Available from: ht tp://news.ibox.bg/news/id_1923069832 Slovo na prezidenta Georgi Parvanov na tarzhestvenoto zasedanie na Narodnoto Sabranie po povod prie- maneto na Balgariya za palnopraven chlen na Evropeiskiya sayuz (address by Georgi Parvanov, President of the Republic of Bulgaria, on the occasion of Bulgaria's accession to the EU). Parliament, 11.01.2007. [online]: Available from: http://www.president.bg/news.php?id=2763 (status 17.01.2007).

24 Dimitrov, G. P. *Kultur im Transformationsprozess Osteuropas. Zum Wandel kultureller Institutionen am Bei- spiel Bulgariens nach 1989*. Munich, 2009, p. 172.

station in Sofia. Invitations were sent promising the museum's opening. The artist stressed how important a museum of this kind is and took the first step towards its establishment. The performance sparked a fierce debate and caused a public scandal.

"Well, that's our country, not entirely indifferent towards culture, but we have decided to identify ourselves with the distant past and its historical legacy… Yes, government policy is currently that the only face it wants to show is linked to the traditions and treasures that have been found in our country, and they must advertise our country. Which in my opinion is entirely wrong. I believe that a country cannot rely exclusively on the past and not invest in its future … In Athens, for instance, a biennale is organized called "Destroy Athens". It's remarkable that a country like Greece, ninety per cent of which is associated with antiquity in people's minds, holds a biennale for contemporary art with the aim of destroying a particular cliché. But we want to start creating one so that one day we can struggle to break away from it. Another point, of course, is that however hard we try we will never be able to create a cliché like Greece's."[25]

The end of the political coalition was inevitable, and in 2009 the GERB party came to power. Its manifesto contained three priorities relating to culture:

- Culture should be returned to the public agenda and cultural policy should concentrate on personality
- The cultural heritage is to be managed in conjunction with tourism, education and science policies
- Introduction of European models of cultural management and development[26]

The programme also offers an ambitious plan for its implementation. In 2012, for example, the Museum of Modern Art, that had already been planned in 2005 as an artistic installation, was actually opened.

2.4 Thoughts on a Declaration, or In Step with the Times

This work intended to examine the development of the artists' associations (unions) from 1995 to 2008. Following the declaration described below, this intention became irrelevant. In the summer of 2011 an idea that could almost be classed as a child's prank was actually carried out, and it immediately became clear on the one hand just how deeply the legacy of the communist regime is rooted in the collective consciousness and, on the other, how polarized Bulgarian society remains. The patent necessity for a debate that had not been held for twenty years, namely

[25] Petkova, S. *Zhivot sled euforiyata* (*Life after euphoria*). Interview with I. Moudov. [online]. In: *Kultur, no.* 8 (2447), 28.02.2008. [viewed 22.02.2012]. Available from: http://sitekreator.bg/svetlapetkova/ivan_moudov.html.

[26] Partiya GERB (GERB party). Programa na partiya GERB za evropeysko razvitie na Balgariya (manifesto of GERB, the Party for the European Development of Bulgaria). [online]: [downloaded 07.01.2010]. Available from: http://www.gerb.bg/uf/pages/upr_programa_gerb_1June.pdf. Sofia, 2009, pp. 63–64.

on the legacy of the communist regime and its symbols in cultural policy, emerged in painful fashion.

One day, Bulgaria's capital city woke up to find an interpretation of our times – in the form of a modified and "new" monument to the Soviet Army.

Photo: I. Tchankov

The newly created work was emblazoned with the title "In Step with the Times". This incident might have been quickly forgotten and have had no great repercussions, had it not been accompanied by a declaration issued by eighteen associations which some found disconcerting, others found amusing and still others saw as an attack on the memory of the dictatorship. Among the signatory bodies were the associations of writers, filmmakers, architects and journalists but also the National Pro-Russia Movement, the Bulgaria-Russia forum, the Federation for Friendship with the Peoples of Russia, the Russian foundation Sustainable Development in Bulgaria, the Bulgaro-Russian Chamber of Industry and Commerce, the Shipka Bulgaro-Russian Society and the Slavic Society in Bulgaria.

The signatories were angry at the desecration and sacrilege that had been committed, holding it to be shameful. One commonly voiced view was that the act was an attempt to incite unrest and so damage relations with the Russian population. Apologies were offered with one voice to the Russian population, along with the assurance that all the signatory associations and societies "loved their brothers, the Russians, and held Soviet soldiers in the highest regard". They also promised that, as in Plovdiv where the Alyosha Monument still stood, steps would be taken in Sofia so "that the memory of the heroes who gave their lives for the victory over fascism is not tainted".[27]

These statements and the declaration itself would be of no particular interest were it not for one remarkable exhortation: "We call upon all artists, associations, public institutions, organizations and foundations that support the preservation of our historical heritage, and all religious organizations, especially the Bulgarian Orthodox Church, to oppose the vandals and affronts." The call noted that "the public authorities and the municipality of Sofia will immediately incorporate the monument in the security concept and install surveillance cameras to prevent a recurrence of such a thing which is unworthy of the nation."

The signatories of the declaration described themselves as the nation's intellectual elite and demanded security measures to protect one of the last symbols of dictatorship in Bulgaria. The declaration is insulting, and what is important about it is not so much the monument it refers to but the views and message it wishes to convey. Are those who wrote and signed it living in the present or the past? However, it subsequently emerged that not every member of the architects' association shared these views, and the same applied to members of the journalists' and filmmakers' institutes. During the dictatorship, when they were part of the privileged caste, they were willing servants of the party machinery which may be why they failed to notice exactly what it was that the political leaders of the Red Army gave to the Bulgarian people. I may be permitted to recall some aspects.

Thousands of murders were committed without anyone ever being brought to trial – days after the border was crossed and when Bulgaria had already declared war on Nazi Germany. In the so-called People's Tribunals, the death sentences passed eliminated the nation's political and intellectual elite.[28] Bulgarian nationals were interned in dozens of concentration camps which extinguished free-thinking in Bulgaria for forty-five years. Delusional industrial programmes, the plunder of the country by means of the "foreign currency programmes" and the Secret Service's foreign companies – robbery, which of course continued with the transition of crime after 1989. The two attempts, ignoring Bulgaria's national identity, to become the sixteenth Soviet republic.[29] Last but not least, the unbelievable "project",

---

[27] Declaration. [online]. Available from: http://pressclub.bg/society/organizations/20110620/news-43346 (status 20.06.2011).

[28] Ognyanov, L. *Darzhavno-politicheskata sistema na Balgariya 1944-1948* (*The state political system in Bulgaria 1944–1948*). Sofia, 1993, p. 32.

[29] Although Valentina Petkova says that the wording "16th republic" does not occur in the records of the two plenary meetings of the central committee of the Bulgarian Communist Party in 1963 and 1973, these documents hint at increasingly close and harmonized economic relations with the Soviet Union. (author's translation). Cf. Petkova, V., 2010. Balgariya – 16- a republika na SSSR. Tova e mit! (Bulgaria as the 16th republic of the USSR. That is a myth). [online].

and the terror it engendered, that is known in Bulgarian history as the "Process of Rebirth" and led to the emigration of 300,000 Bulgarian Muslims and the aggressively enforced change of the names of those who remained.[30]

The declaration bears striking similarities to a telegram sent on 6 February 1974 in which Bulgarian writers also express their extreme indignation at affronts committed against remembrance. In it they offer "Friendship and cooperation to the great Soviet state" and "condemn the atrocities that grieve the movement of mankind and its clear objective and happy future."[31]

At this point, it is appropriate to note that the "Union of Bulgarian Writers" split into various factions in the 1990s. Today there are several registered writers' associations.

Such clear support for the protection of artists and culture in the country can in no way be inferred from press coverage during the transition from 1989 to 2011. Reporting focuses more often on scandals relating to the real estate left to these associations under communist rule because the clichés of the vocabulary used only have meaning in the country's "interior". "Outside" it they are evidently of no importance – and it was important to revive the lies of propaganda as soon as possible. In this way, the bureaucratic status quo was to be complacently maintained at any cost. It may be safely assumed that the painting over of this monument to the Russian Army was in no way intended as a mockery, but as a reminder of lost values; and if mockery was intended, then mockery of an unbearable reality and the young generation's fear of a future without prospects. No other interpretation is possible than that the professional authors of these protest telegrams and objections realized the risk of being unmasked and reacted immediately with an incredible instinct for self-preservation. The way these "elites" think and act appears not to have changed, since their reaction indicates that they are "political chameleons" who do nothing more than change their colours for one night according to the prevailing situation in world politics. This is all too understandable, since, as ever, it is a matter of self-interest and preserving former privileges and social relevance. Today, Bulgarian society is again the recipient of this protest let-

In: *Trud*, 29.10.2010. Available from: http://www.trud.bg/Article.asp?ArticleId=657129 (status 12.07.2011).

30 Dogan, A., 2009. *Doklad na predsedatelya na Dvizhenie za Prava i Svobodi (DPS) – Achmed Dogan pred VII-ta Natsionalna konferentsiya na DPS, 12.12.2009* (*Report of the president of the Movement for Rights and Freedoms, Ahmed Dogan, at the 7th national conference [DPS] 12.12.2009*). [online]. Sofia, p. 4. [viewed 29.01.2012]. Available from: http://old.dps.bg/cgi-bin/e-ms/vis/vis.pl?s=001&p=0037&n=000018& (status 21.01.2010).

31 Sayuz na Balgarskite Pisateli (Union of Bulgarian Writers), 2010. Deklaratsiya na SBP po povod "Archipelag Gulag" na Aleksandar Solshenizin (Declaration of the Union of Bulgarian Writers following publication of *The Gulag Archipelago* by Alexander Solzhenitsyn). [online]. In: *Glasove*. [viewed 22.02.2012]. Available from: http://www.glasove.com/deklaratsiya-na-sbp-po-povod-arhipelag-gulag-na-aleksandur-solzhenitsin-9025 (status 12.07.2010).

ter, and if society and the world in which a person with no talent lives has become more open, if the talentless can publish books freely, draw, paint and take part in competitions without fearing the sanctions of artists' collectives that are affiliated to a political party, they will instead fear for their very survival as artists. And a quick glance at the names of the signatories and the "creative" organizations they belong to shows that most of them are completely unknown. Only couched in the ideological clichés and "in step with the times" does the army of the 1970s become entirely lost in the anonymity of impotent and grey art associations. It is comforting that the telegram against Solzhenitsyn had been signed by the same unions and artists, but that none of them are remembered for their remarkable works. I may be permitted to name only those who did not want to sink in embarrassment and refused to sell the moral face of the nation.

In Bulgaria they are the two poets Valeri Petrov and Blagoi Dimitrov; the satirist Marko Ganchev; the theatrologist Gocho Gochev and the writer Christo Ganev. Their decision is supported by all those people who, though unknown to history, show courage despite their fear. These five artists prove that it is still eminently possible to fight against violence and lies.

The abovementioned monument to the Soviet Army was already an artistic compromise. Before it gained the form it has today it was censored several times. Its creator, Atanas Dalchev, wrote in 1992 that for him the whole thing had been a compromise that enabled him to continue working as an artist during the dictatorship.[32] In reality, this "cartoon" with the painted soldiers hides the actual transition to democracy which occurs in the mind and replaces a hero from one era with others who are similar. The question is what the authors of the modified monument think today.[33] The magazine *Edno* asked them about this, and excerpts from the interview are found below:

Who are you? How many of you are there? Tell us something about yourselves.

We are a group of nine artists who call ourselves "Destructive Creation". Most of us actively produce art, though. In the project as a whole there were some people who painted and some who didn't, but helped in other ways. Not all of them are here now. I myself completed my first year at a university in England, studying interior design. In general, every one of us has some connection with art. I myself will go to the Netherlands to study animation.

Who chose this monument to the Red Army? There are other symbols of communism in Sofia.

32 Dimitrova, B. *Dalchev prenaregda bratskata mogila v Plovdiv* (*Dalchev restructures the monument in Plovdiv*). [online]. In: *Trud*, 30.09.2009. [viewed 18.02.2011]. Available from: http://www.trud.bg/Article.asp?ArticleId=240599.

33 Koi e v krak s vremeto (Who is in step with the times?) [online]. In: *Edno* magazine, 17, 14.09.2011. Sofia. [viewed 19.09.2011]. Available from: http://edno.bg/en/edno_magazine/koy-e-v-krak-s-vremeto/

For us, it isn't a symbol of communism. We chose the monument because it has lost a lot of its value. There are many people who want to put something else up in its place, but in this case that's the stupidest thing that could be done. But isn't that what happened to the mausoleum?

What was the idea behind replacing the Soviet soldiers with figures from mainstream culture?

Our main idea was to show that when the Soviet Union was powerful we tried to be the best communists, but that since we started living in a democracy we've tried to be the best democrats and Americans. Generally, we were inspired by a wide range of opinions, any one of which could have prompted this campaign. In addition, this monument represents the subculture in Sofia because we spent a lot of time here as teenagers. Part of the provocation was the fact that this monument had long since stopped symbolizing what the older generation associates with it. It lost its relevance as a symbol of the Red Army a long time ago. You can see young people here who have had a few drinks, and others who are even less attractive to look at, but it is also a meeting-place for young artists. I'd like to add that this monument possesses the most powerful symbolism. It was placed right in the middle of the city. We specifically chose this spot because twenty years ago it was still guarded and anyone who hung around here was regarded with suspicion. Anyone who had done what we did twenty-five years ago could have been shot. That shows how much has changed in the way we think about historical symbols in the space of just one generation. The figures we chose are the heroes of our generation and they are substitutes for the heroes of the previous generation.[34]

The rethinking of the socialist legacy and the transition from one generation to the next occurred *de facto* at intellectual level. Symbols were exchanged, with no institutional debate, due to a need to test their effectiveness. This woke the spirits of the past. Clearly, the core of the problem regarding the relationship between culture and tradition lies in this discussion, and the task facing the hegemony in the country is to redefine this relationship. Otherwise there will always be events in society that could sweep the structures aside. From a historical, and global, point of view maturity in the exercise of power has always been an exception, which is why it has only ever been possible to gain freedom by means of revolt.

2.5 Overview of the Major Trends in Bulgaria Cultural Policy Since 1989

The time and the process of democratization after 1989 are described as the transition; radical transformations of structures were started. These changes affected every aspect of social and political life in the countries in transition. The people

[34] Koi e v krak s vremeto (Who is in step with the times?) [online]. In: *Edno* magazine, 17, 14.09. 2011. Sofia. [viewed 19.09.2011]. Available from: http://edno.bg/en/edno_magazine/koy-e-v-krak-s-vremeto/

were now able to participate voluntarily in cultural life. The status of intellectuals also shifted, from a central to a peripheral position.

"It is impossible to know which one of these two 'democratizations' is going to prevail. This dilemma is particularly pertinent for the post-socialist countries, which have in the past 15 years been faced with two processes – democratization and globalization – and are still searching for the most effective strategies to overcome the difficulties of this transition."[35]

The structural reorganization meant that many experts in this field lost their jobs when sharp cuts were made in the budget for the culture sector. Many cultural institutions ceased operations. Libraries, cultural centres, theatres, museums and galleries began to suffer a prolonged shortage of funds. There was no money for new productions, or for replenishing or maintaining existing funds.

Culture slumped into a crisis whose consequences were seen in changes affecting whole generations who lost contact with art and did not understand its aims and values. The paradigm for thought and action in cultural policy required a reassessment of the existing model and consisted of abolishing censorship and the ideological dependency of art and artists' organizations, decentralization and the emergence of new subjects for cultural policy – foundations, private cultural institutions, new professional associations (after 2000). New forms of funding emerged, in both the public and the private sector. Part of the newly formulated cultural orientation, with democratization and the population's participation in cultural life, remained rhetoric. Cultural policy and cultural development in Bulgaria were no longer a national priority. In its programme "Bulgaria 2001", the Kostov government that came to power in 1997 set itself the aim of privatizing culture.

The approach taken towards privatization was imprudent, failing to take the preservation of bookshops, cinemas, cultural centres etc. into account. As a result, 1998 saw the destruction of a system that had worked well and served as a network for the dissemination of culture. The Ministry of Culture announced the privatization of bookshops and theatres and transferred responsibility for these to the Ministry of Industry.

In 1999, for example, an act for the protection and development of culture was passed.[36] In it, culture was defined as the act of creating, studying, disseminating and preserving cultural values and the outcomes of this activity.[37] This definition served the cultural institutes, the arts and the activities they performed and referred to culture in the strictest sense.

---

[35] Obuljen, N. *Why we need European cultural policies. The impact of EU-enlargement on cultural policies in transition countries.* Amsterdam: European Cultural Foundation, 2004, p. 9.

[36] Zakon za zakrila i razvitie na kulturata (Protection and Development of Culture Act), 1999. Darzhaven vest- nik no. 50, 1 June 1999.

[37] Dopolnitelni razporedbi (additional provisions), Section 1.1.

The passing of this act triggered a widespread debate in the country, and although it was heavily criticized it became an instrument for the cultural institutions to use. With the act, national cultural policy set itself the aim of safeguarding the national cultural identity and of ensuring state protection of existing cultural institutions and the cultural heritage.

NGOs and artists advocated fixing the national culture budget at 1% of gross domestic product. In addition, they wanted considerable tax incentives for sponsorship and the allocation of a generous percentage of the returns from gambling to culture.

Chapter 1 (General Provisions): Article 1 contained provisions for the principles and priorities of national cultural policy, cultural organizations and institutions for the protection of culture, its national identity and possible ways of supporting and financing artists and cultural activities.

The Protection and Development of Culture Act contained provisions for the creative and economic autonomy of cultural institutions, but in practice the law could not be enforced when it was passed because some institutions, such as the theatres, were not entitled to receive supplementary subsidies. At the end of 1999 and the beginning of 2000, certain passages in the clauses on funding cultural institutions were repealed. For example, § 6 of the provisional and concluding regulations in the Act were brought into line with the provisions of the new stipulations in the tax law. Item 14, Art. 23: The result especially reduced the tax transformation by the level of subsidies granted to cover the costs of activities conducted by cultural institutions in a calendar year.[38] After the reform, a joint system of funding by the state and the municipalities was introduced.

> "The new law on culture of 1999 that stipulated that 30% of all funds should be provided by private sponsors was a condition of Bulgaria's acceptance and the acceptance of its cultural programmes into the European Union itself. The EU made the 'third sector', i.e. the organizations of civil society between the state and the market, a priority. The European Union aims to create a secular, pluralistic and multicultural society. Officially, culture and education remain the remit of the national states, but in the Treaty of Maastricht of 1992 the cultural dimension of the European Commission was established for the first time. Since its accession to the EU in January 2007, Bulgaria has reorganized its cultural policy according to the European model and participated actively in all relevant EU programmes. The Bulgarian laws pertaining to audiovisual media and intellectual property were brought entirely in line with the EU."[39]

[38] Zakon za zakrila i razvitie na kulturata (Protection and Development of Culture Act), 1999. [online]. Darzhaven vestnik no. 50, 1 June 1999. Available from: http://lex.bg/laws/ldoc/2134664704 [19.02.2012].

[39] Bachmaier, P. Der Wertewandel in Ostmitteleuropa. In: P. Bachmaier et al., eds. *Der kulturelle Umbruch in Ostmitteleuropa: der Transformationsprozess und die Bildungs- und Kulturpolitik Tschechiens, der Slowkei, Polens und Ungarns im Kontext der internationalen Beziehungen.* Frankfurt am Main, Vienna inter alia: Lang, 2005.

The Finance Act and the Protection and Development of Culture Act in Bulgaria defined how the partial transfer of funding to municipalities was to be achieved. By concluding specific agreements, the Ministry of Culture contributed 70% of the funds required for salaries, the municipalities 30%. The municipal authorities were obliged to sign contracts with the Ministry of Culture to ensure in particular the best possible division of responsibilities in the funding process. Protection of culture also meant protection from arbitrary measures on the part of the authorities and would have been impossible to achieve without a strategy, continuity, transparency and a guaranteed right to public controls. The official annual reports of the Ministry of Culture were set out accordingly with details on all its receipts and outlay and all the measures taken that could be construed as an essential component of a transparent and democratic process in the culture sector. The parties that took part in the 2008 parliamentary elections described the culture sector as a vision. It is considered a factor for socio-economic development, although a generalizing argumentation for high art is lacking, as are definitions of what should have determined the foundations of the future development of the country's cultural policy.

Principles of Cultural Development

Following the end of communist rule in 1989, the three principal aspects of Bulgaria's transition from a totalitarian system to a democracy in the field of culture were democratization, decentralization and privatization. Underpinned by a political pluralism that was gradually establishing itself and by the structures of the budding civil society, new subjects of cultural policy appeared: private cultural institutions, alternative organizations, professional associations, foundations, religious communities etc.

In the years of transition, the Ministry of Culture was restructured several times. It was headed by a minister with two deputy ministers and secretaries general; the minister's council acted as a supporting committee with an advisory role. The arts centres had stayed faithful to the principle of autonomy, known in 2006 as a good intention from the early years of the transition.

An important step in reorganizing the funding policy for the arts was the abovementioned new body, the "Centre of the Arts" that was established in 1992. The introduction of this "Centre" as a body within the Ministry of Culture soon raised the question of the importance of the individual cultural institutions as assessed on the basis of their activities and – a new aspect – their economic results. The Centre was therefore the first step towards decentralizing the arts in Bulgaria. Everyone was now entitled to submit a project which would then be rejected or approved for funding by a panel of experts.

By 1993, the Centre's development was well advanced. However, in 1995 the question of redistributing the funds for culture from a central authority was raised again, and centralization was a *fait accompli*.[40] At this point there were no private theatres in Bulgaria. All were state-run and funded entirely by the state.

In February 2005, the Ministry of Culture was incorporated into the Ministry of Culture and Tourism. With the parliamentary resolution of 16 August 2005 it was once again reorganized as the Ministry of Culture. The Ministry's plan, long discussed, to turn and integrate its arts centres, which had their own – albeit small – budget, into directorates was finally implemented after a meeting of the Council of Ministers on 6 August 2006.[41]The resulting changes led to a reassignment of responsibilities. The National Centre for Music and Dance became the National Centre for Theatre, while the National Centre for Museums, Galleries and the Arts and the National Book Centre were closed. The Ministry took over all the tasks of these centres, whether these were artistic, administrative or financial.[42]

In the course of the reorganization, administration was divided among eleven departments: two general administration directorates and nine directorates with specific remits. Besides the administrative changes made by the Ministry of Culture there was the concept for cultural development, a policy paper drafted in only two months and the first document that aspired to present the vision for cultural policy in the country and was even audaciously called the "Culture Constitution" by the Ministry of Culture's advisory committee.[43]

The concept was divided into eight sections, two of which defined the priorities of cultural policy and made repeated reference to national values.

The concept's thirty-five pages presented the principles for cultural development and the specific priorities of the sectors. They contained a provisional list of cultural monuments of national importance and targeted the potential for development of cultural tourism and cultural routes, which were also listed. In addition, the gradual withdrawal of the state was planned, as was a shift to the principle of

40 Organization chart of the Ministry of Culture 1990–1995. In: Koprinarov L. *Bulgarian Cultural Policy, 1990– 1995*. Sofia: Institute of Culturology, 1996, p. 38.

41 Familia NPO za izkustvo i kultura (Family NGO for Art and Culture). [online]. Available from: http://familia.cult.bg/?page_id=3 (status 14.09.2006). Ministerski savet (Council of Ministers' resolution on acceptance of the provisions made by the Ministry of Culture regarding the organization and closure of the National Centres for the arts and cultural activities). [online]: Available from: http://www.government.bg/cgi-bin/e-cms/vis/vis.pl?s=001&p=0174&n=000049&g = (status 14.09.2006).

42 Ibid.

43 Mitov, M., 2005. *Predstavyane na konzeptsiya za razvitie na balgarskata kultura* (*Presentation of the concept for developing Bulgarian culture*). [online]: Available from: http://www.slovesa.net/index.php?id=615 (status 07.12.2005).

project promotion. In this connection, tax reductions were planned for all those investing in cultural projects, as already laid down in the coalition agreement.

Passing a new law on cultural funding was also declared a priority. Within clearly defined legal parameters for the interrelationship between the state and the municipalities, a public-private partnership was to be created for the funding of cultural policy and cultural products. The creation of clear criteria and principles for state subsidy was expressly mentioned, according to which projects could be submitted on a competitive basis. Protection of the arts was described as a priority area of government policy.

There can be no doubt that the country's contemporary culture required a law on funding at this time too that would open the door to alternative funding channels and stimulate ideas for tax incentives for grants and donations. However, the law was not put into practice.

What was missing from the "Arts and Culture Constitution" of that time were above all specific details and deadlines. It was not clear which term of office the paper was referring to and what the intentions were behind delaying submission of the "Arts and Culture Constitution" to the Council of Ministers for approval and implementation. The advisory committee, which had written the text, made its own contribution to the fate of the concept, which consisted simply of gracing the archives with a new document. The comments about this concoction, its presentation and the ensuing political hoo-ha provided further proof of a fact that had long been obvious, namely that it was the Ministry's habit merely to prepare such papers without ever seeking coordination with NGOs or at least creating an environment in which public discussion could take place. While it was true that a strategy of this kind had long been wished for – especially since it provides the principles for the entire culture sector since the changes began – there is a risk that without a broad public discussion beforehand it will take on an antiquated character, which is what happened in practical terms in this case.

The Ministry of Culture is directly responsible for cultural development. Following the tempestuous 1990s, the strategy of using culture as an obvious propaganda tool was abandoned. All public relations work and its products are being increasingly geared towards economic considerations, and this naturally also included cultural policy. The Ministry's primary responsibility was therefore to secure the administrative parameters and the vision for sustainable cultural development. This could not happen because the Ministry only very rarely listened to what the non-government sector was saying.

Culture needs heavy investment that is stable over a long period. This investment need not come solely from the public sector, it can also be private. The unique characteristic of culture as a sector that cannot always be organized according to the precepts of free enterprise is that interests and objectives are pursued that the free market cannot always achieve. They should be the government's priorities, but in this case the economic principle that decrees that when the state withdraws, the market occupies the space it leaves, does not apply at all. Left at the mercy of the forces exerted by the free market and faced with unstable or non-existent cultural policy, the culture sector shows numerous flaws. It transforms itself into something incomplete, with the result that certain art forms are in the process of disappearing forever. This is particularly true in Bulgaria, because the number of cultural organizations fell steadily until only those remained that could be marketed to ensure their survival. The market has its selective function, whereas the modern state assumes responsibility in the field of culture for creating or supporting art forms that have no attraction for it and do not yield immediate profits. The first report on the Ministry's work, its spending from the budget and the implementation of all these activities appeared in 2006. Before then, no minister had publicly explained exactly what the Ministry had accomplished and which parts of the budget could be found in a standardized report on its activities. This procedure contravened the law on the protection of culture, but was nonetheless planned by the same Ministry and then implemented.

Laws passed since 2008:

- Law on cultural heritage
- Law on public lending libraries
- Law on theatres is pending.[44]

In recent years, state cultural institutions and the subjects most important for the development of the culture sector have been determined by the dominant role of the state. At the same time, the value of the budget fell continuously in real terms, causing a major crisis for public institutes whose very existence was threatened. The decentralization and division of responsibilities among the municipalities, which has taken place over the years without clear parameters and spontaneously, is an important argument for holding future debates and developing a cultural strategy for the arts and cultural institutions.

[44] Chronology of legislation, State Gazette.

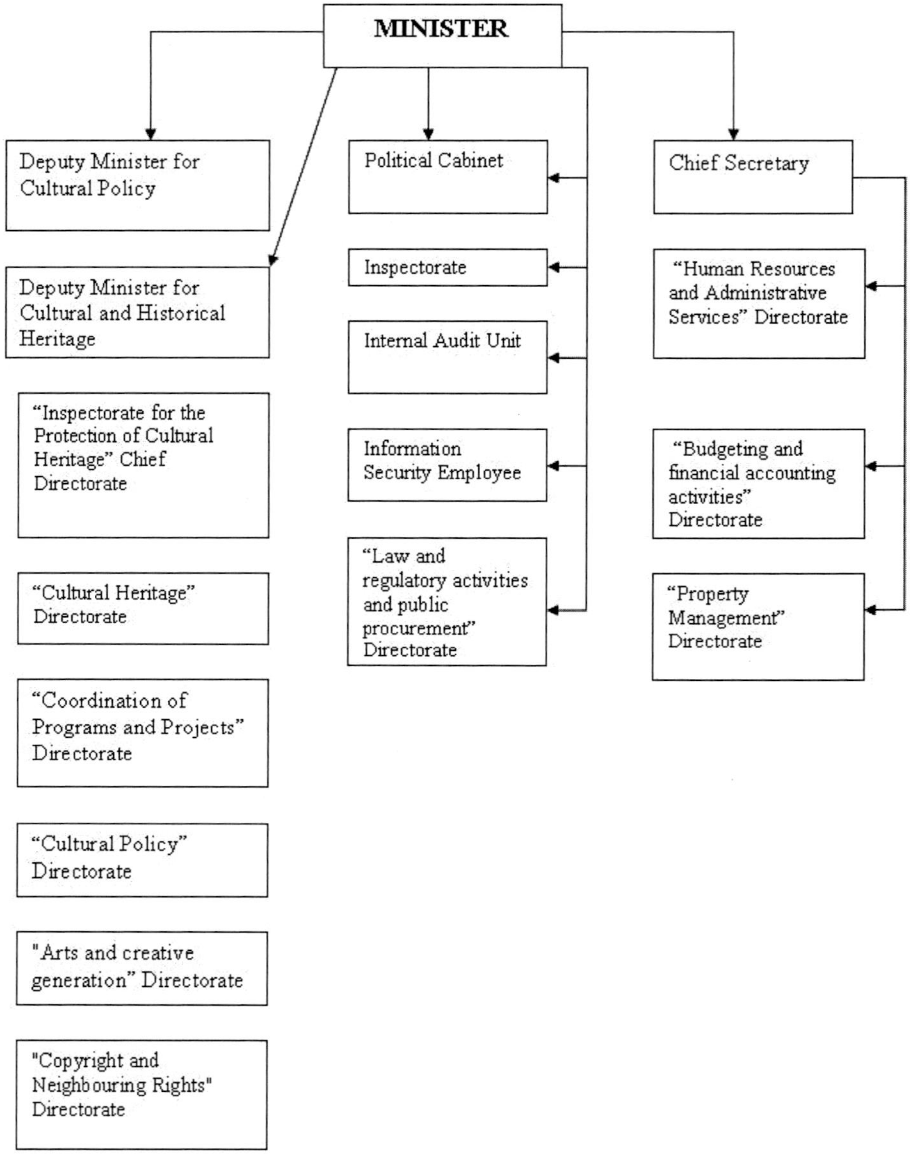

Status: June 2009.

Figure 4: Organization chart of the Ministry of Culture, 2010[45]

[45] Council of Europe. *Compendium of Cultural Policies and Trends in Europe, 2010.* [online]. [viewed 19.02.2012]. Available from: http://www.culturalpolicies.net/web/bulgaria.php?aid=31

Table 4: Budgetary expenditure on culture by category and management levels 2006[46].

	Direct costs	Transfers to institutions	Transfers to other administrative levels	Total	% of total
Cultural goods	10 404 000	4 500 000		14 904 000	4.78
Cultural heritage	7 832 000				2.55
Historical monuments	1 351 000				0.44
Museums and art galleries	6 481 000	100 000			2.11
Archives			4 400 000	4 400 000	1.41
Arts	45 796 000			45 796 000	14.65
Visual arts/design					
Performing arts	45 796 000			45 796 000	14.65
Music	22 986 000			22 986 000	7.35
Theatre and operetta	22 810 000			22 810 000	7.3
Multidisciplinary					
Media	9 411 000	110 300 000		119 711 000	38.27
Books and press	2 553 000			2 553 000	0.83
Books	2 553 000			2 553 000	0.83
Press	-				
Audiovisual Multimedia					
Cinema	6 858 000			6 858 000	2.2
Radio		38 100 000		38 100 000	12.18
TV		72 200 000		72 200 000	23.06
Other	26 043 000	11 200 000	95 400 000	132 643 000	42.38
Interdisciplinary		10 600 000	95 400 000	106 000 000	33.86
Cultural contacts with other countries	94 000	600 000		694 000	0.22
Administration	10 659 000			10 659 000	3.4
Teaching	14 527 000			14 527 000	4.64
Costs not assignable to a particular category	763 000			763 000	0.24
Total	91 654 000	126 000 000	95 400 000	313 054 000	100%

46 Byudzhetni razchodi na ministerstvoto na kulturata po sektori i upravlenski niva (Budgetary expenditure of the Ministry of Culture by sector and government sector). [online]. Available from: http://www.minfin.bg/bg/page/247 (status 05.10.2011).

Table 5: Budgetary expenditure on culture by category and management levels 2007[47]

	Direct costs	Transfers to institutions	Transfers to other administrative levels	Total	% of total
Cultural goods	17 109 456	7 282 000		24 391 456	6.2
Cultural heritage	14 617 176				
Historical monuments	5 226 942				
Museums and art galleries	9 390 234	1 060 000			
Archives			5 300 000		
Arts	2 492 280	922 000			
Visual arts/design	58 171 032			58 171 032	14.6
Performing arts					
Music	58 171 032			45 796 000	14.65
Theatre and operetta	28 968 389				
Multidisciplinary	28 752 808				
Media	449 835				
Cultural goods	9 506 810	112 600 000		122 106 810	30.6
Books and press	1 119 568				
Books	1 119 568				
Press	-				
Cinema	8 387 242				
Radio		44 600 000		38 100 000	12.18
TV		68 000 000		72 200 000	23.06
Other	27 273 910	400 000	166 100 000	19 3773 910	48.6
Interdisciplinary			166 100 000		
Cultural contacts with other countries	4 470 556	400 000			
Administration	4 628 610				
Teaching	17 234 465				
Costs not assignable to a particular category	765 799				
Total	112 061 208	120 282 000	166 100 000	398 443 208	100%

2.6 Assessment

What happened in Bulgaria after 1989 could be seen as both a result and a victim of culture, together with internal conflicts and the inability to solve these cultural contradictions. Regrettably, Bulgarian society remained a closed society, despite

47 Ibid.

the huge opportunities after liberation from dictatorship brought by the political transformation, and despite all the processes that had accompanied this transformation. In contrast to an "open" social system, the individual's right to self-determination was not sufficiently respected here; the attitude towards the rights of the individual was too negative.

Furthermore, the lack of political maturity led to the almost total neglect of the question of what defines Bulgaria as a cultural nation. The fundamental values of the Bulgarian Revival are among the primary factors in this definition. A collection of knowledge and experience, but also the ability to engage consensually in dialogue – in other words, the gathering in of traditions of civil and political culture – can guarantee new social and cultural prospects and define priorities for cultural funding, or identify important aspects in this field.

3. CULTURAL POLICY BY CATEGORY

3.1 Cultural and Historical Heritage

Bulgaria has an enormous cultural heritage with specific characteristics. The country's geographical position means it has constantly been exposed to diverse cultural influences because since antiquity it has stood at a crossroads passed by many peoples. Since its foundation in 681, Bulgaria has been regarded as a link between East and West. Consequently, a role as mediator between the cultures of ancient and advanced peoples can be attributed to Bulgarian culture itself.

Archaeological exploration in Bulgaria in the European context began following liberation from Ottoman rule and the foundation of the new Bulgarian state in the last decade of the nineteenth century.

The travel account by the Austrian Felix Kanitz, who portrayed the country's cultural heritage with great meticulousness in 1882, can be considered the start of exploration of the layers of culture in Bulgaria.[1] Earlier, in 1876, a report written by Konstantin Jireček had been published in Czech and German simultaneously. The first excavations were led in 1878 by the Russian Byzantinist Fyodor Uspensky and the Czech brothers Hermengild and Karel Škorpil. It was they who first described the prehistoric monuments in northern Bulgaria.

In the communist era, decree no. 1608 of the Council of Ministers of 30.12.1951 marks another turning point in measures taken with regard to the cultural heritage: with this decree, regulation of the country's history started. In 1969, a law on cultural monuments and museums was passed that had dramatic consequences. After 1989, this law was amended several times. However, these amendments contradicted each other. In 1995 they tended towards liberalization, but in 2005 were aimed more at tightening the law and maintaining it.[2]Ultimately, it led to restoration of the state monopoly and, shortly afterwards, was again repealed and amended several times.

The biggest problem with respect to Bulgaria's cultural heritage turned out to be not a shortage of money or the prevalence of private grave-robbers, but the absence of appropriate reforms in the field of antiquity studies that also meet the socio-cultural needs of the general public. Further, the cultural heritage system

---

1 Kanitz, F. P. *Donau-Bulgarien und der Balkan, Historisch-geographisch-ethnographische Reisestudien aus den Jahren 1860–1879*. Leipzig, 1882, pp. 7–65.

2 Zakon za pametnizite na kulturata i muzeite (Law on cultural monuments and museums). [online]. Darz- haven vestnik. Available from: mc.government.bg/files/75_10.1.ZAKON_3.doc (status 05.01.2011).

does not comply with the international agreements on culture that Bulgaria has signed[3]

In these international agreements, cultural heritage is not defined simply as the finite number of protected sites, monuments and cultural values, but also as the identity of a place, i.e. the landscape. This is precisely the new concept of landscape contained in the European Landscape Convention (Florence, 2000) that was later also ratified by Bulgaria.[4] According to this Convention, the term "landscape" refers not only to natural beauty, but to the entire integrated area, whose character is the result of the action and interaction of natural and/or human factors. The landscape is judged to an important factor in the formation of local cultures and an important component of the European natural and cultural heritage. In the new draft of the Cultural Heritage Protection Act, archaeological heritage is defined only as "material traces of human activity" (Article 140), with no mention made of the role played by its context.[5]

So that previously neglected cultural values also come under legal protection, the international treaties incorporated the new, unconventional instruments of integrated conservation, structural conversion and preservation into the plans for socio-economic development.[6] However, the Cultural Heritage Protection Act (passed by the National Assembly in July 2008 and in force since 10 April 2009) did not follow this trend.

"The tension resulting from the choice between privileging either the collective interest or the private interest is brought out when one considers the following. In some EU member states, the owner may loose [*sic*] the object altogether in an ad hoc system which declares it nationally protected and hence inalienable; or else, in case a permanent export license is given, the owner may find himself obliged to *pay*, in compensation for what is considered a 'loss to society'. Heritage in such cases is eminently considered as something that regards the entire society; and government, as the representative of the community of moral owners, therefore receives payment *in lieu* from the private possessor."[7]

---

3 Asotsiatsiya ArHea. *Strategiya za opazvaneto i ustoychivo razvitie na kulturno-istoricheskoto nasledstvo v Balgariya, osnovni nasoki* (*Strategy for the preservation and sustainable development of cultural heritage – guidelines*). [online]. Available from: http://archaeology.zonebg.com/strategy.pdf, p. 31 (status 29.12.2006).

4 Council of Europe. *European Landscape Convention*, no. 176, Florence 01.03.2004. [online]: Available from: http://conventions.coe.int/Treaty/Commun/QueVoulezVous.asp?NT=176&CL=ENG (status 26.06.2008).

5 Zakon za kulturnoto nasledstvo (Cultural Heritage Act), 2009. Darzhaven vestnik no. 19, 13 March 2009. Amend. several times. (status 18.08.2011).

6 Zones de Protection du Patrimoine Architectural Urbain et Paysager (Architectural, Urban and Landscape Heritage Protection Zones). [online]. Available from: http://www.vie-publique.fr/documents-vp/zppaup.pdf (status 02.07.2008).

7 Knoop R. Heritage policies in Europe. In: R. Afman and R. Knoop, eds. *Moving Heritage, Managing Mov- able Heritage in the EU, Bulgarian-Dutch Experiences 2005–2008*. Driebergen-Sofia, 2008, p. 194.

The Cultural Heritage Act passed by parliament was supported by 140 members of parliament. Only three voted against it.[8] The Act recognizes the institution of proprietor, preserver and collector of cultural values and provides for the possibility of transactions with movable cultural goods.

No provision is made for conducting transactions with cultural goods of archaeological value.

- A catalogue of all collections is to be compiled.
- Movable cultural goods that have been recognized as having archaeological value and are not part of state assets can, under the law, only be sold at auction in order to guarantee the state right of pre-emption.

"The pre-accession period and the first year of Bulgaria's EU membership have brought significant changes in the field of offences related to cultural objects. The economic development, the opportunity for economic private landowners over their own property cause a withdrawal from crimes related to cultural goods. The legal economic activities become more attractive than looting churches and archeological sites. The people in charge of illicit traffic schemes are still highly motivated to keep their incomes increasing. Mass criminality in the field of cultural heritage is now being transformed into notorious organized criminality. In similarity to other EU countries the new threat can be treated with the existing resources of the Bulgarian government, in close cooperation with other EU countries... The Bulgarian legal market of cultural goods and cultural heritage has developed in the situation of intensive illicit traffic. Collecting in Bulgaria has always been legal, provided the collectors have declared their cultural properties. Some illicit dealers succeed in persuading persons of financial resource to invest in their own collections. After its registration a newly formed collection can be managed as a private museum thus generating legal income. The new collectors today get more interested in the legal than in the illicit market of cultural goods, and in the cultural industries related to it."[9]

The Act led to further nationalization and regulation of cultural goods. Archaeologists, experts and collectors protested against the bill, warning that it would not stop grave-robbers. It cannot protect the identity of a landscape.

---

[8] Parliament. Stenograma ot debata v narodnoto sabranie proveden predi glasuvaneto na parvo tsetene na zakona za kulturnoto nasledstvo (shorthand text of the discussion in the National Assembly before voting on the first reading of the Cultural Heritage Act), 30.07.2008. Doklad otnosno akonoproekt za kulturnoto nasledstvo, Nr. 854-01-84, vnesen ot narodniya predstavitel Nina Cilova i grupa narodni predstaviteli (Report on the project leading to the Cultural Heritage Act no. 854-01-84). Sofia. Krastev, T. *Proektozakonat za kulturnoto nasledstvo krie riskove* (*The cultural heritage bill involves risks*). [online]. [viewed 19.02.2012]. Available from:http://www.icomos-bg.org/filebank/att_28.pdf

[9] Pavlov B. The cultural goods market in Bulgaria from illicit trade to cultural industries. In: R. Afman and R. Knoop, eds. *Moving Heritage, Managing Movable Heritage in the EU, Bulgarian-Dutch Experiences 2005-2008*. Publishers: AO Consultants for Development, Driebergen, Netherlands, 2008, in cooperation with the Ferdinandeum Association for Bulgarian National Heritage with the financial support of the Matra Pro- gramme of the Netherlands Ministry of Foreign Affairs. Driebergen-Sofia, 2008, p. 159.

The archaeological heritage is defined only as "material traces of human activity" (Article 140), with no mention made of the role played by its context (a key concept of the European Convention on the Protection of the Archaeological Heritage of 1991 that Bulgaria ratified). The concept was discussed in detail in the Venice Charter of 1964, Article 1:

> "The concept of a historic monument embraces not only the single architectural work but also the urban or rural setting in which is found the evidence of a particular civilization, a significant development or a historic event. This applies not only to great works of art but also to more modest works of the past which have acquired cultural significance with the passing of time."[10]

The previously used term, "cultural monument" (signifying a site or work protected by law) was replaced by the term "cultural object" which has a broader meaning. Both the protected objects and the respective interests concern only a very small section of the population. The Act shows a lack of understanding of global trends.

From the start of the transition, the Ministry of Culture has adopted the position of existing only on the periphery of the media and public interest. The wording of the Act conveys the following message:

- Only objects listed as worthy of protection are of value; all others are of no importance and consequently not part of the cultural heritage.
- There is a danger that objects are left without protection that play a specific role for the nation's cultural identity.
- The various wordings of the concept of culture include everyday culture. This serves as the basis for the next level of classification into tangible and intangible culture.

The most important factors for preserving this heritage, however, are the value system of society itself, vigilance within society and the status of civil society's development.[11]

3.2 Museums

After liberation from Ottoman rule in 1887, preservation of ancient sites and artefacts became a central topic for the Bulgarian state. The discussions on this topic were inspired by scientists and well-known personalities of public life. Five years

10 The Venice Charter for the Conservation and Restoration of Monuments and Sites, 1964. II. International Congress of Architects and Technicians. [online]. [viewed 18.02.2012]. Available from: http://www.icomos.org/charters/venice_e.pdf

11 Asotsiatsiya ArHea. *Strategiya za opazvaneto i ustoychivo razvitie na kulturno-istoricheskoto nasledstvo v Balgariya, osnovni nasoki* (*Strategy for the preservation and sustainable development of cultural heritage – guidelines*). [online]. Sofia: Sfera IK, 2003, p. 31. Available from: http://archaeology.zonebg.com/strategy.pdf (status 29.12.2006).

later, the first district directives were issued with the aim of preventing the destruction and export of cultural and historical goods. In 1888, the provisional rules for scientific and literary institutions were passed. They determined how the central sources of Bulgarian history were to be located and protected.

In 1911, the Antiquities Act came into effect. This law laid down clear and systematic measures for protection and named the institutions that were to be responsible for implementing them.

Omissions with regard to antiquities in built-up areas and the resources for their preservation and restoration led to the passing of the Preservation of Old Buildings in Built-up Areas Act in 1936.

Table 6: Oldest museums in Bulgaria[12]

Varna	Archaeological Museum	1888
Varna	Marine Museum	1923
V. Tarnovo	Museum of Architecture	1978
Gabrovo	Etara	1976
Gabrovo	Museum of Education	1973
Kazanlak	Shipka Buzludzha Park Museum	1964
Kozloduy	Radetzky Steamship National Museum	1962
Plovdiv	Ethnographic Museum	1917
Plovdiv	Museum of Bulgarian Revival and National Liberation	1961
Plovdiv	Zlatyu Boyadzhiev Art Gallery	1952
Rila Monastery	Holy Site Museum	1961
Ruse	Museum of Transport and Communication	1966
Sofia	Archaeological Museum (BAN)	1879
Sofia	Museum of Military History	1916
Sofia	Ethnographic Museum (BAN)	1906
Sofia	National History Museum	1973
Sofia	Literature Museum	1976
Sofia	Boyana Church Museum	1968
Sofia	Museum of Sport	1959
Sofia	Earth and People Museum	1986
Sofia	Polytechnic Museum	1957
Sofia	Natural History Museum	1889
Sofia	Agriculture Museum	1956
Sofia	Museum of Church History and Archaeology	1921
Sofia	Gallery of Foreign Art	1985
Sofia	National Art Gallery	1948

Although incomplete, these legal documents served as the basis for major activity on the part of the state, which was carried out by the National Museum of Archaeology, the Antiquities Commission, the state museum and the civil society through archaeological and historical societies.

12 National Statistics Institute

Following the coup d'état of 9 September 1944, all these old laws were repealed.

It was only with decree no. 1608 of the Council of Ministers in 1951 pertaining to the measures to be carried out for the "preservation of cultural monuments and the development of the museums in the country" and with the instructions issued for its implementation that the communist government drew attention to Bulgaria's cultural and historical heritage. Some time later, decree no. 165 of the Council of Ministers of 5 August 1958 pertaining to the protection of the cultural heritage, the development of museums and directives for implementation introduced stringent regulation of the discovery, exploration, research, restoration and exhibiting of Bulgaria's cultural heritage. This meant a state monopoly combined with regulation at all levels. Responsibility for cultural and historical goods was transferred to the authorities.

The communist government emphasized that the cultural and natural sights were property of the entire population and were under the protection of the state regardless of whether they were legally state, public or private property. To ensure state control of movable and immovable monuments, a council for preservation of cultural monuments and a council for museums were established. The Monuments Act and other regulations were passed to put the party policy into practice.

After the end of communism in 1989, the priorities of cultural policy with respect to museums were as follows:

- Changes to the legislative framework, reorganization of existing resources and creation of new sources of income
- Study of other countries' experiences
- Creation of the conditions necessary for the preservation and restoration of movable cultural goods
- Organization of scientific research

In the economic report to the President in 2007, the nature of this policy relating to the cultural heritage is described as follows: Bulgarian culture today is no longer determined by the public cultural institutions alone, but also by the "third sector", i.e. non-government organizations (NGOs) which are funded mostly by international foundations. These organizations have the aim of promoting contemporary, mostly abstract and experimental art, literature and culture and of suppressing art propagated before 1989 as "totalitarian" and "pre-modern". The Open Society foundations created by the American billionaire and philanthropist of Hungarian extraction George Soros played a prominent role in the value shift in the Bulgarian population. The national Open Society Foundation Sofia was established in Bulgaria on 5 April 1990 with the express approval of the Bulgarian government. George Soros's programmes were so diverse that practically the entire non-state sector was dependent on funds provided by Open Society. The Foundation's budget, approximately USD 100 million in the years 1990 to 1997, was more than the budget of the Bulgarian Ministry of Culture at the time.[13]

In 1995, the total number of museums and art galleries in the country included thirteen national museums and galleries funded and administered directly by the Ministry of Culture, 193 museums and galleries funded by the municipalities, numerous museums run by the authorities and over four hundred collections belonging to schools, art exhibition centres, public organizations and companies.

These rules were adopted by the Bulgarian museums as a working definition, so to speak. During the transitional period, the biggest problems facing Bulgarian museums and galleries were major obstacles to their growth, legal parameters that were not always clear and the physical protection of movable cultural goods in museum depots and at the exhibitions themselves.

Most of the permanent exhibitions in museums were outdated. In addition, there were no standard procedures for temporary exhibitions (regardless of whether these were a museum's own exhibition or a visiting one). Neither did the museums have annual schedules for temporary exhibitions. The acquisition of a new base of future museum visitors was a wish, but not a priority; no programmes were created specifically for schools or that could have expressed clear objectives.

To the majority of Bulgarian museums, the theory and practice of museum education and programmes of museum education were unknown. The chief criterion for the way a museum is organized is a survey of its visitors; but research of this kind was not conducted at any time during the period, which affected the planning of activities at the museums accordingly.

Table 7: Number of museums and art galleries in Bulgaria in 1995[14].

Overall	206
Historical	53
Memorial sites	47
Specialist museums	83
Galleries	43

The existing museum structure and the museum experts' categories did not reflect the altered circumstances. Conservation and restoration work at most of the museums was of a mediocre standard. It was not carried out by qualified licensed experts. In some cases, valuable exhibits were damaged.
– There was no standardized museum software.

13 Bachmaier, P. Der Wertewandel in Ostmitteleuropa. In: P. Bachmaier et al., eds. *Der kulturelle Umbruch in Ostmitteleuropa: der Transformationsprozess und die Bildungs- und Kulturpolitik Tschechiens, der Slowa- kei, Polens und Ungarns im Kontext der internationalen Beziehungen.* Frankfurt am Main, Vienna inter alia: Lang, 2005.

14 Koprinarov, L. *Balgarskata kulturna politika 1990–1995 (Bulgarian Cultural Policy, 1990–1995).* Sofia: Institute of Culturology, 1996, p. 87.

- The available modern information technologies for cataloguing and conserving movable cultural monuments, information exchange and the promotion of museums were not used.
- There was a lack of motivation among the museum specialists with regard to their work and professional training.
- Complacency and indifference were rife among them. An increase in the average age of the guild members was observed.
- The museums remained detached from and passive towards developments in cultural tourism.
- Museology as a branch of scientific study, and especially applied museology, was unknown to the staff at one museum.

In conclusion, it can be said that there were no strategies for creating synergies in the sphere of museum work, there was a lack of coordination and no consistent museum policy.

"The solution to the problems that have accumulated in the museums depends largely on the initiative of the museum curators. Their priorities must be the same as ours so that we, as a state institution of the Ministry of Culture, do what is necessary to help them overcome their problems and to support their future development."[15]

Table 8: Receipts and expenditure by type of museum 2011[16].

	Museums	Receipts in BGN		Expenditure in BGN
	Number	Total	Budget subsidies	Total
For the country overall	197	38 987 000	26 337 000	33 400 000
General	87	17 254 000	11 950 000	14 655 000
Specialist	110	21 733 000	14 387 000	18 744 000
Art galleries	38	73 440 000	4 895 000	7 063 000

Table 9: Receipts and expenditure by type of museum 2008[17].

Museums		Receipts in BGN Expenditure in BGN		
	Number	Overall	Incl. from budget	Overall
			Subsidy	
Total	222	36 730 000	26 509 000	34 361 000

[15] Ganchev, R., 2006. Sastoyanie, problemi i perspektivi pred balgarskite Musei i Galerii. Doklad na Rumyan Ganchev – direktor na NZMGII, predstaven na Natsionalnata rabotna sreshta na direktorite na muzeite i galeriite v Balgariya (Status, problems and perspectives of Bulgarian museums and galleries. Report by R. Ganchev, Director of the National Centre for Museums and Galleries in the Ministry of Culture. [online]. *National conference of curators of museums and galleries in Bulgaria, Sofia, 20 June 2006*). Available from: mc.government.bg/ . . . /Nacsreshta-dokladG(3).do (status 30.06.2006).

[16] National Statistics Institute. [online]. Available from: http://www.nsi.bg/otrasal.php?otr=24&a1=665&a2=667#cont (status 07.01.2013).

After 2000, steps were taken in Bulgaria to bring museums and galleries in line with the market. For instance, state subsidies were reduced proportionate to a museum's own income. This trend was confirmed in an analysis of the receipts and visitor numbers at museums and galleries. Seen as a whole, the number of visitors to museums and galleries remained unchanged during this period. In 2011 a sharp increase was noted. At the end of this process of adaptation, the receipts of the museums and galleries had increased almost fourfold.

Ultimately this was possible not just because admission prices rose, but more especially because of the sharp increase in the receipts obtained by museums and galleries from activities and subsidies. This is a new facet of the overall picture. The trend towards increasing market terminability and adaptation shows the relationship between subsidies and receipts that the museums and galleries were able to accrue and which generally amounted to one quarter of the overall sum.

The Ministry of Culture made efforts to protect movable cultural goods, but not the material cultural heritage. The following projects and programmes were carried out:

- A complete inventory and clarification of the contents of the museums' collections
- Compilation of public catalogues for the collections of the National Museum, the museums and art galleries in the Republic of Bulgaria and movable cultural monuments
- Digitization of museum collections, computerization of national, regional and local museums and creation of a national IT network for which a grant of over BGN one million was planned in 2007.

The annual increase of subsidies and specific programmes for museums and art galleries should be taken into account here, as should the acquisition in conjunction with the municipalities of over BGN 12 million from the structural fund in the period from 2007 to 2013 for projects to improve the building stock of museums and activities for storing and exhibiting cultural goods.[18]

[17] National Statistics Institute (NSI). [online]. Available from: http://www.nsi.bg/otrasalen.php?otr=34 (status 16.11.2009).

[18] Danailov, S., 2008. Otgovor na ministara na kulturata na vapros na narodniya predstavitel Nikolay Michailov, otnosno politikata na Ministerstvoto na kulturata po opazvaneto na pametnizite na kulturata (answer given by the Culture Minister to a question asked by Nikolai Michailov relating to the preservation of cultural monu- ments). [online]. Available from: http://mc.government.bg/page.php?p=1&s=11&sp=407&t=409&z=0 (status 28.11.2008).

Table 10: Museums and programmes 2002–2008[19].

	2000	2002	2005	2007	2008
Museums – number	224	220	229	227	222
No. of visitors in millions	3 938	3 555	3 925	4 060	4 631
Per museum in thousands	18	16	17	18	21
Lectures and talks – number	42 530	45 631	60 311	63 176	57 595
Incl. those in a foreign language – number	6 664	8 003	11 659	12 839	9 419
Exhibitions – number					
Museum's own	1 447	980	1 044	1 145	1 221
Joint exhibitions		682	589	792	790
Concerts – number	686	597	657	704	696
Book reviews – number	360	347	521	459	448
Video presentations – number	1 646	1 182	1 409	1 292	1 174
Competitions – number	115	104	107	150	160

There was no significant change in the number of museums,[20] although visitor numbers rose by 14.1%. However, cultural and educational work at the museums failed to keep pace with this development. The museum inventories (artefacts, scientific material, resources, material for exchange) increased by approximately 66,000 units in 2008 (1.0% compared to 2007), although the number of artefacts dropped by 0.7%. Compared to 2007, the museums' receipts rose by 8.8% in 2008 (to BGN 36,730), while spending rose by 6.5% to BGN 34,361. Total turnover for 2008 was as follows:

- BGN 26,509 (72.2%) from budget subsidies
- BGN 4,845 (13,2%) from ticket sales
- BGN 986,000 from donations and sponsorship

In 2008, the museums had 2,398 employees on their payrolls, of whom 2,226 were on permanent contracts. Compared to 2007, the number of employees fell by 6.8% (175 individuals).[21] The study *Problems of Museums in Bulgaria* that was presented on 29 September 2005 and had been carried out by a marketing firm for

19 National Statistics Institute (NSI)

20 From 227 in 2007 to 222 in 2008

21 National Statistics Institute (NSI). [online]. Available from: http://www.nsi.bg/otrasalen.php?otr=34 (status 11.11.2010).

the National Centre for Museums, Galleries and Performing Arts was part of a campaign to increase public awareness of Bulgaria's cultural history and heritage. Eighty-one curators of museums and galleries in Bulgaria took part in the survey.

The most commonly cited problems were:

- outdated and inappropriate legislation governing the museums' activities
- obsolete infrastructure combined with theft and illicit trade in valuable museum artefacts
- a lack of interest in funding museums on the part of private enterprise

Most of the curators stated that staff levels at their museums, particularly of specialist employees, were too low. They also stated that the activities of their museums received insufficient support from the existing public institutions. The respondents said that culture and the arts excited the least interest among the general public. Information given on the organization of leisure time confirmed this disappointing situation for culture and museums. One quarter of the museums had no catalogue of the artefacts in their possession. Approximately a fifth of the museums had not conducted an inventory in the last five years. Some museums had carried out their last inventory over ten years previously. According to figures published by the Bulgarian National Bank for 2008, receipts from international tourism (excluding transport) amounted to 2,533 million euros, which was 10.8% more than the year before.[22] If administration of culture is decentralized, then museums really do need a large number of visitors in order to survive. The new act of 2009 regulates this interrelation. The political rhetoric regarding the country's cultural heritage is predominantly emotional and yielded no specific approaches for the practical measurement of indicators which could have led to genuine progress in preserving the cultural heritage and a comprehensive government strategy regulated by subsequent legislation. That the term has become associated with cultural tourism in recent years and has thus found its way into everyday language cannot in itself be a factor. It should also be mentioned here that the monthly pay of employees in state and municipal museums has been subject to an almost unchanging development over the years and remains one of the lowest indicators when compared to average salaries both in the sector itself and in other subsectors. These employees are highly qualified professionals, but the fluctuation in the workforce has a negative impact on the institutions' professional status and is, in consequence, not especially motivating. What is more, museum employees have no protection under labour law, since they are employed as general administrative employees.

Comparison of the investment indicator with other subsectors in the cultural

[22] Darzhavna Agentsiya za turizma (State Agency for Tourism, Dept. of Statistics and Analysis), 2010. *Internatsionalen turizam Balgariya januari–dekemvri 2008* (*International tourism in Bulgaria January – December 2008*). [online]. Sofia, p. 1. [viewed 19.02.2012]. Available from: www.tourism.government.bg/.../file_64_bg.doc (status 15.01.2010).

sphere reveals the urgent necessity of reforms in order to prevent the collapse of the entire system.

3.3 National History Museums

Although the idea of creating a pan-Bulgarian museum was born in the 1840s, it was not until 1869 that its implementation was incorporated in the statutes of the Bulgarian Literary Society as an immediate task. There, the necessity of establishing an institution in the form of a committee was specified for the first time. Construction of the museum began immediately after liberation from Ottoman rule, under the provisional Russian administration and concurrently with the introduction of the structures of the modern Bulgarian state. Following the creation of the public library, a separate museum collection was instituted that soon grew into a museum department. The antique artefacts that constituted it were chiefly donations or the results of the diligence of teachers from the surrounding area and further afield who sent everything to Sofia that they judged to be of historical value and could be seen as part of the history of the country of Bulgaria. In-house regulations and procedures were developed.[23]

- There were areas for which no written regulations existed.
- Most of the internal documents required revision to bring them into line with legal provisions.
- There were no harmonized regulations in the National Museum for accounting, which would have permitted consistent management procedures.
- The regulation governing document circulation chiefly concerned the accounts and personnel departments.

Because there was no general document governing document circulation as a whole, it was not possible to trace the processes from initiation to completion or to monitor the separation of functions.

In its report, the Audit Office stated that:

- the National Museum was not organized in a way that would provide an accurate picture of economic transactions and protection of assets.
- the National Museum still had in its possession a large number of unused admission tickets printed many years previously. So that these could be used, the face value was adapted to current admission prices. There are no records of the number of tickets sold at inflated prices.

The report also stated that donations had been made to the Museum in both cash and kind, but that there were no regulations or records pertaining to the collection

[23] Smetna Palata (Audit Office). *Doklad za rezultatite ot izvarsheniya odit na finansovoto upravlenie na byudz- heta na natsionalniya istoricheski muzei* (*Report on the findings of the inspection of the financial manage- ment of the budget of the National History Museum*), 01.01.2007–31.12.2007. Report no. 0700000208, no. 286, 6.11.2008. Sofia, p. 1–2.

of donations. What is more, the National Museum had no written directives for documenting orders placed with companies.[24]

The National History Museum, which had in its possession great treasures and collections, needed suitable premises in the middle of the city. However, the Bulgarian government was unable to agree to make this search a priority.

3.4 Sofia Municipal Museum

Bulgaria had no concept for adapting the cultural heritage to life in a modern society. The economic conditions in the 1990s were not conducive to creating such a concept.

In 1941, the City of Sofia had created a municipal museum in the building that had housed the thermal baths. However, the museum was destroyed in 1944 in air raids during World War II. Before the raids, however, it had been possible to rescue some of the 120,000 exhibits that tell the story of the city of Sofia. These exhibits included ancient coins and vessels, jewellery, icons, paintings, furniture, clocks, photographs and much more. In 1946, the Museum resumed its work, although it had no building to house it.[25] Since 1952, the Museum of History has existed as an autonomous organization, but has no building in which the exhibits could be displayed. In 1959, construction work in the city centre revealed the foundations of a three-sided tower, a remnant of the fortification walls of the ancient city of Serdica. The municipal authorities in the Bulgarian capital decided to place a permanent exhibition from the Museum of History of the City of Sofia on the site, which was not completed until 2013. Although the Museum had no premises of its own, it was active in collecting and research and was able to organize over one hundred exhibitions in Bulgaria and abroad.[26]

In 1998, Sofia city council decided to place the former thermal baths in the centre of Sofia at the disposal of the Municipal Museum. Renovation of the building, which was built in the late nineteenth century by the architects Petko Momchilov und Friedrich Grünanger, began in 2004. A memorial to the two architects is planned.[27]

---

[24] Ibid.

[25] Dimitrova, G., 2008. Muzeiat na Sofia ostava v tsentralnata mineralna banya (The Museum of Sofia stays in the central mineral baths). [online]. In: *Stroitelsivo Gradat* 4, Feb 2008. [viewed 20.02.2012]. Available from: http://stroitelstvo.info/show.php?storyid=454580 (status 23.02.2008). Lazarova, J. Muzeiat na stara Sofia, Golyamata snimka (The Museum of Old Sofia, The Big Picture: 33 Photographs). [online]. In: *Dnevnik*, 02.09.2009. [viewed 20.02.2012]. Available from: http://www.dnevnik.bg/bigpicture/2009/09/02/778130_muzeiat_na_stara_sofii a/ (status 12.09. 2009).

[26] Authors' collective, Serdica-Sredets Sofia, Vol. 2. *Muzei za istoriya na Sofia* (*National History Museum Sofia*). Sofia, 1994, pp. 7–23.

[27] Museum of the History of Sofia et al... *Österreichische Architektureinflüsse in Sofia um die*

3.5 Performing Arts

3.5.1 Theatre

In the 1990s, the number of visitors to cinemas and theatres fell sharply.[28] A survey conducted in 2005 stated that 78% of the population went neither to the theatre, nor to the cinema. It was at this time that the existential pursuit of a change in the status quo on the part of Bulgarian theatre became reality. Plays censored prior to 1989 and previously banned genres were now performed. Innovative interpretations of the classics were sought, whether these were Bulgarian or works from abroad. The dynamics of the transition were also felt by the theatre, in which individuals also had to come to terms with their past so that they could live with their new souls. Audiences, however, were not interested in the actors' and theatre managers' existential intellectual struggles and were at best aware of the quality of the staged performance. In 1993, the Centre for Theatre in the Ministry of Culture was founded on the basis of recommendations made in Charles Landry's report on the management of culture. Only one year later, a theatre reform began, moving from a funding system that was geared to infrastructure maintenance and salaries to the funding of artistic activities. In this reform, the National Theatre Centre had the role of coordinating the entire transitional process. The necessity of the change was undisputed, and no resistance was offered. Among the projects given priority in this transition of Bulgarian theatre were the change in the funding strategy from centralization to decentralization and the foundation of new theatre companies and their support, as well as changes to the structure of the overdeveloped network of theatres. Repertory theatre was replaced partly by open stages with the aim of making stages available to independent theatre companies who were able to apply to project funding. In the period from 1989 to 1995 there were thirty-six drama stages, twenty-four puppet theatres and six musical theatres.[29]

Jahrhundertwende (German/Bulgarian). 2nd edition, revised and expanded. Sofia, 1998, p. 23. Smetna Palata (Audit Office) (ed.), Doklad za rezultatite ot izvarshen odit na obekt adaptatsiya na tsentralnata mineralna banya za musi na Sofia s aktivno prisastvie na mineralna voda. Stolichna obshtina za perioda ot 01.01.1998 g. do 30.06.2008 g. Nr. 0400001608, priet s reshenie na smetnata palata Nr. 171/23.07.2009 (Report on the findings of the Audit Office's examination of the conversion of the premises of the central mineral baths in Sofia into a museum with active presence of mineral water), Sofia.

28 National Statistics Institute (NSI), 2011. *Satisticheski spravochnik 2009* (*Statistical guide 2009*). [online]. [viewed 06.01.2013]. Available from: http://www.nsi.bg/otrasal.php?otr=24&a1=660&a2=2508#cont. Sofia, pp. 83–85 and p. 446.

29 NSI. Sofia, 1996, p. 440.

As far as politicians were concerned, it was clear that culture was in a bad way and that something had to be done to improve the situation. A survey revealed the need for a first theatre reform which was implemented in 1998 and led to the emergence of three different forms of theatre:

- repertory theatre, which had its own stages
- drama theatre with stages open to all
- the so-called (6 +) theatre in which six people per venue were employed and paid by the state

If a municipality wished a theatre for which it was responsible to move into a different category, it had to take on the necessary funding. A fundamental difficulty at the beginning of the theatre reform was that fifty state theatres were using premises owned by municipalities.[30] The spreading economic crisis and rising inflation meant that the theatres were caught between the two stools of the state and the municipalities. The municipalities' budgets were reduced meaning they could not afford the upkeep of the buildings. The state, for its part, saw no reason to assume these duties since it did not own the buildings. The lack of agreement between the state and the municipalities also applied to the musical theatres, which led to the foundation of a Philharmonic Society. This society was organized in a way very similar to the Viennese model (Musikverein/State Opera). This meant that the city philharmonic orchestra was identical to the orchestra of the musical theatre. The reform process itself was characterized by the double standards of state funding, at a time when the state was under pressure from the economic downturn and was trying to free itself of the obligation to support state theatre companies. Whereas the state theatres could receive subsidies for their infrastructure, the independent companies had to apply for projects that needed approval before support was granted for creating and marketing cultural products.

In 1995, the budget of the Ministry of Culture was allocated as follows:

- 18.0% theatre (20.3% in 1991)
- 11.8% opera (12.3% in 1991)
- 6.6% Philharmonic societies and orchestras (5.5% in 1991)

The rest of the funds went to the media, museums and other institutions. In the opera category the state covered 98% of the costs, for theatre the figure was 56%. The rest of the money came from the municipalities. 93.3% of the total budget of the Ministry of Culture was reserved for payment of overheads, with salaries (76% for opera, 68% for theatre) accounting for the lion's share. Capital investment accounted for 6.4%, with 1–2% being spent on projects outside the existing institutions such as NGOs. The number of subsidized jobs fell dramatically; of the 3,400 employees in 1996, 1,850 – around half – were made redundant.

[30] Vandov, N., 2002. Palno e s martvi zakoni (It is full of dead letter laws). [online]. Interview with Prof. Danailov in: *kultura.bg*, no. 14, 05.04.2002. [viewed 21.02.2012]. Available from: http://www.kultura.bg/media/my_html/2222/cpb-lambo.htm (status 02.07.2006).

From 1998–2002 the number of people working in the culture sector was cut from 41,286 to 28,980.[31] Depending on the municipality they found themselves in, repertory theatres had to reduce the number of planned posts from eighty-five to fifty-two. "Open stages" were permitted to provide between twenty-three and thirty-two jobs, while the so-called "Stages 6" had only six members of staff as the name suggests. As a result of this reform, a group of unemployed people appeared on the job market who had special skills and knowledge, but were unable to find a job: stagehands, directors and actors. At the same time, normal operation of theatres was disrupted owing to the lack of qualified staff.[32]However, the crisis in the country that was deplored by journalists, authors and theatre people, was not reflected on the stage. Besides the chronic under-funding, there was also a lack of producers and directors with political courage.

"Bulgarian theatre is not political, Bulgarians prefer to be entertained at the theatre," says the actor Lubov Mirkenev of the theatre in Ruse. "We concentrate more on interpersonal relationships."[33] Interestingly, there was no artistic contradiction of this statement.

Until the turn of the millennium, five documents determined cultural policy, also in the field of theatre:

- The cultural strategy for decentralizing support of theatres (1997)
- The directives for the structure and activities of the National Centre for Theatre (1997)
- The programme for development of theatres for the budget (1998)
- The Cultural Development Act (1999)
- The 2001 government programme, in the section on culture[34]

"The outstanding presence of Bulgaria in the rich and diverse cultural palette of Europe accentuates strongly the problem of investments in the development, promotion and integration of Bulgarian culture. The Government will set as its main priority the stimulation of the participation of the private and non-government sector in the cultural development by creating favourable conditions for investments and a variety of initiatives. We believe that the fulfilment of this priority requires actions for consolidation and partnership of

31 Agentsiya za ikonomicheski analizi i prognozi (Agency for economic analyses and forecasts). Natsionalen plan za razvitie na Republika Balgariya za perioda 2007–2013 (National development plan of the Republic of Bulgaria for the period 2009–2013). Sofia, 2005, p. 112.

32 Ministry of Culture. Natsionalna programa 2004. Zaetost v podkrepa na balgarskiya teatar (National pro- gramme 2004. Employment at Bulgarian theatres). Sofia, 2004, p. 1.

33 Marcus, D., 2008. Bulgarische Symptome: Auf Gastspielreise in Russe mit dem Theater Osnabrück. Zwischen menschlich und möglich. [online]. [viewed 19.02.2012]. Available from: http://www.nachtkritik.de/index.php?option=com_content&view=article&id=1076:bulgarische-symptome-auf-gastspielreise-in-russe-mit-dem-theater-osnabrueck&catid=419:theaterbrief-aus-bulgarien&Itemid=100060

34 Natsionalno Dvizhenie Simeon Vtori (National Movement Simeon II for Stability and Progress). Pravitelstvena programa (programme of the government of the Republic of Bulgaria). Sofia, 2001, p. 50.

the executive authority at all levels with the nongovernmental sector and the business. The Ministry of Culture will make maximum efforts to preserve the centuries-old cultural traditions of Bulgaria, will promote private investments in Bulgarian culture and in partnership with the Bulgarian citizens will work actively on supporting and optimising the cultural infrastructure."[35]

To define the preferences and incentives for the implementation of investment activities in the various cultural sectors for the development and governmental support of research in the arts field, the following measures were planned:
- Implementation of amendments to the legislation on culture in order to ensure legal provisions that meet the market conditions
- Freedom of action and the creation of market-oriented conduct on the part of cultural institutions and artists
- A new law on the cultural heritage, a law on sponsorship and a new law on the *chitalishta*
- The decentralization of the administration and funding of culture and increased involvement of NGOs in cultural processes
- Cultural diversity as the foundation of dialogue and social integration.

In 2008 there were thirty-nine theatres in which 4,608 performances took place. That was 5.4% less than in 2007.[36]

When a Culture Minister decrees a change in the activities of theatres, a parallel reality appears. This parallel reality is, for example, the critical view taken of the reform by theatre managers and actors. The new theatre reform (2010) created an imbalance between the theatres in small towns and those in large towns because state subsidies were granted on the basis of the number of tickets sold. That means that a theatre was richer the more tickets it sold and this in turn meant that the actors were paid more. The theatre reform as it was worded meant that the theatres in small towns and in towns with a stagnant economy and high unemployment had to be closed. Two examples of this are Vidin and Smolyan. The chief consequences of the last theatre reform were a reduction of state subsidies for the theatres and a reduction of the number of employees and actors reminiscent of 2001 when a similar reform was carried out. In small towns with high unemployment, a cultural policy with tailored objectives would have been necessary because the theatre reform chiefly affected regional theatres in small towns which were closed down. The actors were judged according to how well-known and popular they were; this situation ultimately robbed them of the right to experiment. The result was a drop in the quality of productions and a fear of staging works by new playwrights. In

---

35 Pravitelstvo na evropeiskata integratsiya (Government of European Integration). Programa na pravitelstvoto na evropeiskata integratsiya ikonomicheskiya rastezh i sotsialnata (Programme of the Government of European Integration, Economical Growth and Social Responsibility). Sofia, 2005, pp. 20–40.

36 NSI. *Yearbook 2009*. Sofia, 2009, p. 85.

2012, the government led by the GERB party laid down harmonized spending standards for the funding of state theatres: opera houses, ballets and philharmonic societies. The decree concerned the funding that the cultural institutions received for every ticket sold because it had not changed since 2011. The only exception is the Ivan Vazov National Theatre that will receive BGN 20 per ticket sold in 2013 instead of BGN 15. In future, the drama theatres will receive BGN 12.50 per ticket sold, the dramatic/puppet theatres BGN 15, the puppet theatres BGN 10, the musical-drama theatres BGN 40, the opera houses BGN 60, the operatic-theatre centres, philharmonic and symphony orchestras BGN 50. This resolution was ratified in 2012. The Sofia Opera and the ballet, as well as the Sofia Philharmonic, will each receive BGN 70 each in subsidies in future, the state folklore ensemble will receive BGN 52 and the State Music and Ballet Centre will receive BGN 60 for every ticket sold. The system of delegated budgets in state cultural institutions began with the last theatre reform in 2010 whose aim was to make the subsidies granted to theatres, opera houses etc. contingent on the number of tickets sold, in other words, on audience interest in the performances they staged. On 1 January 2011, the theatres started funding themselves according to the system of so-called delegated budgets, a result of the reform. The table below shows that based on the average number of performances and attendances, opera theatres can attract audiences that equate to a third of the capacity of the halls in which the performances take place. For the entire theatre category, a funding and artistic policy is required so that the drama theatres and musical theatres can attract larger audiences.[37] The dramatic-puppet theatres and the puppet theatres, which attract large numbers of people, are an exception here. The performances for children are particularly popular. The measure most often adopted by the theatres until 2011 to increase receipts beyond their budget was renting out parts the buildings they owned. This trend continued in 2012.[38] Towards the end of 2012, the Minister pronounced the theatre reform to be successfully completed. As usual, however, there is no written analysis.

---

[37] Ministry of Culture. Statement pertaining to state cultural institutions' success in meeting certain figures in specific artistic genres as of 31.12.2012 . [online]. [viewed 28.05.2013.] Available from: http://mc.government.bg/page.php?p=58&s=81&sp=415&t=85&z=0

[38] Ministry of Culture. Strategii i politiki za razvitieto na sektor "kultura" *v* perioda 2011-2020, chast I, analiz na situatsiyata v sektor "kultura" i proiztichashtite ot nego deistviya za optimiziraneto i razvitieto mu (Strate- gies and measures for the development of the "Culture" sector from 2011–2020, part I: Analysis of the situa- tion in the "Culture" sector and the resultant measures for optimization and development). Sofia, p. 6.

3.5 Performing Arts

Organization	Total performances 2012	Visitors 2012	Subsidies for visitors	Total receipts from house productions and co-productions	Transfers under mixed funding with municipalities 2012	Average no. of visitors per production	State subsidy per ticket in BGN	State subsidy according to the formula	Expected total subsidy from municipalities and the state according to the formula if audience figures stay the same - 2013
Theatres	**9 461**	**1 294 270**	**1 247 260**	**7 632 797**	**1 745 890**				
Cultural institutions of national significance									
Ivan Vazov National Theatre, Sofia	618	175 283	174 895	1 532 630	26 220	284	15	2 623 425	4 182 275
Drama theatres	**2 686**	**560 084**	**529 948**	**3 653 300**	**800 920**				
Aleko Konstantinov satirical theatre, Sofia	205	64 349	52 917	535 059	0	314	12.5	661 463	1 196 522
N.O. Masalinov drama theatre, Plovdiv	299	92 548	89 930	816 951	40 000	310	12.5	1 124 125	1 981 076
Sfumato-Sofia theatre workshop	234	12 899	11 683	75 669	22 500	55	12.5	146 038	244 206
Bulgarian Army Theatre, Sofia	316	104 021	98 305	777 961	0	329	12.5	1 228 813	2 006 774
N. Y. Vapstarov drama theatre, Blagoevgrad	131	18 750	18 610	92 549	62 500	143	12.5	232 625	387 674
Adriana Budevska drama theatre, Burgas	180	45 097	45 046	281 089	176 900	251	12.5	563 075	1 021 064
Racho Stoyanov drama theatre, Gabrovo	135	18 733	16 727	80 566	103 600	139	12.5	209 088	393 254
Yordan Yovkov Theatrical Centre, Dobrich	102	19 646	19 139	118 757	40 000	193	12.5	239 238	397 995
Drama theatre, Lovech	201	20 537	19 102	60 040	83 600	102	12.5	238 775	382 415
Anton Strashimirov drama theatre, Razgrad	151	24 123	21 388	90 680	0	160	12.5	267 350	358 030
Sava Ognyanov drama theatre, Ruse	212	41 851	40 637	235 833	43 000	197	12.5	507 963	786 796
Stefan Kirov drama theatre, Sliven	184	34 791	34 621	196 466	64 900	189	12.5	432 763	694 129
Geo Milev drama theatre, Stara Zagora	163	25 876	25 663	133 936	62 100	159	12.5	320 788	516 824
Drama theatre, Targovishte	73	19 339	19 256	72 064	30 000	265	12.5	240 700	342 764
Nevena Kokanova drama theatre, Yambol	100	17 524	16 924	85 681	1 820	175	12.5	211 550	369 051

Organization	Total performances 2012	Visitors	Subsidies for visitors	Total receipts from house productions and co-productions	Transfers under mixed funding with municipalities 2012	Average no. of visitors per production	State subsidy per ticket in BGN	State subsidy according to the formula	Expected total subsidy from municipalities and the state according to the formula if audience figures stay the same - 2013
Puppet theatre	**2 237**	**271 178**	**264 776**	**1 523 553**	**523 750**				
Nikola Binev youth theatre, Sofia	275	44 061	43 131	300 602	0	160	15	646 965	947 567
Valentin Stoychev Theatre 199, Sofia	358	32 965	32 965	276 672	0	92	15	494 475	771 147
Puppet theatre, Vratsa	278	36 870	36 870	156 167	112 150	133	15	553 050	821 367
Dimitar Dimov Drama and puppet theatre, Kardzhali	302	29 038	28 657	115 135	12 000	96	15	429 855	556 990
Konstantin Velichkov Drama and puppet theatre, Pazardzhik	210	23 754	23 124	97 085	100 000	113	15	346 860	543 945
Ivan Radoev Drama and puppet theatre, Pleven	247	30 776	29 912	135 664	173 600	125	15	448 680	757 944
Ivan Dimov Drama and puppet theatre, Haskovo	293	42 506	41 671	325 978	72 000	145	15	625 065	1 023 043
Vasil Drumev Drama and puppet theatre, Shumen	274	31 208	28 446	116 250	54 000	114	15	426 690	596 940
Puppet theatres	**3 920**	**287 725**	**277 641**	**923 314**	**395 000**				
Burgas	330	34 026	31 063	107 213	45 000	103	10	310 630	462 843
Varna	304	34 402	32 048	135 437	50 000	113	10	320 480	505 917
Vidin	253	19 451	19 151	61 098	2 500	77	10	191 510	255 108
Gabrovo	356	16 261	15 873	43 112	30 000	46	10	158 730	231 842
Dora Gabe - Dobrich	227	18 847	17 675	56 277	20 000	83	10	176 750	253 027
Plovdiv	460	28 474	27 700	98 042	45 000	62	10	277 000	420 042
Ruse	240	14 793	14 778	44 735	32 000	62	10	147 780	224 515
Silistra	327	17 089	16 741	51 267	0	52	10	167 410	218 677
Sliven	379	25 244	24 535	79 119	30 500	67	10	245 350	354 969
Stara Zagora	409	35 478	35 365	122 948	70 000	87	10	353 650	546 598
Targovishte	439	25 291	24 463	68 778	30 000	58	10	244 630	343 408
Georgi Mitev-Goro, Yambol	196	18 369	18 249	55 289	40 000	94	10	182 490	277 779

3.5 Performing Arts

Organization	Total performances 2012	Visitors 2012	Subsidies for visitors	Total receipts from house productions and co-productions	Transfers under mixed funding with municipalities 2012	Average no. of visitors per production	State subsidy per ticket in BGN	State subsidy according to the formula	Expected total subsidy from municipalities and the state according to the formula if audience figures stay the same - 2013
Music, Dance, Art	**1 442**	**405 402**	**397 691**	**3 342 230**	**780 370**				
Cultural institutions of national significance	338	114 505	112 629	1 516 770	0				
State Opera, Sofia	199	68 143	66 767	1 069 533	0	342	70	4 673 690	5 743 223
Sofia Philharmonic	96	34 387	34 387	348 999	0	358	70	2 407 090	2 756 089
Filip Kutev State Folklore Ensemble, Sofia	43	11 975	11 475	98 238	0	278	52	596 700	694 938
Drama-musical theatre	463	120 593	117 441	925 295	246 400				
State Music and Ballet Centre, Sofia	139	48 519	47 512	419 738	0	349	60	2 850 720	3 270 458
Theatre-Music Centre, Varna	222	50 212	48 770	356 571	160 000	226	40	1 950 800	2 467 371
Music-drama theatre, Veliko Tarnovo	102	21 862	21 159	148 986	86 400	214	40	846 360	1 081 746
Opera and music centres	391	138 666	138 257	773 486	420 000				
State Opera, Plovdiv	77	25 150	25 150	169 578	50 000	327	60	1 509 000	1 728 578
State Opera, Stara Zagora	106	29 588	29 425	188 453	90 000	279	60	1 765 500	2 043 953
State Opera, Ruse	103	46 257	46 020	219 913	100 000	449	60	2 761 200	3 081 113
State Opera, Burgas	105	37 671	37 662	195 542	180 000	359	60	2 259 720	2 635 262
Symphony and philharmonic orchestras	250	31 638	29 364	126 679	113 970				
Pleven Philharmonic	75	9 578	7 605	44 168	0	128	50	380 250	424 418
Vidin Sinfonietta	84	7 760	7 760	32 344	0	92	50	388 000	420 344
Vratsa Sinfonietta	41	7 362	7 362	26 394	75 732	180	50	368 100	470 226
Shumen Sinfonietta	50	6 938	6 637	23 773	38 238	139	50	331 850	393 861
Performing arts, total	**10 903**	**1 699 672**	**1 644 951**	**10 975 027**	**2 526 260**			**39 084 805**	**52 586 092**

Source: Ministry of Culture, statement on state cultural institutions' success in meeting certain figures in specific artistic genres as of 31.12.2012. [online]. [viewed 24.04.2013.] Available from: http://mc.government.bg/page.php?p=58&s=81&sp=415&t=85&z=0.

3.5.2 Modern and Classical Ballet

From 1944 to 1989, ballet in Bulgaria was governed by loyalty towards Russian-Soviet academicism. Despite this, soloists from the Sofia Opera Ballet founded the Arabesque Ballet Studio as early as 1963. This studio spearheaded a new approach.[39]

The EK Company came third in modern choreography with their production at the 14th International Contemporary Dance Contest in Cologne in 1983. Despite its success, the company received no support and the studio closed down in 1986.

The Arabesque Ballet Studio was led by ballet mistress Margarita Arnaudova from 1972 to 1994. The company was then taken over by Kalina Bogoeva, one of the stars of the Sofia Opera. Since 1998, the director has been R. Markova, a long-serving member of the company. The studio survived the crisis of the transition, but the ballet's programme is modest. In 2009, it had twenty dancers and ten administrative staff. Ballet Arabesque, which used rooms in the State Musical Theatre, is the only contemporary dance company to receive an annual subsidy from the Ministry of Culture. The subsidies granted from 1999 to 2009 amounted to EUR 45,000. Another example of the non-conformity of dance is the Amaranth Dance Studio, founded in 1993 by Krassen Krastev and four dancers from the Arabesque Studio. Ballet critics were unfavourable in their assessment of Amaranth because the studio still had a penchant for traditional rather than modern dance. A project to establish a centre of modern dance was rejected by the Ministry in 1999. In academic circles the hypothesis prevailed that classical dance was sufficient for a dancer's training, which is why the Graham technique and jazz dance were taught only fleetingly at the State Choreography School. The programmes were still influenced by Russian teaching techniques. The only university that taught modern dance as a separate course of studies was the Faculty of Theatre at the New Bulgarian University. However, in the 1980s and 1990s many dancers from Bulgaria chose to take their training into their own hands and participated in the seminars at the Palucca School in Dresden which, owing to visa regulations and the country's relationship with countries with a well-developed democracy, was their only chance. Later, self-education became a practice adopted by young artists who took an active interest in modern ballet, and gradually the world and the diversity of styles opened out before them which, due to censorship, had reached Bulgaria only in part or not at all before 1989. The Sofia Dance Week Festival organized in 2008 by the magazine *Edno* gave Bulgarian audiences to chance to discover the various styles of dance that exist all over the world.

After 1989, the Ministry of Culture failed to recognize the importance of modern dance for the development of the arts as a whole in the country and declined to support it. The funding schemes, both at national and at local level, still focused

---

[39] Ballet Arabesque. [online]. Available from: http://www.arabesque.bg/ (status 21.02.2008).

on folk dance. Similarly, classical ballet at the state-subsidized theatres and the ballet competition in Varna, the oldest competition for classical ballet in Europe, received support.

Table 1: New productions of the State Musical Theatre by genre, 1995–2001[40].

Year	Opera	Ballet	Operetta	Musicals
1995	27	17	5	4
1996	22	10	6	3
1997	22	5	2	3
1998	16	19	8	4
1999	21	14	5	1
2000	17	22	1	5
2001	15	8	1	3

3.5.3 Books

The conditions of the transition have proved risky, both for the middle levels of the old administration and the newly established, higher levels of the new one. The former level was in danger from inner psychological barriers that resisted everything new, and the latter because of inexperience and ignorance. The apparatus of state proved incapable of coming to terms with society's needs in the modern era and the changes that were under way. Svetlozar Zhekov remarked on this subject:

> "The drain of the intellectual elite in our recent history is a good reason to think about this. And in the years before, the emigration of artists of the word and of thought such as Tzvetan Todorov, Julia Kristeva, Dimiter Inkiow, Petar Ouvaliev, Christo Javacheff-Christo and many others who see themselves less as Bulgarians than as citizens of the country in whose language they write is eloquent proof that in the era of globalization, national creative potential can be bought and sold."[41]

In general, however, the "people of the word" feel far more like cosmopolitans than members of a particular nation. The economic boom in the book trade in the first years of the transition was due largely to the curiosity of Bulgarian readers who had up to then been forced to live with the censorship exercised by the repressive regime. The mechanisms of the market clearly revealed the good sides,

---

[40] Biks, R., Yaneva, A. and Karakostova, R. In: *Balgarski muzikalen teatar 1890–2001* (Bulgarian Musical Theatre 1890–2001). Sofia, 2005, p. 315.

[41] Svetlozar Zhekov, Direktor na NZK pri Ministerstvo na kulturata na R. Balgariya, Seminar "Pregled na natsionalnata politika za knigata" s uchastieto na ekspertite na saveta na Evropa, Prof. Dr. Hartmut Walravens i David Kingam, predstaviteli na ispalnitelnata vlast, parlamenta i knizhnata obshtnost, Chisar, 1999. (Svetlozar Zhekov, director of the National Book Centre of the Min. of Culture of the Rep. of Bulgaria. Seminar *Appraisal of the national book policy* attended by experts from the Council of Europe Prof. Hartmut Walravens and David Kingam, representatives of the executive, parliament and the literary community). Sofia, 1999.

but also the bad sides, of the book trade. Private publishing companies freed themselves from state interference, while state-run publishers went to the wall or were almost completely absorbed by the market. After this first boom period for private editors came the collapse of the population's purchasing power and consequently the number of books printed. The new publishers emerged from the circle of former state publishers, editors, translators and authors. By pursuing decentralization, as was natural, the book publishers lost the chance of centralized sales and distribution. The demand for books was high, new editions were continually printed. The changes that took root and the new market mechanisms meant that the private publishers released the state from its thankless task of disseminating knowledge and thought, and in return it destroyed one of its sub-functions – the book distribution system. This blow against intellectual activity in Bulgaria was worse than many of the unpopular measures of the economic reform. Bureaucracy ignored the voices coming from the circles of the intelligentsia with recommendations for saving books and bookshops. The loss of the state-run book distribution system necessitated unforeseen investment, and this took money away from other areas. The state abandoned the bookshops, which were part of intellectual existence and the national identity. During the years of the transition, support of bookshops and libraries was no longer a national priority. The Ministry of Culture and the National Centre for Books were powerless in their struggle for intellectual identity and were faced with the reality that the sale of state printing shops, bookshops and libraries brings in capital that can be used for other purposes. The democratic and market-oriented Bulgarian state had done much to enable publishers from abroad to sell their books in Bulgaria, but had done little for Bulgarian publishers and authors who did not have the same status.

The most important question arising from this is: What did the state contribute to give them a chance in the race between the intellectual sphere, culture and the mass market? The answer is: It was firstly the wasted time, but also the generation of the transition who had grown up with different intellectual needs owing to the lack of dialogue between the state and the highly qualified people of the word and the book who remained on stand-by, as it were, waiting for their time to come and relying on realization dawning of the importance of preserving the country's intellectual wealth.

Having been liberated from the totalitarian state, the literary community hoped that Bulgarian literature and its authors would become partners in a dialogue with the new democratic and market-oriented state. The Ministry of Culture privatized publishers, libraries, printers, bookshops and cinemas and transferred the responsibility for them to the Ministry of Industry. From 1995 to 2000 the number of libraries fell from 8,069 to 5,669, in other words by 2,400.[42] Of these closures,

[42] NSI. *Yearbook 1996*. Sofia, 1996, p. 442.

757 were libraries in *chitalishta* and 638 were school libraries. These closures went ahead without any supervision whatsoever, with the result that many national treasures were lost, depriving citizens, and particularly children, of their right to have access to cultural, educational and information services.[43]

The biggest problem in this situation was the absence of a national strategy for the territorial library network and library services and the fate of those people who had devoted their lives to books.

The monthly magazine for book publishers and bookselling, *Knigite dnes* (April 2005), published data from a small but very good bookshop in Sofia, including details on the shop itself and the number of books sold. The magazine asked questions such as:

- Where is the courage of influential people who claim that their book reviews are genuine and representative?
- Why do they not openly show the extent of their commercial power by revealing the number of copies that have actually been sold?

The other key question asked in the article is that of information on the number of copies of a book that are printed. Publishers reveal these figures only when they are required for a subsidy. According to information supplied by the National Centre for Books, Bulgarian books are printed in runs of 500.[44]

However, many publishers claim they have printed more copies than they actually have in order to increase the value of the project. Authors and translators in particular are interested in knowing how many copies have been printed, but information about additional runs is often withheld from them.

For most publishers of subsidized books, it is of no import whether the books are sold or not because they have already received their share. The subsidies are granted by the Directorate for Books in the Ministry of Culture. Elsewhere in the article in *Knigite dnes*, Plamen Doynov writes:

> "The writers' guild is led by people who are not interested in marketing books. The marketing of books is a matter of essential importance neither to the publishers, nor to the writers' guild. This is why the sale and distribution of books is in the state it is in – because it is left to fend for itself."

In 2004, the Bulgarian Book Association carried out a sociological study with the National Book Centre in the Ministry of Culture. The study, titled "Books and Readers in Bulgaria", uncovered several particularly detrimental facts that

---

43 Sayuz na biblioteknite i informatsionnite rabotnitsi (Union of Librarians and Information Sector Employees). *Za neobchodimostta ot neotlozhni merki za reshavane na osnovnite problemi na bibliotekite v Balgariya* (*On the necessity of solving the problems of libraries in Bulgaria*) [online]. Publ. 21.04.2004. [viewed 21.02.2012]. Available from: http://www.lib.bg/za_neob.htm (status 11.06.2007). NSI. *Yearbook 2005*. Sofia, 2005, p. 448.

44 Doynov Plamen. Knigi bez tirashi (Books with no circulation). In: *Knigite dnes*, no. 4. Sofia 2005, p. 17.

are responsible for the falling interest in reading among the population. The most striking negative trends were found among children and teenagers. In April 2006, the Bulgarian Book Association published a memorandum in conjunction with the Librarians' Association with the title "Reading Bulgaria."[45]

The Bulgarian President, Georgi Parvanov, supported the memorandum and, in the St. St. Cyril and Methodius National Library in May 2006, announced a national campaign called "Make a book a gift " with the aim of inviting the population to revive the old family tradition of giving books as gifts to relatives and friends and to call on publishers, authors and intellectuals to help school libraries and the *chitalishte* libraries by donating books.

In 2007 the following sentence appeared in the economic report to the President:

> "It is obvious that, besides protection, culture also needs support as part of the conscious strategy and national policy. While we contribute part of our income in the form of tax relief or other economic activity, the state could create incentives for the participation of business and industry in culture and for investment therein. In this way, social and private interest would grow proportionate to our continual development."[46]

In 2008, the number of publications held in the St. St. Cyril and Methodius National Library accounted for 21.8% of the entire stock of publications held in libraries in Bulgaria.[47] The regional libraries held 34.0% of the overall stock of publications, specialist libraries 25.0%, university libraries 16.2% and *chitalishte* libraries 3.0%. In 2008, the number of people employed in libraries fell by 105 compared to the previous year. This figure gives cause for concern and raises the question of the role and importance of the *chitalishta* in the country. One of their most important roles is that of a library. This is a tradition linked to Bulgaria's past – the Bulgarian Revival. The *chitalishta* and libraries accounted for 59.2% of all 4,552 libraries in the country with over 2,000 books, and they were used by 41.1% of all library users. Over the last few years their number has fallen by approximately 15%. In 2005, libraries' income was BGN 36.5 million, 74.4% of which came from the national budget. In 2008, the number of readers dropped to 253,000. This represents a drop of 5.2% compared to the previous year. This trend continued in the following years.[48]

---

45 Text of the memorandum "*chetyashta Balgariya*" ("Reading Bulgaria"). [online]. Available from: http://www.lib.bg/kampanii/4bulgaria/memorandum_4B.htm (status 18.04.2006).

46 President's office. *Ikonomicheski doklad za prezidenta-2007, Balgariya: sotsialni predizvikatelstva i evro- in- tegratsiya* (*Economic report to the President 2007, Bulgaria: Social Challenges and Euro-integration*). Sofia, 2007, p. 133.

47 NSI, 2008.

48 NSI, 2009. [online]. [viewed 06.01.2013]. Sofia 2009, pp. 81–89. NSI, 2011. Available from: http://www.nsi.bg/otrasal.php?otr=24&a1=584&a2=585#cont

Table 2: Published books and brochures in thousands, 2000–2011[49].

	2000	2001	2002	2003	2004
Books					
Titles	4 233	4 200	5 117	4 679	5 516
No. of copies in millions	8 051.8	5 392.8	4 690.1	3 662.8	3 489.1
Average no. of copies per title	1 900	1 300	900	800	600
Brochures					
Titles	794	784	901	832	916
No. of copies in millions	1 311.4	1 174.3	926.1	820.7	797
Average no. of copies per brochure	1 700	1 500	1 000	1 000	900
Books and brochures per capita	1.2	0.8	0.7	0.6	0.6

	2005	2006	2007	2008	2011
Books					
Titles	5 221	5 666	5 943	6 023	4 525
No. of copies in millions	3 186.3	3 358.7	4 106	4 023	2 717
Average no. of copies per title	600	600	700	700	600
Brochures					
Titles	808	896	705	744	496
No. of copies in millions	730	778.9	691	623	496.1
Average no. of copies per brochures	900	900	1 000	800	900
Books and brochures per capita	0.5	0.5	0.6	0.6	0.4

The table shows the effects of cultural policy on the publication of books. Whereas in the year 2000 the average number of copies printed per book was 1,900, this figure had fallen to 600 in 2011, meaning that 6% fewer books were being published. Books were a victim of the transformation. A report from the Association of Librarians says:

"Funding for libraries took a drastic downturn due to the absence of legal provisions. In the report *Millennium 2000* of the European library economics project LIBECON, Bulgaria ranks last among 29 European countries in terms of financial indicators. Together

[49] NSI

with the reduction of the number of libraries, acquisition of new books fell by half compared to 1994 and to 20% compared to 1989. Acquisition of new books in the *chitalishta* fell to 10%. Libraries have no recourse to alternative sources of funds such as fees and saleable services, but are for the most part dependent on the state budget. Donors receive no tax relief."[50]

Table 3: Libraries with more than 200,000 library documents in 2008[51].

	Libraries	Stock of publications		Readers	Items loaned out	
	Number	Total in millions	Incl. books	Tsd.	Total in millions	Incl. books
TOTAL	47	34 987	18 411	253	6 842	4 868
National Library	1	7 639	1 683	130	495	118
Regional libraries	27	11 867	10 117	125	3 735	2 890
Art centres	4	1 063	999	9	338	230
Universities	11	5 666	4 223	100	2 221	1 618
Specialist libraries	4	8 752	1 389	6	53	12

Table 4: Libraries with more than 200,000 library documents in 2011[52]

Libraries 2011		Publications in libraries in millions		Readers	Items loaned out	
	Number	Total	Books	Tsd.	Total	Incl. books
Total	47	32 758	18 427	218	6 201	4 558
National Library	1	7 809	1 730	13	476	75
Regional libraries	27	11 778	10 028	127	3 857	3 031
Art centres, municipal libraries	4	1 039	977	9	335	261
University libraries	11	5 762	4 296	66	1 496	1 182
Specialist libraries	4	6 369	1 396	3	36	9

50 Sayuz na biblioteknite i informacionnite rabotnitsi (Association of Employees of Libraries and Information Services), 2004. *Za neobchodimostta ot neotlozhni merki za reshavane na osnovnite problemi na bibliotekite v Balgariya* (*On the necessity of solving the problems of libraries in Bulgaria*). [online]. [viewed 21.02.2012]. Available from: http://www.lib.bg/za_neob.htm (status 11.06.2007).

51 NSI. Sofia, 2009, p. 89.

The legislative framework for the operation of libraries was not laid down until 2009. Article 1 of the act read: "This Act governs the foundation, the types, the roles, the management and the financing of public libraries."[53]

With this act, the foundations were laid for the further development and operation of libraries.

3.6 Media and Current Developments

3.6.1 The Film Industry

Film industry professionals in Bulgaria were, like their counterparts in Poland, the Czech Republic and Hungary, unable to adapt to the new circumstances. In Bulgaria, filmmaking is strongly influenced by global culture. The country is in a vacuum caused by its traditional culture.

Table 5: Number of cinemas, 1990–2000[54].

1990	1991	1992	1993	1994	1995	1996	1997	1998	1999	2000
2,174	979	383	270	247	232	219	216	205	191	179

Table 6: Number of cinemas, 2003–2012[55]

	2003	2006	2007	2008	2009	2010	2011	2012
Number of cinemas	149	66	62	57	56	42	43	41
In towns					52	42	42	40
In villages					4	-	1	1
Showings/hours					173 140	20 727.5	25 519	272 400
In towns					172 120	20 727.5	25 418.3	241 883
In villages					1 020	-	1 007	817
Visitors in tsd.	3.531	2.580	2.631	2.429	3.041	4.157	4.649	4.257
In towns					3.029	4.157	4.636	4 248
In villages					12	-	12	8
Average no. of showings per cinema					3 091.8	4 935.1	5 934.7	5 919.5
Average no. of visitors per cinema					54 300	98 900	108 100	103 800
Average audience figures per film					17 600	20 100	18 200	17 500

52 NSI. [online]. [viewed 11.12.2012]. Available from: http://www.nsi.bg/otrasalen.php?otr=34&a1=1497&a2=1498#cont

53 Zakon za obshtestvenite biblioteki (Public Libraries Act). Law Gazette 42, 23 December 2010.

54 President's office. *Ikonomicheski doklad za prezidenta-2007, Balgariya: sotsialni predizvikatelstva i evro- in- tegratsiya* (*Economic report to the President 2007, Bulgaria: Social Challenges and Euro-integration*). Sofia, 2007, p. 128.

In the period 1990 to 2010, the number of cinemas in Bulgaria fell, in keeping with the Europe-wide trend. In 2008, the number had fallen by a factor of 2.6 compared to 2003. In 2008, the number of cinemagoers fell by 202,000 compared to the previous year, which equates to 7.7%, while ticket receipts rose by BGN 2.6 million, or 24.2%.

After 1989, the film industry received no more state support. In consequence, 80% of film industry professionals are unemployed.[56]

In 1991, the National Film Centre was founded as a mediator between the state, politics and cinemas. The state monopoly was abolished. Apart from introducing market principles and criteria, the Centre's objective was to create, at the same time, possible ways of obtaining subsidies to safeguard future productions. Thanks to the reform of the film industry, the number of companies working in the sector grew from 44 in 1997 to 86 in 2011.[57]

The situation of the state film studio is also deteriorating more and more. The number of feature films produced by the studio fell from 21 in 1985 to 7 in 1995.[58] From 1997, cinemas were privatized and quickly converted into shops, amusement arcades or chemists'.

To prevent the Bulgarian industry's being left behind by its European counterparts, the state offers subsidies amounting to 25% of cinema receipts for international co-productions in which Bulgarian film professionals are involved. These subsidies can amount to a maximum of 50% of the total production costs. Under the provisions of the Film Industry Act, cinemas with a small seating capacity can apply for state funds. State funding of the production of Bulgarian films amounts to not less than 30% of production costs, and a not unimpressive 80% of the films' budgets.[59]

Boyana Film was the biggest film studio in the entire Balkan region.[60]

The economic crisis from 1994 to 1998 also affected the number of people going to the cinema, which fell by 30%.

Until 1989, 90% of all films shown came from the Soviet Union. Since 1990,

55 NSI, Sofia 2009, p. 85. *Yearbook 2010.* Sofia, 2011, p. 433. [online]. Available from http://www.nsi.bg/otrasalen.php?otr=34&a1=1497&a2=1498#cont [viewed 11.12.2012] and from http://www.nsi.bg/otrasal.php?otr=24&a1=644&a2=645#cont [viewed 30.06.2013].

56 Tomova, B. and Andreeva, D. Balgarskata filmova industriya v usloviata na transformatia (The Bulgarian film industry during the transformation process). Sofia: Observatoriya po ikonomika na kulturata (Observatory of Cultural Economics), 2007, p. 2.

57 Ibid.

58 Koprinarov, L. *Balgarskata kulturna politika 1990–1995* (*Bulgarian Cultural Policy, 1990–1995*). Sofia: Institute of Culturology, 1996, p. 143.

59 Film Industry Act, 2007. Law Gazette 98, Section 5.

60 Dimitrova, G., 2005. *Boyana veche ne e studioto na Balkanite (Boyana is no longer the studio of the Balkans*). [online]. In: *Kultur*, 6, 18.02.2005. [viewed 20.02.2012]. Available from: http://www.kultura.bg/bg/article/view/10660

American movies have had an almost equal share at Bulgarian cinemas as Russian ones.

The Ministry of Culture's film industry bill of 2001 guarantees state funding. The state declares itself willing to support five feature films, ten documentary films and 120 animated films per year, and to allot 10% of the national television company's budget to the Bulgarian film industry. This measure was intended to place Bulgarian film production on a stable financial footing.[61]

The act, when passed, worded this as follows: Annual subsidy for the company of an amount based on the average budgets of the previous year for up to seven feature films, fourteen full-length documentaries and 160 minutes of animated film.

Since 1992, Bulgaria has been a member of Eurimages. So far, more than thirty productions with Bulgarian involvement have been supported by this fund. Furthermore, Bulgaria is working with its neighbouring countries Greece, Turkey, Serbia, Macedonia and Romania. Chronology:

- In 1996, the National Film Centre issued grants of USD 260,000 – thus reaching rock bottom.
- In 2001, subsidies paid out by the Bulgarian National Centre for Film amounted to USD 1.26 million.
- In 2002, these subsidies amounted to USD 1,080,000.
- In 2001, the average amount granted for a feature film was USD 500,000.[62]
- In 2005, a new marketing strategy was launched in association with the newspaper *24 Chasa* to increase the popularity of Bulgarian films.
- In 2006, the newspaper *Capital* started a similar venture.

In Bulgaria, three major international film festivals are held:

- Sofia International Film Festival
- Festival of European Co-productions, Sofia
- Love is Folly Festival, Varna

France, Germany and the USA are the principal partners on co-productions.

Table 7: Films Produced 1997-2012[63].

Films produced	1997	1998	1999	2000	2003	2012
	44	32	88	79	86	111
TV films	26	15	75	62	76	80
Feature-length films	9	6	8	13	12	–
Short and medium-length films	35	26	80	66	74	80

61 Film Industry Act, 2007. Glava treta Finansirane (Law pertaining to the third funding). State Gazette 98, 27 November 2007.

62 [online]. news.bg, 13.07.2006.

In 2008, ninety-one films (feature films, short films and medium-length films) were produced. Compared to 2007, the number of films produced rose by a factor of 1.3 and the number of feature films fell by five.

The proportion of films produced for the cinema in 2008 accounted for 16.5% of all films produced. Compared to the previous year, this represents an increase of 0.8%.

The biggest change for cinema in the last ten years is the change in the system of state funding. Funding is not granted solely to the necessary infrastructure, but also the implementation of film projects. This means that independent producers now have the same opportunities as the former filmmaking monopoly to participate in the production of films.

The efforts undertaken aim to create a film industry capable of establishing its own domestic market and then gradually becoming integrated in the pan-European criteria, structures and market for audiovisual products.

The law on the film industry passed in 2003 governs the relationships connected to the production, distribution and showing of films in Bulgaria as well as the creation of conditions for its development and regulates state funding of the Bulgarian film industry.

The priorities of state policy laid down in the law are as follows:

- the right of the general public to enjoy free access to various forms of cinematic art
- protection of the rights and interests of cinema audiences
- support of new talents and young writers working in the cinematic sector
- presentation of Bulgarian cinema in the country itself and abroad
- creation of conditions for foreign film productions in the country.

An executive agency, the National Film Centre of the Ministry of Culture is founded with advisory and specialist bodies:

- the National Film Council draws up a national programme for the development of the film industry and suggests it to the Minister, lobbies for the amount of state funds needed for productions and proposes an annual quota for the production of Bulgarian debut films;
- the National Arts Commission, consisting of nine members, discusses film projects and puts them forward for state support.

The National Film Centre is state-funded and subject to the jurisdiction of the Ministry of Culture. It performs the following tasks:

- supporting the development, distribution and showing of Bulgarian films in the country itself and abroad
- developing laws relating to the film industry

[63] NSI *Yearbook 2005*. [viewed 04.06.2013]. Available from: http://www.nsi.bg/otrasal.php?otr=24&a1=648&a2=649#cont. Sofia, 2005, p. 448.

– maintaining the archives.

Additionally, the National Film Centre offers free guidance and specialist assistance to:

– the National Film Council
– the National Committee for the Arts
– the National Board of Classification
– the National Technical Committee
– the Finance Committee for subsidies from the national budget, the body responsible for deciding on the financing of film projects.

The National Commission for the Issue of Film Categories suggests a category to the agency's executive director for every film slated for distribution or showing in Bulgaria.

The level of financial support for projects is at least 30% of the average budget for films of this kind in the previous year and no more than 80% of the submitted project's budget.[64]

The act contains detailed directives for supporting the showing and for distributing Bulgarian films and films co-produced with European countries and countries with which Bulgaria has signed agreements pertaining to the film sector.

The discussions organized in 2008 by Sofia Press on Bulgarian cinematography tried to answer the questions relating to Bulgarian cinema. In this connection, Professor Alexander Grozev, director of the National Film Centre said: "Filmmaking in our country is not yet an industry; it is a craft. The Bulgarian cinema lives within the territorial boundaries of our country. (…) To date, we have managed to sell precisely two films abroad – to Poland … "[65]

In his view, the main reason for the collapse of Bulgarian cinema after 1990 is the lack of distribution channels.

"Because after the end of communist rule, Bulgarian cinema disappeared – literally. Bulgarian cinema was robbed of many things, most importantly of its means of subsistence, the material basis was destroyed for a few years. We have certainly experienced one or two odd things, as when not a single Bulgarian film appeared in the space of a calendar year and filmmaking was a question of personal outlook, if not obstinacy. Because it is not normal that an artist carries the idea for a work inside for six, seven, eight years and is not in a position to bring it to fruition. Fortunately, four years ago (2003) the Film Industry Act was passed and provided a legal basis for the development of the film industry in our country. In the last three years, cinema has begun to breathe, to live. Last year at the National Film Festival seven new premieres were shown (…) Currently, shooting is under way on twelve new feature films. A whole generation has been given the opportunity to find complete expression, and last year Bulgarian cinema took shape.

64 Zakon za filmovata industriya (Film Industry Act), 02.12.2003.

65 Grozev, A. *Praveneto na kino u nas vse oshte ne e industriya* (*Filmmaking is not yet an industry in our country*). [online]. In: News.bg [viewed 19.02.2012]. Available from: http://news.ibox.bg/news/id_271135103 (status 25.07.2008)

"But another generation is emerging – those young people who only recently passed their school-leaving exams and I place all my hopes in them because they are equipped with a new way of perceiving the world, supply an entirely new perspective and consequently will contribute to bringing about changes in Bulgarian cinema. Several years ago, the main topic was the transition, this painful transition, looking back into the past and simultaneously (feeling) dissatisfaction with the present. But already there is serious interest in the psychological problems of the modern-day person. The individual has already reacted to the fact that the world has opened its eyes. It is literally possible to communicate with the whole world. These are all existential topics facing the new generations of filmmakers and I am expecting several interesting films over the coming years."[66]

Georgi Cholakov, chairman of the National Film Council, expressed the view that distribution is a very serious problem: "Legislators have laid down a specific number of quotas for Bulgarian and European films which are simply being ignored. Before 1989, Bulgarian directors did not need to think about the market. They concentrated on the audience (...)"[67]

And according to Alexander Donev, film critic and head of the Department of Film, Advertising and Show Business at the New Bulgarian University, the state has no interest in enabling audiences to see Bulgarian films: "There is far too little money for making films in Bulgaria, but even less is available for advertising them."[68]

Table 8: Subsidies applied for and granted for the National Film Centre in the budget of the Ministry of Culture, figures in BGN[69].

Year	Subsidies applied for	Subsidies granted	Difference
2005	7 266 046	6 200 000	– 1 066 046
2006	8 041 733	6 200 000	– 1 841 733
2007	8 234 842	6 600 000	– 1 634 842
2008	10 237 812	10 900 000	+ 662 188
2009	16 101 968	16 000 000	– 101 968
2010	19 000 000	8 100 100	– 10 900 000
Total:			– 14 882 401

This is further evidence of the fact that the formula used for calculating the subsidies (which was not part of the Film Industry Act) was not adhered to, and

66 Ilieva, S. and Kolev, P. In: *Bulgarian Diplomatic Review*. [online]. Available from: http://www.diplomatic-bg.com/c2/content/view/1402/47/ (status 27.10.2009).

67 Grozev, A. *Praveneto na kino u nas vse oshe ne e industriya* (*Filmmaking is not yet an industry in our coun try*). [online]. In: News.bg [viewed 19.02.2012]. Available from: http://news.ibox.bg/news/id_271135103 (status 25.07.2008).

68 Ibid.

69 Cited in Tomova, B. and Andreeva, D. *Balgarskata filmova industriya v usloviyata na pazarna ikonomika* (*The Bulgarian film industry under the conditions of the market economy*). [online]. Observatoriya po iko- nomika na kulturata (Observatory of Cultural Economics). Sofia 2010. Available from: http://ncf.bg/wp-content/film_industry_observatory.pdf (status 07.02.2010).

as a result the film industry was deprived of BGN 14,882,401 during this period. B. Tomova and D. Andreeva write on this subject:

"Where is the solution? A solution of this kind lies in the new method stipulated by the National Film Council and the next step would be to transfer this method to the Finance Ministry and so connect the last link in the chain of decision-makers close to the Bulgarian film industry (Bulgarian cinema)."[70]

Table 9: Feature films produced in Bulgaria, 1995–2008[71]

1995	1996	1997	1998	1999	2000	2001
6	7	3	3	2	4	3
2002	2003	2004	2005	2006	2007	2008
3	3	7	5	7	5	5

Table 10: Feature films produced in Bulgaria, 2011[72]

		Films produced in 2011							
					Television				
					Total		Series		
Total	Total	Video films	Cinema		Television films	Number	Episodes	Other	Cost in BGN
	91	75	16	72	65	7	117	3	22 515.8
Full-length	21	10	11	9	8	1	22	1	12 846.5
Feature films	14	3	11	3	2	1	22	-	12 398.1
Documentary films	7	7	-	6	6	-	-	1	448.4
Short films	70	65	5	63	57	6	95	2	9 669.2
Feature films	7	6	1	6	-	6	95	-	8 360.3
Documentary films	54	54	-	53	53	-	-	1	815
Animated films	8	4	4	4	4	-	-	-	493.3
Others	1	1	-	-	-	-	-	1	0.53

3.6.2 Television and Radio

The development of the radio and television sector in Bulgaria has been characterized in recent years by the predominance of economic interests and the media

70 Ministry of Culture, statement pertaining to state cultural institutions' success in meeting certain figures in specific artistic genres as of 31.12.2012 . [online]. [viewed 28.05.2013]. Available from: http://mc.government.bg/page.php?p=58&s=81&sp=415&t=85&z=0

71 Cited in Tomova, B. and Andreeva, D., 2007. *The European Cinema Yearbook 2007.*

72 NSI. [online]. Available from: http://www.nsi.bg/otrasalen.php?otr=34&a1=1497&a2=1498#cont (status 11.12.2012).

presence of the ruling political parties while initiatives for legislation and decisions have remained in the background. The setting-up of funds to finance public service broadcasters and the regulative body was provided for in the Radio and Television Act passed in 1998. The fund has still not come into effect due to the absence of a system for collecting the licence fees that, under the 1998 act, households are obliged to pay.

"Bulgaria has one public TV station: *Chanel 1*. It has few viewers and suffers from a lack of technical resources that prevents it from competing with the two main commercial TV channels: *Nova TV*, owned by the Modern Times Group (MTG) and *BTV* (owned by Rupert Murdoch's News International). The Economedi group launched a new channel, *Replay TV* (*RE:TV*), in late 2008."[73]

Once again, diversity of information and investigative journalism in Bulgaria are under serious threat. That is the conclusion reached by the report published by Reporters Without Borders on the situation of press freedom in the southeast European country two years after it joined the EU in January 2007.[74]

In the Reports Without Borders press freedom index for 2008, Bulgaria was ranked 59th out of 173 countries, lower than any other member of the European Union. Organized crime and various forms of pressure exerted on the media by politicians and business circles are, according to the report, the main reasons for Bulgaria's negative showing with regard to freedom of speech.

According to the report, the press freedom situation worsened considerably in the two previous years (2006 and 2007). Mafia-like groups increased their influence on the media. Several journalists had already capitulated and begun to censor themselves. Others, though, were able to resist the pressure exerted by political and business lobbies. Bulgaria emerged from more than four decades of centralized news control and censorship when Todor Zhivkov's Soviet regime collapsed in 1989. Twenty years later, the country has many national and regional publications. *Trud* and *24 Chasa* are the two most popular and widely distributed dailies. *Sega* is growing in importance but faces competition from other newspapers such as the daily *Dnevnik* and the weekly *Capital*. The other newspapers are tabloids similar to those in Germany and the United Kingdom. *Express*, *Monitor* and *Politika* are the most widely read. Free newspapers such as *19 Minuti* and *Za Grada* are beginning to appear in Sofia.[75]

---

73 Basille O., 2009. *Resignation or resistance, Bulgaria's embattled press hesitates.* [online]. Reporters Without Borders, For Press Freedom, Bulgaria. Available from: http://www.rsf.org/IMG/pdf/rsf_rep_bulgaria_en.pdf (status 05.02.2009)

74 Ibid.

75 Indzhev I., 2009. *Zapochva li jurnalisticheski bunt sreshtu tiraniyata v mediite?* (*Are journalists starting to oppose the tyranny in the media*?). [online]. Available from: www.ivo.bg (status 19.11.2009). Parliament. Da vdignem zavesata (Commission for the records of former employees of the Bulgarian Peo- ple's Army's secret service and intelligence service). [online]. [viewed 26.01.2012]. Available from: http://www.comdos.bg

Reporters Without Borders see that the opening of the communist-era archives, approved in 2006 to facilitate entry into the EU, showed that the Bulgarian political class is largely comprised of former officials and heirs of the Zhivkov regime. In September 2008, the commission ended its work.[76] The development of the radio and television sector in Bulgaria has been characterized in recent years by the predominance of economic interests and the media presence of the ruling political parties.

Changes in legislation on radio and television in 2005 further complicated the implementation of the fund for radio and television and put it back until the end of 2008, after which there were still no signs that it would come into effect. The fund, and the collection of licence fees from households, was intended to facilitate financing and release resources that the Ministry of Culture could then use for artistic projects.[77]

The solution to this problem partly entails the end of the continually increasing subsidies from the national budget which represent the most important source of funds for these institutions. Since it was passed, the Radio and Television Act has been amended several times, most probably to postpone the commencement of the fund's effectivity. After the media community had tried to reach a consensus on a new law for radio and television in 2004 and 2005, which was redrafted several times causing the pressure exerted by media professionals in this regard to diminish, a paradoxical situation emerged: the driving force behind the legislative procedure is the desire to be represented by the media proprietors' business interests.[78]

In 2006, two commissions were set up and tasked with supervising conformity with the code of ethics on the part of the media in Bulgaria.

The two most important changes in the Bulgarian media sector in the years 2005 to 2008 were the reintroduction of the approval procedure and the introduction of a system of self-regulation for the Bulgarian media. The media began to work with well-managed business structures which allowed them greater editorial autonomy. Unlimited access to international news led to an improvement in the quality of the content produced by media professionals, and the sector enjoyed continuous growth. The business interests of the media proprietors and en-

---

76 Deliyska, A., 2008. *Koristta izyade glavite na jurnalistite agenti* (*The minds of the journalist agents were consumed by self-interest*). [online]. Interview with Metodi Andreev. *Novinar* magazine, 03.12.2008. [viewed 22.02.2012]. Available from: http://novinar.bg/news/metodi-andreev-koristta-iziade-glavite-na-zhurnalistite-agenti_MjgxNzs0MQ==.html

77 State Gazette no. 96, Radio i Televiziya (Radio and Television), Section 98, 07.11.2008. Zakon za radioto i televiziyata (Radio and Television Act), 2011. Law Gazettes 133 and 28, 05.04.2011.

78 Strategiya za razvitie na radio- i televisionnata deinost chrez nasemno radioraspraskvane (Resolution of the National Assembly of the Republic of Bulgaria of 28 September 2005 relating to television and radio). [online]. State Gazette 82, 14 Oct 2005. Effective from 1 Jan 2006. Available from: http://www.cem.bg/r.php?sitemap_id=100 (status 14.08.2010).

trepreneurs often compromise the independence of news reporting, while editors and reporters tend to censor themselves as a means of self-preservation.

In the commercial media, the lack of transparency in the ownership structure at state level was never considered a serious matter, which explains where their capital comes from. The law allowed a concentration of the media market in the hands of a few groups and consequently insufficient demarcation when consolidating the property.

Nearly half of the funds come from the Ministry of Culture's culture fund for national radio and television stations. This is to the detriment of the arts. One example of this is the percentage of funds assigned to culture by the Ministry of Culture for the year 2003.

Table 11: Expenditure on Culture 1997–2008

Expenditure	1997	A	1998	A	1999	A	2000	A	2001	A	2002	A
BNTV	15.53	1.29	20.63	1.01	50.72	1.69	29.67	1.08	65.80	2.64	60.03	1.43
BN Radio	14.36		19.04		21.22		23.90		41.03		33.94	
Culture Ministry	23.14		39.09		42.68		49.68		40.40		65.70	

Expenditure	2003	A	2004	A	2005	A	2006	A	2007	A	2008	A	Increase
BNTV	82.57	2.39	66.07	2.27	67.80	1.36	72.20	1.69	68.00	1.25	94.90	1.38	15%
BN Radio	18.37		33.71		36.30		37.70		44.60		54.00		194%
Culture Ministry	42.24	B	44.01	B	76.30	B	65.10	B	90.00	B	108.10	B	156%
C	48.56	2.08	62.40	1.60	287.50	0.36	319.80	0.34	382.80	0.29	60.90	0.32	849%

Expenditure	2009	A	2010	A	2011	A	2012	A	Increase 2008–2012
BNTV	80.8		75		72.2		67.1		-30%
BN Radio	53.7	1.13	51.3	1.21	51.4	1.05	42.1	0.93	-22%
Culture Ministry	119.5	B	104.2	B	117.3	B	117.9	B	+ 9%
C	440.5	0.31	403	0.31	409.8	0.3	*	*	*

A: Share BNTV + BNR of Culture Ministry expenditure

B: Share BNTV + BNR of total expenditure on culture

C: Total expenditure on culture in Finance Ministry's Final Report

Acceptance of a strategy for radio and television stations allowed the restoration of the approval procedure in 2003. The strategy, developed by the two media regulators CEM and KRS, was presented to Parliament in 2003 and voted in in 2005.[79]

In 2006, the situation was made even more complicated by the inadequate regulatory parameters, the limited frequency range and the impossibility of collecting radio and television licensing fees.

The general economic and social development of the country after 2006 supported the sustainable development of the Bulgarian media. Following amendment of Bulgarian legislation, which mirrors the provisions of the EU Treaty of 01.01.2007, foreigners and foreign companies were able to be directly involved in issuing licences.

Cable television coverage increased slightly in 2006 to 61.3% of households compared to 58.4% in 2004. The use of satellite signals showed a faster increase, from 8% of households in 2004 to 9% in 2006. In 2006, approximately 30% of households were still watching terrestrial analogue television.[80]

The national channels are joined by Chanel 1 of Bulgaria National Television and the commercial broadcasters bTV and NTV. The other four terrestrial channels are regional channels broadcast by BNTV in Varna, Ruse, Plovdiv and Blagoevgrad.

In 2008, there were 119 licensed television broadcasters.

Table 12: Number of television broadcasters 1997–2008[81].

	1997	*1998*	*1998*	*2000*	*2003*
Number	30	31	32	86	98
Hours of programming	261 816	506 698	177 760	395 369	498 091

	2006	*2008*	*2009*	*2010*	*2012*
Number	102	119	113	100	114
Hours of programming	599 135	747 036	694 779	660 775	732 731

[79] Zacharieva, J. Litsenzirane i registratsiya na radio i televizionnite operatori (Licensing and registration of radio and television broadcasters). Balgarska mediina koalitsiya (Bulgarian Media Coalition). Sofia, 2006, p. 28.

[80] NSI. Sofia, 2009, p. 91. *Yearbook 2005*, Sofia, p. 454. * Financing of the media regulators (Natsionalen savet za radio i televiziya) was included in the Final Parliamentary Report for 1999 and 2000. Subsequently, and despite its size and importance, the body was not included again until 2008. In 1999, the regulators' budget was BGN 329,227; in 2000 it was BGN 500.3 tsd.; cf. Narodno Sabranie (parliament). Otchet za sa ispalnenieto na byudzheta na Republika Balgariya za 1999, p. 6; Narodno Sabranie, (parliament) Otchet za ispalnenieto na byudzheta na R. Balgariya za 2000, pp. 3–4.

[81] NSI. *Yearbook 2005*, p. 452. NSI. *Yearbook 2010* (2009–2011), p. 439. [online]. Available from: http://www.nsi.bg/otrasalen.php?otr=34&a1=1497&a2=1498#cont (status 11.12.2012)

Table 13: Number of radio broadcasters 2003–2008[82].

	2003	2006	2007	2008	2011	2012
Radio stations	89	95	107	114	87	87
Hours of programming	523 311	591 834	843 365	797 763	640 198	657 037

Table 14: Television programmes by genre 2000–2008[83].

	2000	2003	2006	2007	2008
Total no. of programmes	395 369	498 091	599 135	661 872	747 036
Sport, weather	25 288	31 462	46 920	41 716	53 841
Information programmes	13 068	18 412	20 846	21 025	22 873
Live broadcasts from parliament	353	116	426	564	851
Information / Entertainment	14 384	15 969	17 948	21 152	22 712
Current affairs	8 905	16 148	20 030	21 833	25 796
History	2 669	3 948	3 814	4 071	6 074
Life sciences	12 917	9 361	8 361	9 677	9 746
Educational programmes	6 831	7 690	7 874	14 866	17 651
Religious programmes	1 704	1 324	1 631	5 582	2 657
Sport programmes	20 421	12 110	20 855	27 394	28 742
Arts programmes	144 592	211 774	203 992	202 415	230 497
Feature films		119 601	113 703	107 131	124 900
TV films and video		92 173	90 289	95 284	105 597
Entertainment programmes	27 376	19 450	19 626	25 288	30 798
Music programmes	47 800	65 380	77 332	128 059	145 089
Children's programmes	12 919	14 133	11 343	1 623	14 886
Adolescents' programmes	6 560	8 510	6 110	4 933	6 801
Documentaries	11 918	15 021	15 882	26 432	25 070
Local interest	5 700	8 294	8 589	11 520	9 520
Advertising	16 698	24 300	75 061	31 786	36 361
Teleshopping		6 811	21 135	29 456	33 475
Unclassified	15 266	7 878	11 360	22 480	23 596

and from http://www.nsi.bg/otrasal.php?otr=24&a1=655&a2=656#cont (status 30.06.2013).

82 NSI 2009, p. 90. NSI, 2011. [online]. [viewed 06.01.2013]. Available from: http://www.nsi.bg/otrasal.php?otr=24&a1=650&a2=651#cont NSI, 2012. [online]. [viewed 30.06.2013]. Available from: http://www.nsi.bg/otrasal.php?otr=24&a1=650&a2=651#cont

83 NSI

The time that young people spent watching television fell, because after 2007 they turned their attention increasingly to other media such as the internet and magazines.

In 2005, a survey with semi-structured interviews was conducted on behalf of the National Culture Fund to find out the population's attitude towards consumption in the field of culture. Questions were asked about national cultural preferences and values, how often services were used, the motivation and role of education in this process. The survey was the beginning of a series of studies leading to a comprehensive examination of the cultural reality.

The first part contains the findings from 1,000 interviewees in eighty-six towns. Television is the most widely used medium, being consumed as a leisure activity by 57.4% of Bulgarians.[84]

Table 15: Opinion poll III. In your opinion, does this have cultural value?

	Yes	No	Don't know	Total
Brass band music	77.9%	11.2%	10.9%	100.0%
Pop music, folk music	9.4%	80.9%	9.7%	100.0%
Television	57.9%	31.3%	10.9%	100.0%
Radio	64.9%	23.8%	11.4%	100.0%
Video or DVD	40.8%	42.9%	16.3%	100.0%
Internet	52.5%	33.2%	14.3%	100.0%
Computer games or entertainment software	11.1%	78.9%	10.0%	100.0%
Ethnographical museums and complexes	96.9%	1.0%	2.0%	100.0%
National customs	96.2%	1.8%	2.0%	100.0%
Architecture	96.4%	1.0%	2.6%	100.0%
Natural attractions	73.1%	18.5%	8.5%	100.0%
Fashion design (clothing)	37.2%	46.6%	16.1%	100.0%
Furniture design	40.8%	40.8%	18.4%	100.0%
National dishes	52.2%	30.7%	17.1%	100.0%
Used bookstores	64.7%	14.1%	21.2%	100.0%

"Citizens' journalism" started in 2007 in Web 2.0.

Today, most media offer the chance to post comments.

There are two models for such publications: fee-based internet platforms, and free internet platforms.

Both can be described as a network system of social activity. "Citizens' journalism" may not have the resources needed to replace professional media work, but it can often add to and correct it.

[84] Tomova, B. Gledaneto na televiziya e nai-masovoto natsionalno zanimanie (Television is the most popular leisure activity). In: *Informatsionen Byuletin Kultura* N1. Sofia, 2005, p. 5.

Another important element of the media sector's development after 2006 is the constantly dynamic development of the internet and the broadcast of programmes on it which enables many Bulgarians to view national television channels.

The question of whether the large number of television channels and their continuing growth offers greater variety and quality to Bulgarian viewers remains unanswered.

Table 16: Main channels' share of viewers as a percentage, 2004–2006.[85]

ÒV	2004	2005	2006
bTV	36.5	37.8	37.5
Nova TV	18.8	27.1	21.9
Kanal 1	26.6	19.5	19.8
Planet	2.5	3.6	3.2
Diema+	3.5	3.3	2.7
Fox Life	n/a	n/a	1.8
Skat	n/a	n/a	1.6
Eurocom	1.9	1.5	1.1
Others	8.2	10.8	10.4

The "Radio and Television" Fund was set up under the provisions of the Radio and Television Act. The funds granted as support should be composed of the following payments: annual licence and registration fees for radio and television, interest accruing on the capital already in the fund and monthly fees for television and radio.

The National Media Council decides on the support granted to concepts of importance to the nation that are linked on the one hand to the introduction of new technologies in BNT and BNR, and on the other, to important cultural education projects.

The Radio and Television Act also covers channels' ratings. At least 50% of the annual broadcasting schedule must consist of European and Bulgarian programmes, with the exception of news broadcasts and advertising. Bulgarian National Television is obliged to allocate 10% of its budget to Bulgarian films. The "Financing" section of the act relating to BNR and BNT stipulated that from 2003 subscriptions should account for 50% of the budget. However, this is still not the case. The fees payable for radio and television were to amount to 0.6% of the consumer's monthly salary.[86] The full wording of the section pertaining to the financing of radio and television is as follows:

---

85 IP International Marketing Committee, Television. International Key Facts, October 2006. Luxembourg, 2006, p. 101. IP International Marketing Committee, Television. International Key Facts, October 2007. Luxembourg, 2007, p. 105.

86 Zakon za radio i televiziya (Radio and Television Act), 2007. Law Gazette 41, § 44 (1). Section 4, Financing of BNR and BNTV. § 70.

"Bulgarian National Television receives a subsidy from the state budget for the preparation, development and dissemination of national and regional programmes. The subsidy will be calculated on the basis of the hours of programming and require the approval of the Council of Ministers. BNTV receives confirmation from the Ministry of Finance for subsidies granted for specific purposes. Any excess receipts will be included in the balance at the end of the year and offset against expenditure. The balance will be deducted from the budget for the following year pursuant to § 70 Item 6 of the Television and Radio Act."[87]

Although, in theory, state subsidy is a risky form of funding since it can compromise the independence of public service broadcasters, it is currently the only way of ensuring their survival. The government was reluctant to introduce licence fees for radio and television, fearing a loss of popularity since they would be regarded as a kind of additional tax.

Under the provisions of the 2008 State Budget Act, state subsidies for BNT amounted to EUR 34.1 million. This sum includes the funds required to produce nearly 22,000 hours of programming on Chanel 1, BNTV's regional stations and Bulgaria's satellite TV channel.[88]

Table 17: Output of Bulgarian National Television, 2005.[89]

Genre	Number of hours	Percentage of total programming
Fiction	3 404	45.1
News and information	1 636	21.6
Entertainment	1 048	13.9
Arts/science/culture	475	6.3
Sports	456	6.0
Promos	404	5.3
Advertising	81	1.1
Other	48	0.7
Music	0	0
Total	7 552	100

The Act was also intended to give commercial operators the chance to apply for public funds for the production of programmes with a public character along

87 Smetna Palata (Audit Office) ed. *Doklad za rezultatite ot isvarsheniya odit na finansovoto upravlenie na byudzheta i imushtestvoto na Balgarskata natsionalna televiziya, Nr. 1000000805*, 2.06.2006 (*Report on the findings of the Audit Office inspection of the management of the budget and assets of Bulgarian National Television, no. 1000000805*, 02.06.2006), 2006, p. 2.

88 Ministry of Finance. Doklad po zakona za darzhavniya byudzhet, byudzhet na ustoichivost i razvitie, 2008 (Report for the State Budget Act on the implementation of the state budget of the Republic of Bulgaria 2008), [online]. Available from: http://www.minfin.bg/bg/page/516) (status 05.02.2011).

89 European Audiovisual Observatory. *Yearbook 2007. Film, Television and Video in Europe No. 1. Television in 36 European Countries*. Strasbourg, 2007, p. 34.

with public service networks and to provide incentives for them so that they would develop a stronger interest in producing more programmes with social relevance.

The concentration of the media continues since there are, as mentioned above, no restrictions under law. However, from 2005 to 2006 a discussion took place in the Commission for the Protection of Competition (KZK) that came out in favour of a concentration of ownership in all media sectors. Chomsky reminds us of what a media concentration can lead to:

> "In this respect, the United States represents the form towards which capitalist democracy is tending; related tendencies include the progressive elimination of unions and other popular organizations that interfere with private power."[90]

One of the biggest problems that Bulgarian society has been unable to solve and that dominates the whole period of the transition is political pressure and interference in the work of electronic media.

In 2004, the reality TV format, including programmes such as *Big Brother* on Nova TV, appeared for the first time and aroused great interest, particularly among young viewers. The success of *Big Brother* encouraged the station to produce two further series of the show. In 2006, bTV followed suit with the reality shows *Survivor* and *VIP Brother*.

> "There is no conspiracy behind *Big Brother*. There are commercial interests. This interest is callous, but extremely adept at identifying particular media niches that allow profits to be made. No one is forced at gunpoint to watch *Big Brother*. But people do so, regardless of the fact that they have another eighty or a hundred channels that they could watch. It would be easy to claim that they are misguided, uneducated voyeurs, victims of a hidden political agenda aiming to keep them far away from real life. But it is obvious that such explanations do not work. They have become clichés that betray our inability to understand the appeal of such programmes. The first series was broadcast in the Netherlands in 1999. It evolves into a media spectacle uniting TV, internet and other media to which viewers leap and use mobiles to cast their votes. All this turns *Big Brother* into a subject that many people can discuss simultaneously. And what is more important is that these people are united by a decision-making procedure. A community is created which is closer than that of a standard TV broadcast because it is based on participation (...)"[91]

TV formats of this kind offer viewers the chance to empathize through personalized participation and a series of choices in which they are involved. Added to this are competitive elements and games woven into the programme content that support the claim to authenticity. Viewers are given the opportunity to gain access to publicity – the social component, to conduct experiments, along with the media, into what constitutes a community that knows it is sharing the same emotions and is part of a democratic administrative procedure outside the political context.

---

[90] Chomsky N. *Necessary Illusions*. Boston, Mass.: South End Press, 1989, p. 21.

[91] Spasov, O. Vreme e za pogled otvad Web 2.0 (It is time to look outside Web 2.0). [online]. In: *Kultur* 1. [viewed 19.02.2012]. Available from: http://www.kultura.bg/bg/article/view/13688

Table 18: Media spending in Bulgaria as a percentage, 2003–2006.[92]

Medium	2003	2004	2005	2006
TV	70.0	68.1	67.9	70.8
Printed media	22.6	25.2	21.7	19.2
Radio	7.2	6.4	4.7	4.6
Internet	0.2	0.3	0.7	1.3
Others				
Total spending on advertising	193	210	251	320

Overall, the programmes of the national television channels in Bulgaria do not offer a wide choice. This is especially true for young people since they primarily use the internet to obtain information about events that interest them such as films and music events.

During the entire period under review, no television broadcaster began operating that specialized first and foremost in programme formats providing information solely on cultural and arts events in Bulgaria.

3.7 The Creative Industry in Relation to the Copyright Industry

In Bulgaria too, the creative industry is a new economic sector whose companies are profit-oriented enterprises working with artistic and cultural commodities. In 2004, an EU-funded in-depth study of the creative industry's economic potential was presented in Vienna. A key component of this industry is the copyright industry. In Bulgaria, a survey was conducted on the government initiative that used the methods of and was financially supported by the World Intellectual Property Organization and produced the first-ever analysis of the industries' contribution to the Bulgarian economy on the basis of copyright law. In 2005, the economic sector in Bulgaria that is based on copyright law and related industrial property rights produced commodities of a value of BGN 4.2 thousand million and created added value of BGN 1.2 thousand million. The most important branches of industry protected by copyright produce the largest economic contribution in the sector – a gross output of EUR 2.5 thousand million and added value of EUR 672 million and are an industry in every sense of the term. Measured against GDP, the total share of the copyright-protected branches amounts to 2.8% and that of basic industry to 1.6%. The conclusion reached by the study's authors is that compared to other sectors of the Bulgarian economy the copyright industries (API) are

[92] Kavrakova, A. Television across Europe: Follow-up reports 2008: Bulgaria. [online]. In: *Television across Europe. More channels less independence*. Monitoring Report of the OSI/EU Monitoring and Advocacy Program. Budapest/New York: Open Society Institute, 2008, p. 138. Available from: https://www.opensocietyfoundations.org/sites/default/files/1fullpublication_20080429_0.pdf (status 12.01.2016)

a small but significant sector. Taking growth rates as an indicator, the copyright industries even emerge as those that have developed fastest. In 2005, their gross value, calculated according to the index of current prices, had risen by 50% since 2003, outstripping overall economic growth by 11.5%. In the next few years the copyright branches could, with appropriate public support, become a motor of economic growth.

In 2005, approximately 100,000 people were employed in activities connected to copyright and associated industrial property rights in Bulgaria. Approximately 55,000 people work in the cultural industry alone; this figure represents over half the total number of employees in this sector.[93]

The two biggest copyright industries are publishing and printing, and software and databases; in 2005, they contributed 0.51% to the country's gross value added. The highest value added per employee was achieved in the radio and television industry.

In 2003, film was part of an economic sector that grew by 225% along with areas such as theatre, music and opera, visual and graphic arts, and photography. After only three years, the film branch left this category, subsequently becoming an industry in every sense of the word.

The second-fastest-growing sector is software and databases, with a growth rate of 93%. Its basic activity (web design and development of original software according to customers' specifications) increased by 108%.[94]

The third-fastest-growing sector is architecture, which partly falls in the copyright businesses category.

In the period under review, added value grew by 81%, gross domestic product by 23% and employment by 16%. In real terms, this sector contributes BGN 15.3 million. The sector's importance should not be underestimated since it represents hidden potential that is not recorded in the national statistics owing to several peculiarities.

Seen in isolation, the added value of the essential "copyright companies" amounted to 2.12% of GDP in Bulgaria in 2005. It therefore outstrips the share provided by industry as a whole and approaches the share of added value provided by the hotel and restaurant sector. With the software and databases and advertising performance sectors, the seven other important branches contribute a share of 1.27% of GDP.[95]

---

93 Cholakov, I., Borisova, V. and Keskinova, D. *Ikonomicheski prinos na avtorskopravnite industrii v Balgariya, Varchu danni za perioda 2003–2005* (*Contribution to the economy of the copyright industries in Bulgaria, data for the period 2003–2005*). [online]. Sofia: Univ. Izd Stopanstvo, 2007, p. 7. [viewed 22.02.2012]. Available from: http://mc.government.bg/images/NEWS/bro6ura_wipo_02%2007%202007bg.pdf

94 Ibid.

95 Ibid., p. 9.

The increase in the number of employees in the copyright industries is three times the increase in industry overall. At the same time, subsidies in the state budget for culture in 2005 amount to only 0.72% of gross domestic product: they are only a third of the contribution to the economy of the most important copyright industries (API) and almost half the contribution of the seven sectors immediately associated with culture. These results are directly linked to state policy on the organization and administration of subsidies for cultural activities and are a further argument for their support.

3.8 Internet and Art Networks

The internet is the newest global means of communication, and it began to gain ground in Bulgaria in the 1990s.

One day before EU Commissioner Neelie Kroes visited Bulgaria on 18 September 2012, the magazine *24 Chasa* quoted her as saying, "Almost half of the Bulgarians have never used the internet."[96] According to the Bulgarian Internet Society, 46% of Bulgarians regularly used the internet in 2012 (at least once a week). This was below the then EU average of 68%. The latest survey, conducted in 2013 by the Market test institute, shows that 58.9% of the population over the age of fifteen regularly use the internet. This figure again falls short of the EU average, but only by eight percentage points. In comparison, the figure was 44.69% in 2009, so an upward trend is unmistakable. On the other hand, according to the EK's data, 46% of the population have never been on the internet at all. However, this figure is not reliable and the true figure is likely to be around 30%. The question now is why this should be. Would the structure of the population and the economic development not have widespread internet use as a logical consequence? Examination of other studies shows that Bulgaria was already leading the field for frequency of internet use as early as 2009. This is not widely known, but the explanation lies in the circumstance that the EK does not count internet connections with a speed of over 10 Mbit / second, and most people in Bulgaria have an internet connection that is faster than this. This data corroborates the conclusions of this year's report on the EU index. According to this, Bulgaria ranks first, since 85% of internet users use a connection faster than 10 Mbit / second. Close on Bulgaria's heels in second place is Portugal with 78%. According to a survey carried out by the Council of Europe, 10% of households in Bulgaria with an internet connection are connected to a fibre optic cable or local sticks. This figure puts Bulgaria in fourth place in the EU for this type of connection. In summary it can be said that the internet in Bulgaria is accessible and inexpensive.

96 *24 Chasa*. [online]. Available from: http://www.24chasa.bg/Article.asp?ArticleId=1547809, 18.09.2012 10:53 (status 07.01.2013).

Internet is available everywhere, for example via WiFi. This is not the case in every other EU country. In Greece, for instance, wireless internet is extremely rare, and in Italy WiFi use in cafés, hotels and the like even requires the provision of personal details before a password for the connection is issued. One explanation for the situation in Bulgaria could be that there are over 2,000 internet providers in the country offering a fast connection at low prices. In western European countries, the opposite is the case; there is a small number of providers offering slow connections at high prices.[97]

Table 19: Internet use in Bulgaria, 2008.

	Total	Women	Men	15–19	20–29	30–39	40–49	50–59	60–69
Internet users	44.69%	45.11%	44.26%	74.64%	59.91%	53.94%	42.06%	26.18%	11.57%
At home	35.50%	35.63%	35.37%	60.16%	48.11%	43.88%	34.03%	19.01%	7.61%
Per cent	100.00	100.00	100.00	100.00	100.00	100.00	100.00	100.00	100.00

2005 by subject	
Skype and telephone conversations	45.20%
Music MP3	44.23%
Mailbox	38.37%
Newspapers/news reports	38.00%
MP3 music downloads	36.11%
Search engines	31.94%
Others	28.20%
Weather forecast	25.09%
Sport	24.22%

2005 by subject	
Travel	23.81%
Health	23.44%
Chat	22.86%
Job search	19.20%
Television	18.92%
Online games	17.95%
Radio	17.85%
Online directories	17.29%
Erotic sites	11.74[98]

In 2008, 44.69% of the population are recorded as internet users. In practice, this figure is higher because many children under the age of fifteen are online, and that regularly. Bulgaria is top of the EU rankings for high-speed internet (over 10 Mbit / second). According to the relevant data, 46.5% of internet users in Bulgaria use a connection faster than 10 Mbit / second. Sweden comes second in this ranking with 36%.[99] According to a survey conducted by the Universities of Ox-

[97] Internet Society Bulgaria (ISOC). [online]. Available from: http://isocbg.wordpress.com/category/uncategorized/ (status 07.01.2013).

[98] Internet Society Bulgaria (ISOC Bulgaria), 2009. Palna statistika za Internet potreblenieto v Balgariya (Full statistics on internet use in Bulgaria), cited in the blog by V. Markovski, chair of ISOC Bulgaria. [online]. Available from: http://isocbg.wordpress.com/2009/ (status 16.10.2009).

[99] European Commission, European Economic and Social Committee and the Committee of the Regions. *Progress report on the Single European Electronic Communications Markets 2008.* [online]. Brussels, 2009, p. 141. [viewed 19.02.2012]. Avail-

ford and Oviedo, nine countries – South Korea, Japan, Sweden, Lithuania, Latvia, Bulgaria, the Netherlands, Denmark and Romania – have access to the quality of broadband internet necessary for future web applications such as HD internet TV which are likely to be standard in the near future. In 2008 this was only true of Japan (see the blog by Veni Markovski, chair of the Bulgarian Internet Society). The term "web portal" has no fixed definition; what all attempts to find a definition have in common is simply that such a portal is a website that tries to unite various regularly used services or to create an overview of various topics that can be accessed. Often the term is erroneously used for web applications themselves. Furthermore, a clear distinction must be made from the word "portal" as it is used in informatics. The artist Javor Gardev carried out the first examination of the internet culture scene in Bulgaria. The internet portals for culture and certain topic groups open up a new dimension in the communication of art and require in-depth documentation and research. The findings of this research can influence the future perspectives of cultural institutions. The setting-up of mini-portals can be classified as a separate art category. A network contains mini-portals that share a common theme. Together they form a larger information unit. The Bulgarian networks are relatively weak. A network generally consists of three to ten platforms. Whoever enjoys the support of an institution plays the leading role within the network. The data cited below refers only to 2008. After that year and up to 2012, the figures come from new portals for music, literature, electronic news, theatre, photography, cinema and web design and are evidence of rapid growth. Their number changes constantly. New portals are continually emerging, while others cease to exist. The three largest networks in the arts sector in Bulgaria were for music, literature and electronic periodicals.

Until 2008, the music network consisted of the following mini-portals: z-d.org, techno.orbitel.bg and tekno.cult.bg. The literature network included several important addresses: slovo.orbitel.bg, liternet.bg, litclub.dir.bg, hulite.bg etc. Electronic newspaper and magazines are numerous, with Mediapool.bg being the first Bulgarian website that analysed information. It was updated daily. It is worth mentioning that the proprietor of the information portal news.bg is the founder of the Razvitie (development) foundation, which started in 1997 and organizes a nationwide literature competition. To date, approximately four hundred novels by Bulgarian authors have been registered, one of which has already won the award for eastern European literature. The networks for Bulgarian art and their portals were created over the past few years.

able from: http://ec.europa.eu/information_society/policy/ecomm/library/communications_reports/annualreports/14th/index_en.htm

3.9 Music Networks

Much of the music network is made up of portals that specialize in techno music because this type of music has its roots in the internet. Some very influential mini-portals can be found in this sector since the representatives of these projects directly influence the music scene by also disseminating this music on the internet. A characteristic of this network is that no portal is the same as another and conscious efforts are made to avoid copying concepts. The large amount of information disseminated and the limited resources have resulted in the various mini-portals' establishing distinct identities by becoming highly specialized. They see themselves as information platforms in the music scene, lead discussions on the distribution and promotion of music and also serve as a platform on which the musicians can present themselves.

So great is the variety of portals that it is now virtually impossible to keep track. However, these portals do not exist for classical music, which typical internet users evidently do not look for.

3.10 Literature Networks

The Bulgarian literature network consists of several projects which, unlike the portals in the music network, are not specialized. This network aims to provide virtual libraries with a view to preserving and disseminating Bulgarian literature on the internet. Works by young authors, both Bulgarian and non-Bulgarian, are published online every day. This should help young authors to reach an audience even though funds are scarce.

The advantages of the portal are obvious. They allow the information to be systematically sorted and made available, so the circle of readers is larger. The portals are updated with a minimum of effort and expense. Because the works in the virtual libraries can be viewed free of charge, these web portals are extremely popular. They also provide a panel of experts who list recommended new releases. Readers themselves also have the opportunity to review texts.

Table 20: Works of literature published on the internet in a portal.

Since	2003	Month	2004	2005	2006
Nov.	10	January	627	1,728	1,785

hulite.bg is a website for literature on which the progression of published works in the genres of poetry, novels and novellas can be followed (see Table 30 above). From its inception to 2003, 114,446,907 works were read.[100] There are

[100] [online]. Available from: http://www.hulite.net/modules.php?name=Statistics (status 12.05. 2006).

many examples of literature forums. Stichove ("Poems") was started in 2004 and has since published approximately 100 million works.[101]

Other important literature portals are the *Slovoto* ("The Word") virtual library at slovo.orbitel.bg which has set itself the goal of putting all major works of Bulgarian literature online. Apart from works of classical literature, authors can publish their own work on the internet free of charge. The literature network liternet.bg has an extensive database of Bulgarian and international literature. A large number of volunteers work on this project. The portal literclub.dir.bg was launched in 1998 and could be found on the web under the name *Bodil* until 2001. To date it has served as a combination of a virtual library and an electronic magazine. Despite the small team running the portal, it provides a respectable amount of material and texts. The start page is visited by over 6,000 people per month, from eighty countries: http://dojh.hit.bg/. *Otkrovenia* was launched in 2003 and has approximately 80,000 members: http://otkrovenia.com/main.php?action=mainpage.

3.11 Visual Arts

Before 2008 there was no recognizable network in the field of visual arts. Several projects can be found at www.cult.bg. A very good and clearly laid-out site was www.imagestories.com.

3.12 Theatre

The situation for the theatre is similar to that of the visual arts. A leading website was www.triumviratus.org which presented critical articles in the fields of art and videos and had a very good textual basis.

The site www.redhouse.bg provides information on the free art scene and the debate on art and cultural policy. The site www.casting.hit.bg with information for performing artists is also part of this network. A wealth of portals supply information on a wide variety of events with dates, programmes, ways of buying tickets, details of productions and in some cases films. One example is www.neti nfo.bg, http://bpm.cult.bg. The authors of this site say:

> "We've reached our aim – we've created an image of the future, virtual palettes of galleries, animations, electronic music, and a site combining in it the qualities of a community which by the will of fate is outgrowing the ideas of its generation."

The web counter in Bulgaria provides the following figures on visitors to art and culture websites as of 20 August 2006: [102]

---

[101] [online]. Available from: http://www.stihovebg.com/stats/ (status 30.09.2011).

[102] Webcounter. [online]. [viewed 20.08.2006]. Available from: http://bfcounter.com/?vcat,year,,,,8

No.	+/-	Share	Site	Visitors	Updates	Total
1.	--	11.69%	Cinema	679	99	778
2.	-2 ↓	11.38%	Lessedra Art Gallery	661	233	894
3.	-1 ↓	9.54%	Bulgarian Photo Gallery	554	88	642
4.	+3 ↑	7.04%	Rogger Dojh - Creativity, Foolishness, Normal Literature	409	685	1,094
5.	-2 ↓	6.58%	Literature newspaper	382	65	447
6.	--	6.44%	Official website of the photographer Ivajlo	374	56	430
7.	+4 ↑	6.11%	Paintings by Hitler	355	423	778
8.	-6 ↓	5.99%	Jambol - cult	348	154	502
9.	-4 ↓	5.46%	ewigesarchiv - project by Peter Putz	317	1,008	1,325
10.	-2 ↓	5.39%	Valerys Worlds	313	122	435
11.	-2 ↓	3.75%	Literary forums	218	91	309
12.	3 ↓	2.53%	Literature of the forgotten people	147	67	214
13.	--	2.45%	cult.bg - Server for art and culture	142	103	245
14.	+3 ↑	1.39%	Marina Valčeva - Homepage	81	3	84
15.	-1 ↓	1.22%	drogacultura	71	23	94
16.	--	1.03%	Plovdiv Concert Hall and Theatre	60	24	84
17.	+12 ↑	0.74%	Young talents	43	10	53
18.	-3 ↓	0.67%	cult.bg - search	39	72	111
19.	+3 ↑	0.64%	Jewellery, bonsai, photography	37	9	46

Various art categories from photography to computer graphics to literature

No.	+/-	Share	Site	Visitors	Updates	Total
21.	-2 ↓	0.29%	Valerys Worlds	313	122	435
22.	-2 ↓	0.20%	Literary forums	218	91	309
23.	--	0.18%	Fantastic Photo Worlds. Galleries	188	17	205
24.	-3 ↓	0.14%	Literature of the forgotten people	147	67	214

25.	--	0.13%	cult.bg - Server for art and culture	142	103	245
26.	+3 ↑	0.08%	Marina Valčeva - Homepage	81	3	84
27.	-1 ↓	0.07%	drogacultura	71	23	94
28.	--	0.06%	Concert Hall and Theatre	60	24	84
29.	+12 ↑	0.04%	Young talents	43	10	53
30.	-3 ↓	0.04%	cult.bg - search	39	72	111
31.	+3 ↑	0.03%	Jewellery, bonsai, photography	37	9	46
32.	-1 ↓	0.03%	Fine Art Photo Gallery	34	6	40
33.	+4 ↑	0.03%	Official site of Christo Nikolov	33	10	43
34.	+10 ↑	0.03%	Plamen Rusev	33	4	37
35.	-2 ↓	0.03%	Deine Gobelins	32	22	54
36.	+4 ↑	0.03%	Canko Lavrenov	29	15	44
37.	-2 ↓	0.03%	Vesela Lutăkanova Publishers	29	9	38
38.	-2 ↓	0.03%	Karkelanov Photographic Studio	27	7	34
39.	-9 ↓	0.02%	cult - error	26	3	29
40.	+6 ↑	0.02%	ArtNet - Dora Slavova's virtual gallery	24	0	24

No.	+/-	Share	Site	Visitors	Updates	Total
61.	+6 ↑	0.00%	Homepage	3	0	3
62.	+8 ↑	0.00%	Drug culture questionnaire	3	0	3
63.	+5 ↑	0.00%	About Everything	3	2	5
64.	+2 ↑	0.00%	Red Wing Nest	2	2	4
65.	-2 ↓	0.00%	DiscoveryBG	2	0	2
66.	-9 ↓	0.00%	Haemus	2	0	2
67.	+2 ↑	0.00%	My photo networks	2	1	3
68.	-14 ↓	0.00%	Chemus. The magazine for Bulgarians in Hungary	2	0	2
69.	+2 ↑	0.00%	Wisdom, axioms, thoughts	2	0	2
70.	+3 ↑	0.00%	Miss Beauty on the Internet	1	1	2
71.	-21 ↓	0.00%	Literature Club	1	1	2
72.	-7 ↓	0.00%	Gobelins - Tapestry	1	2	3
73.	+1 ↑	0.00%	Art	1	2	3
74.	-2 ↓	0.00%	Broken Videos	1	0	1

124

The examples show that the literature portals are enormously popular. The table also shows that the hulite.bg portal registered 3,813,061 visitors in the space of only one year. The internet is the medium that allows art and culture to reach a huge audience.

4. THE BUDGET OF THE MINISTRY OF CULTURE

The frequent changes at the head of the Culture Ministry up to 1997 made it difficult for cultural policy to be implemented with any consistency. Although putting the blame on previous governments is a common political tactic, it cannot be completely dismissed in the face of the frequent comings and goings in the Ministry of Culture.

Table 21: Ministers of Culture in Bulgaria, 1989–2009.

Name	Tenure	Occupation
Georgi Robev	28.07.1989–21.02.1990	Conductor
Krastyo Goranov	21.02.1990–22.09.1990	Philosopher
Dimo Dimov	22.09.1990–08.11.1991	Musician
Elka Konstantinova	08.11.1991–30.10.1992	Literary expert
Marin Todorov	30.12.1992–23.06.1993	Education Ministry
Ivaylo Znepolski	23.06.1993–26.01.1995	Cultural scientist
Georgi Kostov	26.01.1995–10.06.1996	Composer
Ivan Marazov	10.06.1996–12.02.1997	Art historian
Emil Tabakov	12.02.1997–21.05.1997	Conductor
Emma Moskova	21.05.1997–25.07.2001	Art historian
Bozhidar Abrashev	25.07.2001–23.02.2005	Composer
Nina Cilova	23.02.2005–16.08.2005	Jurist
Stefan Danailov	16.08.2005–06.2009	Actor
Vezhdi Rashidov	27.06.2009–02.2013	Sculptor

Close examination reveals discrepancies between the figures cited by a confidential source in the Ministry of Culture and the total expenditure on culture cited in the final report of the Ministry of Finance and the Compendium of Cultural Policies and Trends in Europe, 12th edition. There could be a very simple and plausible reason for this. But the key question remains: What value do these figures really have? Because the data comes from different sources, it would be necessary to gather all the reports together in one report.

Table 22: Public spending on culture, 2009[1]

Level of government	Central	Regional	Municipal	Extraordinary capital allocation	Total
1998	40 461 28.29%	7.2 0.007%	49 935 45.33%	29 051.3 26.38%	110 166 100%
1999	42 679 39.66%	n/a	58 041 53.94%	6 891.1 6.40%	107 611 100%
2000	49 704 49.94%	n/a	49 375 49.60%	449.3 0.46%	99 529 100%
2001	49 812 48.91%	n/a	51 274 50.35%	754.4 0.63%	101 841 100%
2002	53 771 46.53%	n/a	60 122 52.04%	1 670.6 1.43%	115 564 100%
2003	64 936 44.98%	n/a	77 122 53.44%	2 275.8 1.58%	144 334 100%
2004	72 855 44.59%	n/a	88 224 54.01%	2 275.8 1.40%	163 356 100%
2005	89 989 45.67%	n/a	104 800 53.19%	2 247.3 1.14%	197 036 100%
2006	92 337 42.11%	n/a	125 286 57.14%	1 633.2 0.75%	219 256 100%
2007	115 053 40.23%	n/a	166 128 58.10%	4 782.5 1.67%	285 964 100%
2008	138 480 42.28%	n/a	187 476 57.25%	1 465.1 0.47%	327 422 100%
2009	120 895 39.80%	n/a	183 128 60.20%	n/a	304 024 100%

As Table 32 shows, a stable process of decentralization was under way as a continual trend from 1998. In 2009, the share of spending at central and regional budget level was 39.80% and the central levels accounted for 60.2% at municipal level. This confirms to the executive authorities that after the stabilization of the Bulgarian economy in 1997 the system of cultural funding should be decentralized. The Currency Board was introduced as an instrument for the stabilization of taxation and the economy. Although this form of funding is becoming more widespread, it nonetheless remains a constant factor in GDP. After 1999, per capita spending on culture stayed relatively stable. Some local authorities began introducing regional structures for supporting cultural projects.

[1] Council of Europe. *Compendium of Cultural Policies and Trends in Europe, 2011.*

4. THE BUDGET OF THE MINISTRY OF CULTURE

Table 23: Spending on culture by level of government 1996 and 1998.[2]

Funding level	1996		1998	
	Total spending	As a percentage	Total spending	As a percentage
Central	4 750 322	62.3	73 924 081	58.0
Regional	1 000	0.01	7 200	0.01
Municipal and others	2 877 400	37.7	49 935 800	42.0
Total	7 628 732	100	123 867 081	100

Table 24: Total spending on culture in the Final Report of the Ministry of Finance and Parliament in millions[3]

Spending	1997	1998	1999	2000	2001	2002	2003	2004	2005	2006	2007	2008
BNTV	15 525 414	20 627 246	50 716 400	29 668.4	65.8	31.9	82 570.2	66 073.8	67.8	72.2	68.0	94.9
BN Radio	14 359 887	19 036 807	21 219 810	23 897.2	29.4	40.8	18 374.7	33 712	36.3	37.7	44.6	54.0
Ministry of Culture	23 135 704	39 094 699	42 679 442	49 684.4	40.4	38.5	42 240.6	44 012.0	76.3	65.1	90.0	108.1
Culture as a budget item	*	*	*	*	*	211.1	485 56.0	508 84.1	287.5	319.8	382.8	460.9

Table 25: Total spending of the Ministry of Culture in millions, 1997–2011[4]

Year	2000	2001	2002	2003	2004	2005	2006
Receipts	10 811 234	10 369 334	9 282 462	10 263 968	11 296 485	13 212 652	14 842 454
Expenditure	49 704 427	49 812 235	53 771 503	64 936 014	72 855 669	89 989 553	92 337 002
Personnel	28 673 101	29 438 978	32 177 476	36 033 931	41 030 656	49 213 624	53 090 513
Maintenance	14 375 467	16 477 313	17 735 424	21 165 216	22 545 427	29 667 249	29 172 776
Grants	281 094	266 723	263 514	261 282	286 013	378 757	440 523
Investments	6 374 765	3 629 221	3 595 089	7 475 585	8 993 573	10 729 923	9 698 190

Year	2007	2008	2009	2010	2011
Receipts	15 448 928	19 644 927	21 122 000	17 182 981	19 728 000
Expenditure	115 053 732	138 480 910	119 500.670	104 215 050	117 370 730
Personnel	57 906 126	64 847 710	*	*	*
Maintenance	38 464 953	46 746 547	*	*	*
Grants	445 708	499 636	*	*	*
Investments	18 236 945	26 387 078	*	*	*

Unfortunately, no other or more detailed comparative analysis for this period, such as the Ministry of Culture's annual report, was available, nor were there any

2 [online]. Available from: http://www.culturalpolicies.net/web/bulgaria.php?aid=622. Ministry of Finance 1998–2009. Figures in BGN. (status 19.02.2012).

3 Parliament,. Final account of the budget of the Republic of Bulgaria, 1997, p. 6. (status 14.11.2011).

4 Ministry of Culture, Finance Department, estimate.

source citations. These would have made it possible to present a more complete and accurate picture. Reference is made to the report of the Audit Office for the year 2003 as an example of the difficulty of making comparisons.[5]

The report concluded that the financial management of budget funds and assets of the Ministry of Culture was far from satisfactory. This inadequate management prevented the fact that those in charge at the Ministry were not actually fulfilling their social-political tasks at all from coming to light. However, no more specific figures were revealed, except that the Ministry had spent a total of BGN 26,133 on flowers. It proved enormously difficult to carry out correct analyses for the theatre category in the period under review, as the Audit Office's report for 2004 shows. The management of the National Theatre was unable to explain a missing amount of BGN 459,100 from a budget of BGN 2,232,747.

Table 26: Report on the examination of the financial management of the budget of the Ivan Vazov National Theatre, 01.01.2004–30.09.2004.[6]

Indicators	Budget for 2004 as originally approved	Corrections made by the Audit Office as of 30.09.2004	Approved annual plan
Receipts in BGN	543 010		543 010
Outlay in BGN	1 773 647	459 100	2 232 747
Transfers in BGN	1 230 637	459 100	1 689 737

The report clearly showed that the final accounts relating to the implementation of the budget of the Ivan Vazov National Theatre up to 30.09.2004 as compared to the figures presented by the Ministry of Culture did not provide an accurate or clear picture of the National Theatre's financial position.

The reports of the Audit Office and the activities of the cultural missions revealed unclear and irresponsible procedures. The concept of cultural diplomacy as practised by the Bulgarian state is thrown into doubt when one considers that their missions in Moscow, Rome and Paris kept no accounts before 2006.[7] No final report of the Ministry appeared for these years, the figures were guarded like state secrets. The figures published in the following years can be regarded as a record of the limited impact that cultural policy had on political life.

5 Smetna Palata (Audit Office) ed., *Doklad za rezultatite ot izvarsheniya odit na finansovoto upravlenie na byudzheta, isvanbyudzhetnite smetki i fondove na ministerstvoto na kulturata za perioda ot 1.01.2003 do 30.09.2003* (*Report on the findings of the examination of the financial management of budget funds and accounts of the Ministry of Culture for the period 01.01.2003 to 30.09.2003*), Sofia, p. 6. [online]. Available from: http://www.bulnao.government.bg/index.php?lang=&p=archive&y=2006&id=18 (status17.02.2009).

6 Ibid.

7 Ibid. [online]. Available from: http://www.bulnao.government.bg/index.php?lang=&p=archive&y=2005&id=18 (status 17.02.2009).

Table 27: Budget of the Culture Ministry, 1997.[8]

Receipts	Expenditure	Subsidies
1 695 453	20 358 587	18 663 134

Hyperinflation meant that the budget was unrealistic and therefore provided no secure foundation for the continued existence of cultural institutions.

Bulgarian National Bank, statistics relating to the exchange rate BGN / USD

30. 09.1996: USD 1.00 = BGN 229.98
17. 12.1996: USD 1.00 = BGN 509.42
04. 06.1997: USD 1.00 = BGN 1,603.60
15. 07.1997: USD 1.00 = BGN 1,792.40
24. 07.1997: USD 1.00 = BGN 1,831.00
25. 07.1997: USD 1.00 = BGN 1,829.80

1995: Budget of the Ministry of Culture in BGN as cited in the official gazette: BGN 1,605,131 million[9]. The budget is defined as an overall figure.
1996: Budget of the Ministry of Culture in BGN as cited in the official gazette: BGN 1,005,882 million[10]. The budget is defined as an overall figure.

In absolute numbers, the subsidies have doubled, but in relation to the USD and the galloping inflation, the budget of the Ministry of Culture no longer has any real value.

Bulgarian National Bank, statistics relating to the exchange rate BGN / USD

30.09.1996: USD 1.00 = BGN 229.98
17.12.1996: USD 1.00 = BGN 509.42 (330% inflation)

A comparison of the budget of the Culture Ministry in the official journal for 1997 with the final accounts of the state budget of the Finance Ministry for the same year reveals great discrepancies.[11]

---

8 Ibid. no. 52. Sofia,1997, p. 21. The Darzhaven vestnik (State Gazette) is prepared, compiled and edited under the supervision of the Na- tional Assembly. New laws are published in it. Darzhaven vestnik was first published on 28 July 1879 and appeared from 1950 to 1962 as *Journal of the Chair of the National Assembly*. It appears every Tuesday and Friday. Additional editions are published if major events occur or urgent issues are to be resolved. The official site of the State Gazette is: http://dv.parliament.bg/DVWeb/index.faces

9 Law Gazette. Budget Project. 3, 140/90. Sofia, 1995, p. 1. Ibid. 46, Sofia, 1995, p. 4.

10 Ibid. 16, Sofia, 1996, p. 4.

11 Minsisterstvo na finansite. *Doklad za ispalnenieto na darzhavniya byudzhet na Republika Bulgariya*. Sofia. (Ministry of Finance: *Report on the implementation of the national budget of the Republic of Bulgaria for 1997*. [online]. Budget Archive. [viewed 19.02.2012]. Available from: http://www.minfin.bg/bg/page/247 (status 25.11.2010).

Table 28: Balance of the state budget of the Ministries of Culture and Finance, 1997.

Receipts	Expenditure	Subsidies
3 845 551	23 135 704	19 310 478

Table 29: Budget of the Culture Ministry, 1998.[12]

Receipts	Expenditure	Subsidies 1998
2 824 005	28 328 205	25 504 200

After 1997, the hyperinflation gradually fell, slowly returning to normal levels. Compared to the year before, subsidies rose by 37%. The discrepancies between the statements and information in *Darzhaven vestnik* and the report of the Ministry of Finance on implementation of the national budget of the Republic of Bulgaria for 1998 must be taken into account.[13]

Table 30: Balance of the state budget of the Ministries of Culture and Finance, 1998

Receipts	Expenditure	Subsidies
6 030 610	39 094 699	29 753 200

Table 31: Funding by category, 1996 and 1998[14]

Cultural activity	Total expenditure 1996	As a percentage	Total expenditure 1998	As a percentage
Museums and archives	186 506	3.3%	2 639 159	3.3%
Monuments	14 910	0.3%	216 169	0.3%
Literature		0		0
Libraries	143 276	2.6%	1 296 885	1.6%
Press		0		0
Music	209 080	3.7%	3 456 855	4.3%
Performing arts	1 093 168	19.6%	16 485 293	20.5%
Visual arts		0		0
Film / national film archive	13 745	0.2%	275 000	0.3%
Radio / TV	3 005 250	53.8%	275 000	49.8%
Socio-cultural work	215 431	3.9%	2 903 765	3.6%
Training	518 034	9.3%	6 408 019	7.9%
Administration	59 145	1.1%	4 523 748	5.6%
National arts centres	127 882	2.3%	2 249 419	2.8%

12 Law Gazette, no. 123 (1998). Sofia, p. 4.

13 Capital budget of the Bulgarian government. [online]. [viewed 25.11.2011]. Available from: http://www.minfin.bg/bg/page/247.

Table 31: Funding by category, 1996 and 1998[14]

Total	5 583 427	100	80 607 617	100

Table 32: Budget of the Culture Ministry, 1999[15]

Receipts	Expenditure	Subsidies 1999
5 480 622	39 092 078	33 611 456

In July 1999 the exchange rate between the German mark and the Bulgarian lev was fixed at BGN 1.00 = DM 1.00. From this year, the budget again appears realistic. For a long time, the Ministry of Culture had scarcely any financial resources. But this year marks the start of a period of stabilization which is reflected particularly in the Protection of Culture Act.

The section of the report on the implementation of the national budget of the Republic of Bulgaria for 1998 issued by the Finance Ministry contains different figures from those in the official gazette.[16]

Table 33: Final account of the national budget, Ministry of Culture, 1999 (based on the report of the Finance Ministry for 1999)

Receipts	Expenditure	Subsidies 1999
9 916 888	42 679 442	28 798 793

4.1 Funding by Category 2000–2008

The development of the Culture Ministry's budget from 2000 to 2008 reflects different tendencies in the distribution of funds according to category.[17] A general trend to be noted is the overall increase in the Ministry's budget, both for receipts and expenditure.

In the year 2000, expenditure amounted to BGN 49,704,427 and then gradually increased until it reached BGN 138,480,981 in 2008. This represents an increase of 278%. Over the same period, however, receipts only rose by 181.7%, significantly more slowly. This means that the Ministry spent more, or had more funds available for the development of the individual categories, even though there

[14] Dossier Bitsritsa-BG, Cultural Policy. Seminar, 18–20 January 2001. European Culture Foundation, Amster- dam, European-Bulgarian Culture Centre, Open Society Foundation, p. 42.

[15] Law Gazette, no. 155 (1999). Sofia, p. 21.

[16] Minsisterstvo na finansite. *Doklad za ispalnenieto na darzhavniya byudzhet na Republika Bulgariya.* Sofia, (Ministry of Finance. *Report on the implementation of the national budget of the Republic of Bulgaria for 1999.* [online]. Available from: http://www.minfin.bg/bg/page/247 (status 25.11.2010).

[17] Ministry of Finance. Budget 2000–2008. [online]. Available from: http://www.minfin.bg/bg/page/247 (status 05.10.2011).

was a shortfall of receipts. The share of expenditure caused by personnel costs was 57.7% higher in 2000; by 2008 this share had dropped to 46.83%. It is also noteworthy that funds for the maintenance and development of infrastructure rose from BGN 14,375,467 to BGN 46,746,547, which represents a threefold increase.

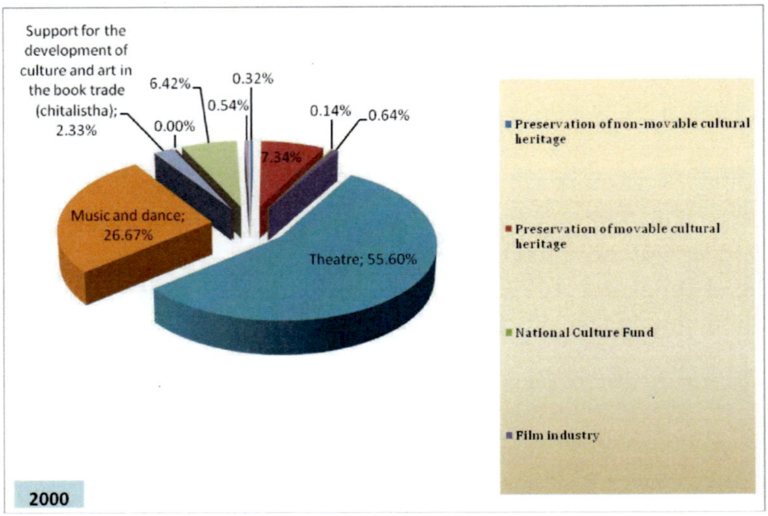

Figure 1: Receipts and share of total receipts in the budget of the Culture Ministry for the year 2000

Figure 5 shows the relation between the receipts and the contributions of the individual sectors in the year 2000. The most receipts came from the theatre category, followed by music and dance.

Figure 6 shows that the share of receipts in the budget decreased. The categories theatre, music and dance were particularly affected by this. Conversely, other sectors benefited from this development. The receipts and costs in the budget are shown as percentages in figures 6 and 7. It is of note that the costs in the theatre category amount to only 26.14% although theatre is a sector that accounted for over half the receipts in the budget for the year 2000.

The composition of spending remained almost unchanged from 2000 to 2008. On the one hand, this is of course ideal, but on the other it meant that unprofitable sectors were stimulated, and this did nothing to support the development of those sectors with low revenue. A look at how each category developed allows the following conclusions to be drawn:

In the music and dance categories, the receipts and expenditure produced a positive trend. As with the overall costs, the costs in these categories increased disproportionately until 2008 and registered a decrease due to steadily rising spend-

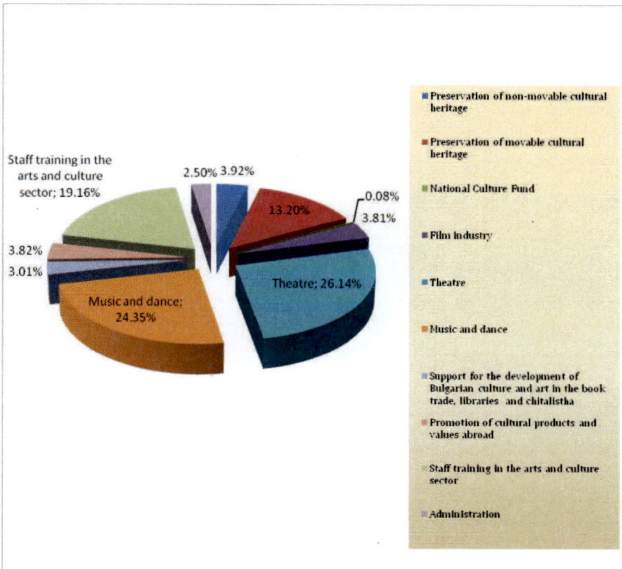

Figure 2: Expenditure as a share of total costs in the budget for the year 2000

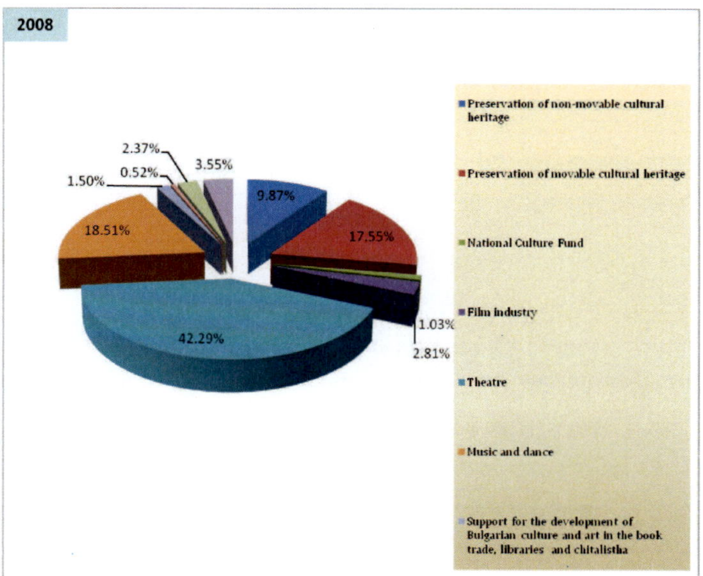

Figure 3: Receipts as a share of total costs in the budget for the year 2008

ing while receipts stayed static. This means that money alone was insufficient to support the sectors. A comprehensive concept for music and dance would have been required if they were to have had a better chance to develop and flourish.

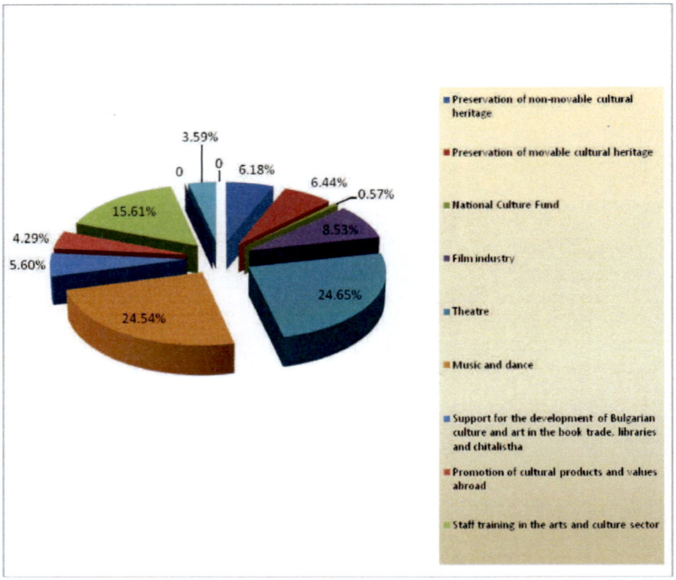

Figure 4: Expenditure as a share of total costs in the budget for the year 2008

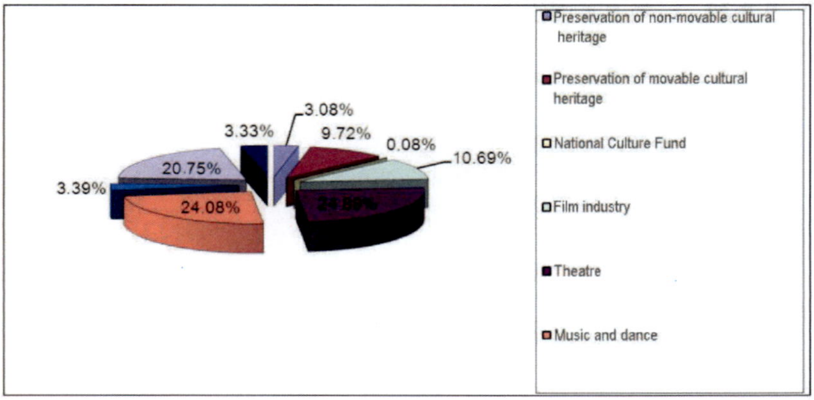

Figure 5: Expenditure as a share of total costs in the budget for the year 2011

Similar trends can be observed in the field of theatre:

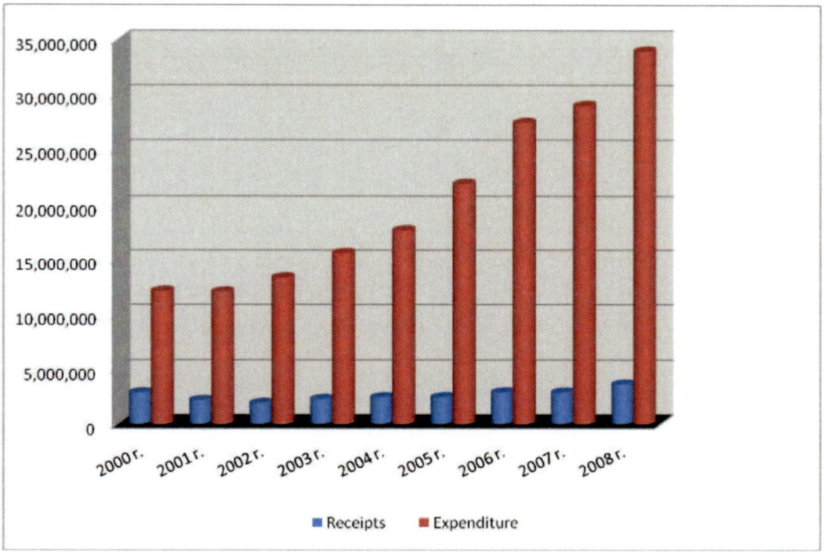

Figure 6: Music and dance: receipts and expenditure

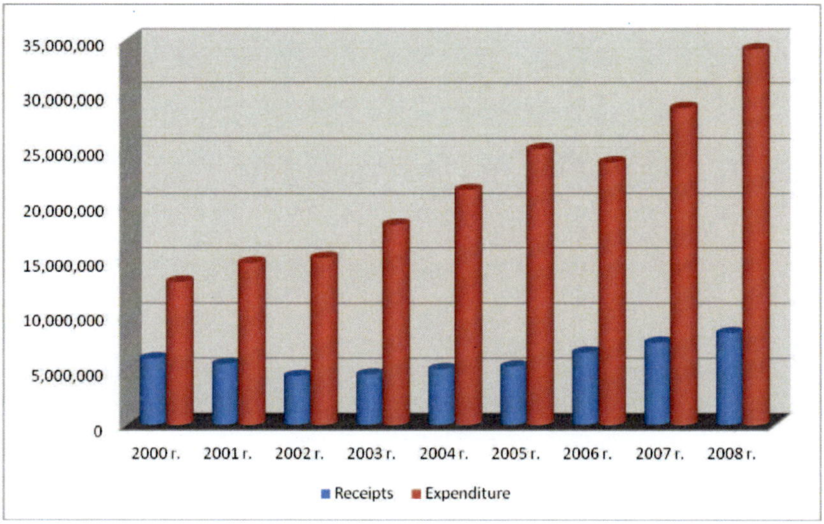

Figure 7: Theatre: receipts and expenditure

Here, the costs have increased markedly although they were an important item in the budget balance. In the nine years from 2000 to 2008, receipts amounted to only 38%, whereas expenditure increased by 162.3%. The increase in receipts can be explained by increased admission prices. It is interesting that there was no significant change in audience figures. The decision to provide more funds for the preservation of the historical cultural heritage in 2007 and 2008 also contributed to increased receipts.

It can be concluded that implementation of the strategy and planning up to this point is unsatisfactory. The increase of 5000% shows unequivocally that this sector had enormous potential for development which was still a long way from being realized. From 2009 to 2012, expenditure on theatres was cut in the Culture Ministry budget. Taking the data of the National Statistics Institute as a basis, receipts in the period from 2008 to 2011 were increased by BGN 3,743,044, i.e. by 40%. These figures show that the theatre sector had enormous economic potential, but at the same time needed a different concept in order to realize it.

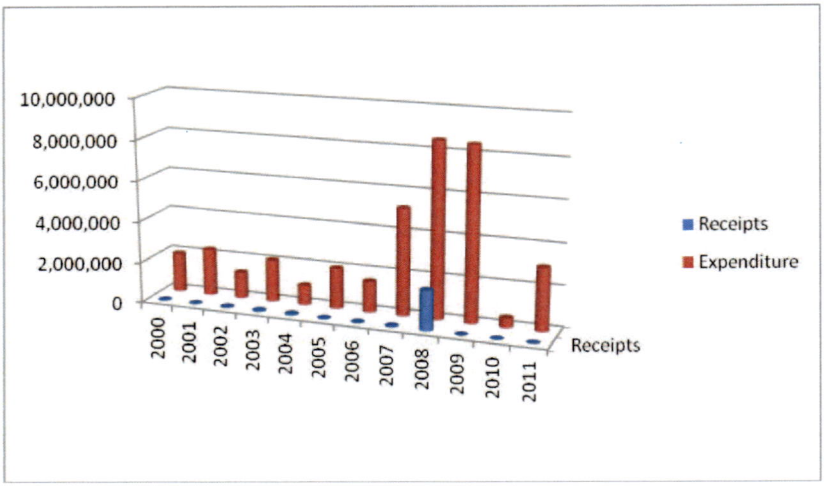

Figure 8: Preservation of non-movable cultural heritage

A trend can be observed in protection of movable cultural heritage, namely an almost parallel increase in costs and revenue. From 2009 to 2012, no figures are available for receipts.

The general trend of falling visitor numbers at the surviving cinemas and the falling number of film productions is clearly reflected in the budget. Spending was conspicuously higher than income. Dedicated funds amounted to BGN 11,808,013 for 2008, while the receipts amounted to only BGN 552,590. The trend nonetheless clearly shows that, thanks to legislation, the film sector received subsidies which in 2008 amounted to 8.53% of the Culture Ministry's budget. The question that remains is how the film industry could raise more funds. The trend unmistakably shows increasing subsidies, but no significant increase in receipts.

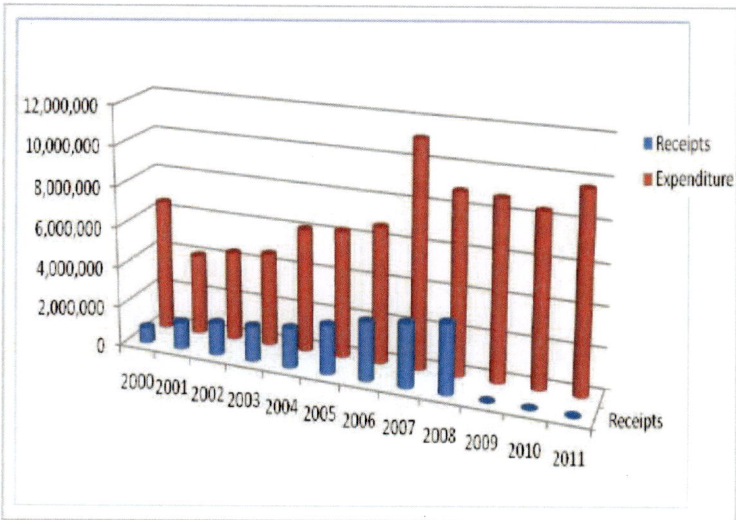

Figure 9: Preservation of movable cultural heritage

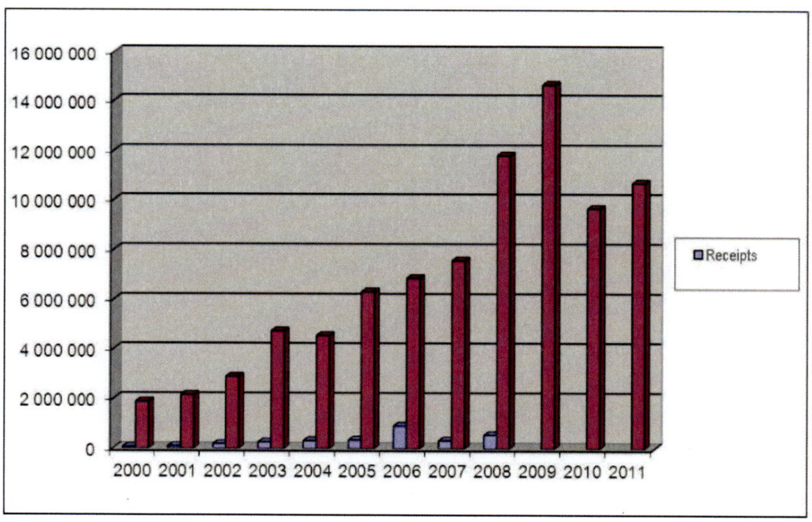

Figure 10: The film industry 2000-2011, receipts and expenditure

In conclusion it can be said that the entire sector will have to step up its efforts to promote its activities or that activities will have to be launched that have a positive effect on receipts.

The following tables clearly show the trends with regard to receipts in the

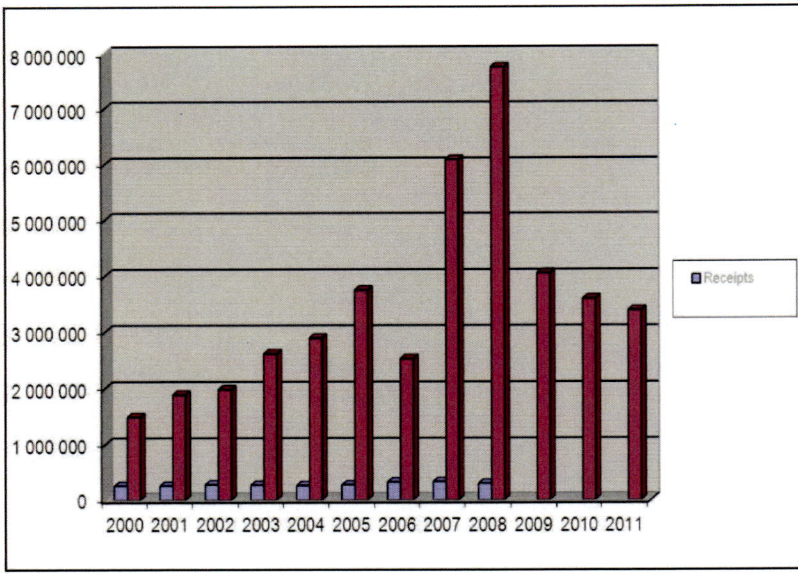

Figure 11: Support for the development of Bulgarian culture and art: Bulgarian book trade, libraries and chitalishta

budgets for 2000 and 2008. During this period, it was theatres and music that had the highest percentages.

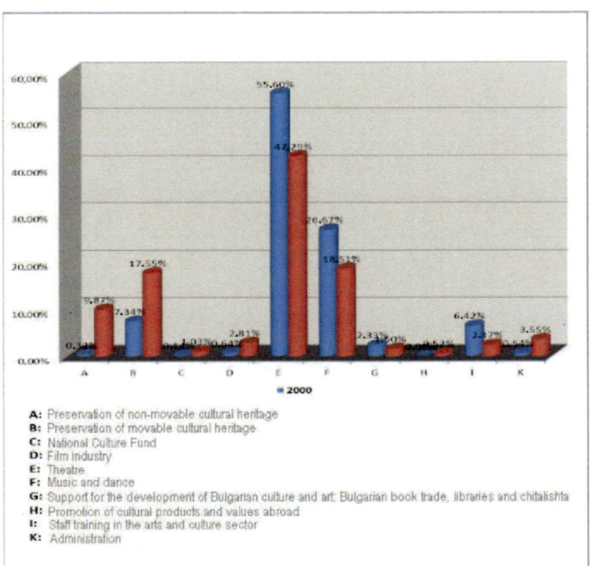

Figure 12: Receipts as a percentage in the budgets for 2000 and 2008

In the year 2000, funding was focused on the theatre, dance and music. In

2008, their share of falling receipts decreased markedly to the detriment of other sectors; these are labelled A and B in the table. A negative trend was also apparent in the development of the book trade including *chitalishta* and libraries as well as in the training of staff in the art and culture sector.

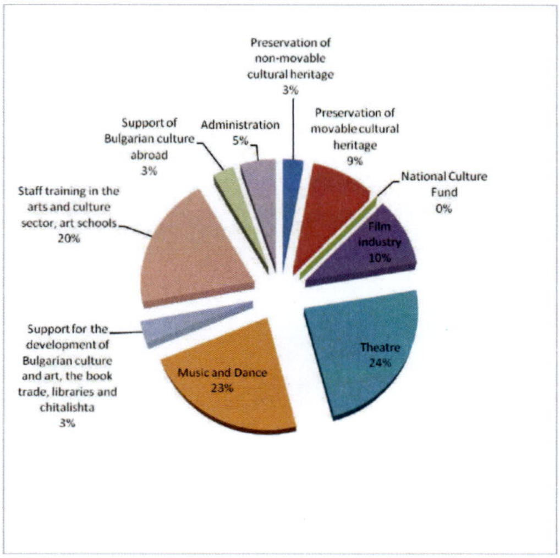

Figure 16.1: Expenditure as a percentage of the Culture Ministry's budgets for 2011

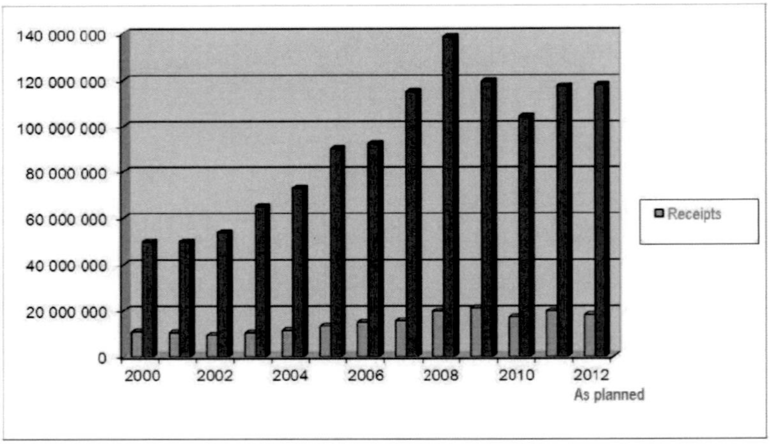

Figure 13: Receipts and expenditure of the Culture Ministry 2000-2011

4.1 Funding by Category 2000–2008

Table 34: Development of the budget for culture by category 2000–2011

Preservation of non-movable cultural heritage									
	2000	**2001**	**2002**	**2003**	**2004**	**2005**	**2006**	**2007**	**2008**
Receipts	34 529	26 861	39 594	43 447	67 930	35 031	36 793	41 151	1 938 637
Expenditure	1 949 280	2 312 426	1 312 040	2 091 994	980 041	2 019 032	1 541 687	5 204 077	8 564 747
Personnel	296 070	347 988	366 825	391 331	436 330	456 021	426 126	645 000	745 571
Investments	1 568 338	1 888 149	867 349	1 610 073	462 878	1 490 522	1 011 742	4 448 856	7 712 190

According to plan			
	2009	**2010**	**2011**
Receipts	-	-	-
Expenditure	8 490 834	470 319	3 073 525
Personnel	549 700	49 869	4873.33
Investments	*	*	*

Preservation of movable cultural heritage									
	2000	**2001**	**2002**	**2003**	**2004**	**2005**	**2006**	**2007**	**2008**
Receipts	793 365	1 349 425	1 617 861	1 751 647	1 965 498	2 431 035	2 905 227	3 135 295	3 448 144
Expenditure	6 560 801	4 058 807	4 463 860	4 651 385	6 149 514	6 298 931	6 759 409	11 167 900	8 911 330
Personnel	1 692 218	1 845 832	2 049 088	2 347 077	2 540 323	2 664 639	3 281 403	3 553 600	3 894 013
Maintenance	2 063 727	1 665 383	2 223 832	2 201 059	2 954 867	2 690 115	3 187 521	4 897 000	4 033 764
Grants	0	0	0	0	0	0	0	0	0
Investments	2 804 856	547 592	190 940	103 249	654 324	944 177	290 485	2 717 300	983 553

	According to plan		
	2009	**2010**	**2011**
Receipts	-	-	-
Expenditure	8 830 820	8 455 894	9 710 963
Personnel	3 727 998	3 863 298	2 901 017
Maintenance	3 837 367	2 505 993	4 084 946
Grants	*	*	*
Investments	*	*	*

4. THE BUDGET OF THE MINISTRY OF CULTURE

National Culture Fund in thousands									
	2000	2001	2002	2003	2004	2005	2006	2007	2008
Receipts	15	40.75	50.825	48.619	56.393	272.668	85.744	269.739	202.402
Expenditure	39.863	468.472	525.047	530.286	527.829	758.952	1 347.640	765.799	783.055
Personnel	7.126	21.886	34.311	34.799	44.367	50.534	180.163	93.126	71.063
Maintenance	32.737	445.809	490.736	495.487	483.462	708.41	1 166.214	564.438	711.992
Grants	0	0	0	0	0	0	0	0	0
Investments	*	777	*	*	*	*	1 263	108 235	*

	According to plan		
	2009	2010	2011
Receipts	-	-	-
Expenditure	1 415 749	63 649	84 955
Personnel	94.47	0	0
Maintenance	0	0	0
Grants	0	0	0
Investments	*	*	*

Music and Dance									
	2000	2001	2002	2003	2004	2005	2006	2007	2008
Receipts	2 883 460	2 188 830	1 911 338	2 289 962	2 447 737	2 458 247	2 909 461	2 893 145	3 636 864
Expenditure	12 104 184	12 023 746	13 336 165	15 598 196	17 745 026	21 953 377	27 406 974	28 968 400	33 987 805
Personnel	8 986 460	9 416 283	10 620 633	12 229 657	14 678 357	18 816 267	19 442 461	20 809 400	22 613 076
Maintenance	2 481 860	2 366 323	2 326 308	2 940 362	2 762 354	2 994 804	3 127 693	4 106 400	4 190 759
Grants	0	0	0	0	0	0	0	0	0
Investments	635 864	241140	389 224	428 177	304 315	142 306	4 836 820	4 052 600	7 183 970

	According to plan	Report 31.12	According to plan
	2009	2010	2011
Receipts	-	-	-
Expenditure	31 143 761	25 390 646	24 070 222
Personnel	23 025 924	20 873 484	19 625 151
Maintenance	4 970 052	4 171 245	3 544 204
Grants	0	0	0
Investments	*	*	*

4.1 Funding by Category 2000–2008

Theatre									
	2000	2001	2002	2003	2004	2005	2006	2007	2008
Receipts	6 011 489	5 500 244	4 428 105	4 571 553	5 058 472	5 296 932	6 543 959	7 449 820	8 306 956
Expenditure	12 991 951	14 710 420	15 160 324	18 169 907	21 327 351	25 058 372	23 841 865	28 790 300	34 141 325
Personnel	8 478 179	9 011 367	9 286 839	9 969 163	11 431 318	13 854 623	15 343 832	16 586 800	17 936 940
Maintenance	4 235 001	5 337 107	4 898 182	4 581 399	5 446 948	5 641 731	6 757 447	7 545 100	8 739 800
Grants	0	0	0	0	0	0	0	0	0
Investments	278 771	361 946	975 303	3 619 345	4 449 085	5 562 018	1 740 586	4 658 400	7 464 585

	According to plan	Report 31.12	According to plan
	2009	2010	2011
Receipts	-	-	**12 050 000***
Expenditure	29 402 351	26 141 778	24 872 907
Personnel	16 362 049	17 677 133	12 917 526
Maintenance	8 355 011	7 495 877	11 098 425
Grants	0	0	0
Investments	*	*	*

Ministry of Culture — Total									
	2000	2001	2002	2003	2004	2005	2006	2007	2008
Receipts	10 811 234	10 369 334	9 282 462	10 263 968	11 296 485	13 212 652	14 842 454	15 448 928	19 644 927
Expenditure	49 704 427	49 812 235	53 771 503	64 936 014	72 855 669	89 989 553	92 337 002	115 053 732	138 480 971
Personnel	28 673 101	29 438 978	32 177 476	36 033 931	41 030 656	49 213 624	53 090 513	57 906 126	64 847 710
Maintenance	14 375 467	16 477 313	17 735 424	21 165 216	22 545 427	29 667 249	29 172 776	38 464 953	46 746 547
Grants	281 094	266 723	263 514	261 282	286 013	378 757	440 523	445 708	499 636
Investments	6 374 765	3 629 221	3 595 089	7 475 585	8 993 573	10 729 923	9 698 190	18 236 945	26 387 078

	Ministry of Culture — Total		
	2009	2010	2011
Receipts	21 122 700	17 182 981	19 728 000
Expenditure	119 500 670	104 215 055	117 370 737
Personnel	*	*	*
Maintenance	*	*	*
Grants	*	*	*
Investments	*	*	*

4. THE BUDGET OF THE MINISTRY OF CULTURE

Budget of the Ministry of Culture according to the official gazette			
2009 г.	**2010**	**2011**	**2012**
121 899 600	102 543 400	104 569 103	117 903 100

Support of Bulgarian culture abroad									
	2000	**2001**	**2002**	**2003**	**2004**	**2005**	**2006**	**2007**	**2008**
Receipts		196 606	156 674	204 953	156 100	128 205	130 407	104 830	102 842
Expenditure	1 901 148	1 935 047	2 527 209	2 451 059	2 289 009	2 279 071	2 572 301	4 470 654	5 937 440
Personnel	915 643	377 682	196 576	205 234	216 267	251 393	289 141	487 300	610 373
Maintenance	973 993	1 529 925	1 687 486	2 092 842	1 779 605	1 982 390	2 033 208	3 821 400	5 083 518
Grants	0	0	0	0	0	0	0	0	0
Investments	11 512	27 440	643 147	152 983	293 137	45 288	249 952	161 954	243 549

	According to plan	**Report 31 Dec**	**According to plan**
	2009	**2010**	**2011**
Receipts	-	-	-
Expenditure	1 491 480	172 461	3 330 927
Personnel	9 300	5 000	281 518
Maintenance	207 700	167 461	2 984 960
Grants	0	0	0
Investments	*	*	*

4.1 Funding by Category 2000–2008

Staff training in the arts and culture sector (schools of the arts)									
	2000	**2001**	**2002**	**2003**	**2004**	**2005**	**2006**	**2007**	**2008**
Receipts	693 914	495 215	481 968	571 804	538 402	629 939	595 728	488 947	465 105
Expenditure	9 524 981	8 787 931	9 765 928	11 707 795	13 315 154	13 443 616	15 228 972	16 009 408	21 622 927
Personnel	6 545 448	6 502 027	7 526 307	8 348 681	8 978 862	9 492 161	10 410 946	11 692 800	14 598 492
Maintenance	1 647 489	1 477 383	1 610 811	2 046 350	2 248 954	2 252 783	3 232 623	3 489 400	4 545 058
Grants	281 094	266 723	263 514	261 282	286 013	378 757	440 523	445 708	499 636
Investments	1 050 950	541 798	365 296	1 051 482	1 801 325	1 319 915	1 144 880	381 500	1 979 741

	According to plan	**Report 31.12**	**According to plan**
	2009	**2010**	**2011**
Receipts	-	-	-
Expenditure	23 698 133	21 401 596	20 735 567
Personnel	16 890 812	16 976 028	15 307 343
Maintenance	5 545 996	3 415 772	4 975 166
Grants	453 058	221 223	453 058
Investments			

Administration									
	2000	**2001**	**2002**	**2003**	**2004**	**2005**	**2006**	**2007**	**2008**
Receipts	58 182	225 973	135 289	260 138	428 717	1 337 342	398 533	412 753	696 725
Expenditure	1 240 409	1 456 121	1 796 082	2 377 530	3 074 146	3 436 898	4 242 949	6 017 594	4 965 834
Personnel	712 154	799 584	894 785	1 104 196	1 238 017	1 498 139	1 788 638	1 990 000	2 047 979
Maintenance	512 267	649 471	759 123	961 912	1 053 256	1 598 635	2 121 823	2 441 194	2 188 570
Grants	0	0	0	0	0	0	0	0	0
Investments	15 988	7 066	142 174	311 422	782 873	340 124	332 488	1 586 400	729 285

	According to plan	**Report 31.12**	**According to plan**
Administration	**2009**	**2010**	**2011**
Receipts	-	-	-
Expenditure	5 411 558	4 190 857	5 413 685
Personnel	2 972 237	2 019 745	2 714 650
Maintenance	2 236 521	2 072 489	2 699 035
Grants	0	0	0
Investments	*	*	*

4. THE BUDGET OF THE MINISTRY OF CULTURE

Support for the development of Bulgarian culture and art: Bulgarian book trade, libraries and *chitalishta*									
	2000	**2001**	**2002**	**2003**	**2004**	**2005**	**2006**	**2007**	**2008**
Receipts	252 186	252 030	274 872	264 983	257 946	269 684	320 927	326 699	294 662
Expenditure	1 498 436	1 891 813	1 983 721	2 619 135	2 895 623	3 749 127	2 529 971	6 090 100	7 758 495
Personnel	993 086	1 062 875	1 150 533	1 306 755	1 336 455	1 541 001	1 616 518	1 772 300	2 050 714
Maintenance	496 864	815 625	811 532	1 207 971	1 355 047	1 637 879	888 479	4 196 100	5 617 576
Grants	0	0	0	0	0	0	0	0	0
Investments	8 486	13 313	21 656	104 409	204 121	570 247	89 974	121 700	90 205

	According to plan	**Report 31.12**	**According to plan**
	2009	**2010**	**2011**
Receipts	-	-	-
Expenditure	4 058 586	3 597 973	3 389 172
Personnel	2 036 934	2 086 590	1 776 515
Maintenance	787 490	538 574	439 739
Grants	0	0	0
Investments	*	*	*

Ministry of Culture Budget 2009- 2012[245]							
	State Budget Act	Final Report	State Budget Act	Final Report	State Budget Act	Final Report	State Budget Act
Receipts	2009	2009	2010	2010	2011	2011	2012
	17 700 000	21 122 700	17 700 000	17 182 981	17 700 000	19 728 000	18 000 000
Expenditure	121 899 600	119 500 670	102 543 400	104 215 055	104 569 103	117 370 737	117 903 100

[18] Ministry of Finance. Report on the implementation of the capital budget of the Republic of Bulgaria 2009. [online]. 2010, p. 85. Available from: http://www.minfin.bg/bg/page/247 (status 27.11.2012).

Table 35: Expenditure on media: BNTV, radio and Culture Ministry, 1997–2008 in millions

Expenditure	1997	**A**	1998	**A**	1999	**A**	2000	**A**	2001	**A**	2002	**A**
BNTV	15.53	1.29	20.63	1.01	50.72	1.69	29.67	1.08	65.80	2.64	60.03	1.43
BN Radio	14.36		19.04		21.22		23.90		41.03		33.94	
Culture Ministry	23.14		39.09		42.68		49.68		40.40		65.70	

A: Share BNT + BNR of Culture Ministry expenditure
B: Share BNT + BNR of total expenditure on culture
C: Total expenditure on culture in Finance Ministry's Final Report[19]

Expenditure	2009	A	2010	A	2011	A	2012	A	Increase
	80.8	1.13	75	1.21	72.2	1.05	67.1	0.93	-30%
BNTV									
BN Radio	53.7		51.3		51.4		42.1		-22%
Culture Ministry	119.5	B	104.2	B	117.3	B	117.9	B	9%
C	440.5	0.31	403.0	0.31	409.8	0.3	*	*	*

This data comes from the archive relating to the Finance Ministry's final report. From 1997–2008 there was a trend for the media to receive almost twice as much in subsidies from the national budget as the Ministry of Culture. A further observation is that the costs to the Culture Ministry of national radio and national television rose. Seen as a whole, the following points are important for culture as an item in the state budget:

- Spending on Bulgarian National Television was increased by 15% until 2008, and spending on radio by 194%.
- The costs of the "Culture" group as a whole rose by 849% between 2002 and 2008.
- For the period 1997 to 2001, the final report of the Finance Ministry did not cite the costs in the category "Culture overall".

A further point to mention is the difference between the data in the Finance Ministry's report and the figures in the law gazette relating to the Culture Ministry's budget for the following years: 2003, 2004, 2005, 2006, 2007, 2008.

Table 36: Spending on culture in millions, 2003–2008, budget of the Ministry of Culture[20]

2003	2004	2005	2006	2007	2008
53 973.4	10 500.0	73 674.6	11 656.8	93 360.02	103 942.0

[19] Parliament and Finance Ministry. Final report 1997–2012

[20] Law Gazette, no. 120, 29 December 2002. State Budget Act of the Republic of Bulgaria.

The law gazette contained several provisions which explained the different figures it cited compared to the Finance Ministry's final report.

For the year 2007, the law gazette contained the following passages:

§ 35. (1) Following a decision by the municipal council pertaining to the municipal budgets for the year 2007, and in accordance with contracts concluded between the Ministry of Culture and the municipalities pursuant to Article 5, subparagraph 2 of the Protection and Development of Culture Act, monies for maintenance, including salaries and social security payments, can be used in the section for "local activities" such as public theatrical performance, puppet theatres, philharmonic societies, opera and other cultural institutions.

(2) In accordance with contracts under Section 1, the Minister of Culture approves the hiring of additional personnel under consideration of the average monthly gross salaries already approved and the amount of funds allocated for the maintenance of each cultural institution.

(3) The money saved from monthly salaries under item (2) can be used for creative projects, specific programmes and financial support of activities of the cultural institutions.

§ 51. The draft bill for the state budget of the Republic of Bulgaria for the year 2008 has been registered by the Council of Ministers at Parliament for assessment and approval of the draft programme budget (...), the Ministry of Culture, (...) as part of the legislative project in 2008.

§ 52. The Finance Minister carried out amendments and concurrent corrections in keeping with the provisions of the law pertaining to the state budget, and corrections to budgets already approved by the Council of Ministers by programme (...).[21]

Provisions such as these may shed light on the discrepancies in the figures in the law gazette and the final report of the Finance Ministry for the years 2007 and 2008, but an overall summary and a harmonized document are missing nonetheless. The figures are cited in the official journal for 2007 and 2008, but again they differ from those in the Finance Ministry report. Total spending by the Ministry of Culture for the year 2007 is given as BGN 93,360,226.

Table 37: Spending from the culture budget of the Culture Ministry in 2008[22]

Total expenditure	10 394 200
Preservation of non-movable cultural heritage	1 072 118
Policy on protection of cultural heritage and the dissemination of cultural products and services	74 961 777
Preservation of movable cultural heritage	7 346 650
National Culture Fund	598 480
Film industry	7 832 692

[21] Law Gazette, no. 108, 29 Dec 2006. Effective from 01.01.2007, amend. No. 52, 29 Jun 2007. Decree no. 20, 2 Feb 2007, on the implementation of the state budget of the Republic of Bulgaria for the year 2007.

Table 37: Spending from the culture budget of the Culture Ministry in 2008[22]

Theatre	24 490 808
Music and dance	30 256 551
Protection of intellectual property	
Support for the development of Bulgarian culture and art: Bulgarian book trade, libraries and *chitalishta*	3 279 278
Policy on promoting culture	3 846 900
International cultural cooperation	120 000
Promotion of cultural products	3 726 900
Policy on the promotion of high-quality education in the arts and culture	19 285 672
Protection of children with special talents	*
Administration	5 847 651

Table 38: Per capita spending on culture 2002-2011 in BGN million[23]

	2001	2002	2003	2004	2005	2006	2007	2008
Expenditure		43 005.9	48 556	62 397.2	287.5	319.8	382.8	460.9
Population	7 928 901							
Per capita		5.42	6.12	7.87	36.26	40.33	48.28	58.13

	2009	2010	2011
Expenditure	440.5	403	409.8
Population			7 364 570
Per capita	55.56	50.83	55.64

Population on 01.03.2001: 7,928,901
Population on 01.02.2011: 7,364,570[24]

Although an increase had been promised in the election manifestos, the culture budget remained between 0.6% and 1.2% of GDP and fell by 0.6%. However, if spending on the media is deducted from this amount and it is adjusted for inflation, the percentage of arts funding is significantly lower: There are four different sources for the Ministry of Culture's budget in the period 1995–2012: the law gazette, a confidential source within the Culture Ministry, the final report of the

22 Law Gazette, no. 113, 28 Dec 2008. [online]. Available from: http://dv.parliament.bg/DVWeb/index.faces (status 05.12.2011).

23 Basis: Final Report of the Ministry of Finance. Figures in BGN million. (status 14.11.2011). Author's calcula- tions.

24 NSI. *Naselenie po godini na preproyavaniya za perioda 1900–2011* (*The population in the years 1990–2011*). [online]. [viewed 22.02.2012]. Available from: http://www.nsi.bg/census2011/index.php (status 23.12.2011).

Finance Ministry and the Compendium for Cultural Trends in Europe. All of these give different figures.

Table 49.1: Per capita spending on culture in USD, 1995–2008[25]

Year	1995	1996	1997	1998	1999	2000	2001	2002	2003	2005	2006	2007	2008
Per capita	9.69	5.26	5.63	10.54	11.88	15.05	16.86	13.94	16.65	22.32	26.68	38.04	44.03
% of GDP	0.6	0.4	0.4	0.7	0.8	0.6	0.7	0.75	0.66	0.74	0.64	0.7	0.72

As stated above, there were serious discrepancies between the budget as it was approved by parliament and as it was published in the law gazette and the report of the Finance Ministry. Here, the figures from the Finance Ministry report have been used since it calculates them to be 0.4% of GDP for 1996, for instance. If the budget of the Culture Ministry cited in the *Darzhaven vestnik* (State Gazette) is taken as the basis and compared, its percentage share of GDP is significantly lower. Furthermore, the per capita spending does not tally. The same is true for the years 1996 and 1997.[26] According to information given orally by the Ministry of Culture, its budgets for the years 1995 to 1999 were destroyed in the year 2000 by a computer virus called Chernobyl, and the Ministry was no longer able consult this data which would have been useful for comparison. Public spending on culture at central level in 2008 went to the cultural institutes of the Ministry of Culture, national radio, Bulgarian National Television, regional departments of the archives, as a grant to the Ministry of Education and Science for the museum of the same name, and as investment in social projects run by the Ministry of Labour and Social Welfare.

The funds that the Culture Ministry had traditionally allocated as support for the media led to a shift of emphasis, and traditional sectors such as theatre, music and books were faced with a drastic reduction in the level of interest.

4.2 The National Culture Fund

With the passing of the Protection and Development of Culture Act and as part of decentralization of the administration and funding of the culture sector in the year 2000, the National Culture Fund was set up.[27] Initially, the fund was established as a legal entity with an account separate from the budget to "promote cultural development, to gather, manage and distribute resources for the implementation

[25] Council of Europe. *Compendium of Cultural Policies and Trends in Europe, 2010.* [online]. Available from: http://www.culturalpolicies.net/web/bulgaria.php?aid=31 (status 19.02.2012).

[26] Funding by category

[27] Law Gazette, no. 50. Zakon za zashtita i razvitie na kulturata (Protection and Development of Culture Act), 01.06.1999.

of national policy in the culture sector". It operates autonomously by storing additional resources from the budget and the market.

Centralization of the National Culture Fund and the conversion of the arts centres to departments of the central administration set the culture sector back during the early phase of the transition.

Table 39: Ministry of Culture budget plan 2008 Programme 3: National Culture Fund 2008, in BGN thousand[28]

Financing	BGN
Ministry of Culture	606 493
Dedicated endowments	97 792
Receipts under the Protection and Development of Culture Act	64 603
Returns from projects	9 404
Receipts	778 292
Outlay	769 047

Table 40: National Culture Fund, Annual Report 2008, in BGN thousand[29]

Financing	BGN
Ministry of Culture	496 060
Dedicated endowments	231 508
Receipts	
Receipts under the Protection and Development of Culture Act	38 231
Returns from projects	7 350
Receipts	773 149
Outlay	773 149

Table 41: National Culture Fund: Annual Report 2006 in BGN thousand[30]

Financing	BGN
Ministry of Culture	481 201
Boyana Film	26 224
Restoration EAD	12 236
Orfei audio-video	10 041
Receipts – § 25	17 031
Other receipts	67
Interest	2.92
Returns from projects	3 700
Receipts	69 303
Outlay	538 080

Table 42: National Culture Fund: Annual Report 2005 in BGN thousand[31]

Financing	BGN
From the Ministry of Culture	486 284
Donation from Kram Komplex GmbH	200 000
Boyana Film	41 909
Restoration EAD	8 107
Vreme Film Studios	1 353
Receipts § 25 from ZÀPÑD	17 031
Other receipts	3 937
Interest	1. 65
Returns from projects	1 224
Receipts Outlay	760 176 774 352

With respect to funding, the Ministry of Culture adopted a policy which was also less than far-sighted. Although the level of funds allocated to creative projects was kept relatively stable, there was, for example not even a minimum of protection against rising consumer prices.

For the art directorates — the former arts centres — these amounts remained

26 Budget of the Ministry of Culture 2008, Programme 3, National Culture Fund.

27 National Culture Fund, Annual Report, 2006.

28 National Culture Fund, Annual Report 2005, 2006, 2007, 2008. [online]. Sofia. Available from: http://ncf.bg/?page_id=7 (status 05.12.2011).

29 National Culture Fund, Annual Report, 2005.

stable: BGN 300,000 per year in the period from 2000 to 2008, compared to BGN 500,000 allocated by the Ministry of Culture to the National Culture Fund for creative projects from 2004 to 2008. Taking the average annual rate of inflation since 2000 into account, however, the value of subsidies granted to the arts directorates for projects was halved, while the value of those granted to the National Culture Fund fell by a third. The conclusion drawn is that during the transition, centralization of the administrative agenda of the Ministry of Culture and a transformation of the fund for culture in the programme took place, while a commentary was delivered from an ideological standpoint on the drift away from the principle of autonomy.

The politicians in the country recognized this discrepancy and set up an experts' commission in 2006 which was tasked with developing a ten-year national strategy for culture. One of the steps in the process of drafting a policy paper for a national strategy for culture was the survey of the population's attitude towards consumption of culture that was carried out on behalf of the National Culture Fund.

The survey was a nationwide investigation and was conducted using semi-structured interviews. Until 2005 it was the only in-depth analysis of national cultural preferences and values, the demand for cultural goods and services, frequency, motivation and limits and the role that education plays in this process. It ushered in a series of three consecutive studies that aimed to produce a comprehensive overview of the domestic cultural status quo.

Table 43: Opinion poll I[30]

In your view, what are the most important objectives of the strategy for the development of Bulgarian culture?				
	important	not especially important	not important at all	cannot say
Changes to legislation on culture, art centres, museums, copyright, cultural monuments, cultural industries	84.8%	12.1%	0.5%	2.6%
Increasing the role of education as a factor in promoting culture	88.5%	10.5%		1.0%
Financing projects for the promotion of Bulgarian culture	89.1%	9.6%	0.8%	0.5%
New financing instruments (art lottery fund, loan and pledge schemes)	49.5%	38.8%	4.0%	7.7%
Renovation of cultural institutions' infrastructure	90.1%	9.2%	0.3%	0.5%
Other	55.8%	5.8%	1.9%	36.5%

30 Natsionalen tsentar za izuchavane na obshtestvenite naglasi (National centre for research into public opinion). Sofia, 2005, pp. 10–29.

All the creators interviewed believed that the national cultural strategy was a priority for the development of Bulgarian culture and should be defined and accepted as soon as possible. Consequently, culture was vital for the nation and national identity and for this reason a cultural strategy should not be the result of the efforts of cultural specialists alone, but of the general public in Bulgaria. The conviction was that the national cultural strategy would have a positive effect on Bulgarian culture: specifically, the way culture and cultural processes are organized within the country on the one hand, and global justification of the nation's culture as a whole and of Bulgarian cultural products on the other.

Against this background, a key question was how the national cultural strategy would influence the cultural products, artists and creators and the market mechanisms related to cultural products. More than three quarters of those surveyed assumed that the cultural strategy would increase the quality of cultural products, raise the prestige of creators and improve their working conditions, and lead to greater market opportunities for the performing arts, the cultural industry and the creative industry and the popularization of the cultural heritage. The consensus, therefore, is that the creation of a national cultural strategy would have positive effects on the entire cultural process which would increase the value of Bulgarian culture and make it part of the worldwide cultural heritage.

The state has the role of ensuring that cultural values are maintained. This was the view expressed by more than three quarters of those surveyed who work in the culture sector. Ranked second in importance were the municipal authorities, with society itself ranked only third. The replies clearly show that creators have a primarily conservative and traditional attitude towards cultural values and cultural products. Most of them had not yet fully adjusted to the dynamic cultural environment of the last fifteen years, not just in Bulgaria but worldwide. It was principally traditional cultural assets such as ethnographic museums and complexes, national customs, architecture and the like that were deemed to have cultural value, with little value being placed on today's popular culture. The same applies to products such as the internet, video and DVD, computer games and entertainment software, fashion design, furniture design and other cultural achievements, all of which were seen as the results of mere trends in culture and consumer preferences. It is revealing that radio was more often considered as having cultural value than television was. This may be because radio became common across the world before traditional television.

The question was: "What are the most important forms of support for state and municipal institutions so that they can create cultural products and services?" The table below shows the answers to this question.

Table 44: Opinion poll II[31]

	important	not especially important	not important at all	cannot say	total
Capital subsidy	80.4%	13.4%	1.6%	4.7%	100.0%
Subsidy for maintenance of cultural institutions	86.0%	12.4%	1.0%	0.5%	100.0%
Project subsidies	76.5%	19.0%	1.3%	3.2%	100.0%
Alternative financing instruments (lottery fund, loan and pledge schemes)	35.3%	48.5%	6.9%	9.3%	100.0%
Tax incentives for sponsors and donors	88.0%	10.2%	1.5%	0.3%	100.0%
Grants to individual artists	65.9%	27.1%	5.2%	1.8%	100.0%
Provision of facilities (studios, workshops, galleries, technology)	68.2%	25.0%	2.9%	3.9%	100.0%
Information and advice	54.0%	36.4%	7.2%	2.4%	100.0%
Marketing projects for the promotion of Bulgarian culture	76.2%	18.5%	1.8%	3.4%	100.0%
Prestigious projects abroad	69.5%	23.6%	2.4%	4.5%	100.0%
Other	40.9%	4.5%	1.5%	53.0%	100.0%

According to the creators, it is the state that is at the centre of efforts to maintain and popularize Bulgarian culture. The state should therefore maintain culture by guaranteeing the continued existence of state-funded cultural institutions. This could be achieved in the following ways:

- State support (88% of respondents)
- Introduction of tax incentives for benefactors (who sponsor or donate to culture)
- There was a broad consensus that a change to legislation of this kind would significantly increase the amount of funds available to culture because many companies are not just interested in supporting cultural events and institutions, but can also benefit from it.
- Subsidies for the preservation of cultural institutions, capital subsidies, project subsidies and others.

Least popular among the respondents were alternative financing instruments such as a lottery, loan and pledge schemes. This shows the guild's reserve towards innovation and entirely corroborates the previously identified traditional attitudes. Artists see the role of the state as primarily a provider of subsidies and funds. More than half the respondents believed that the biggest problem facing Bulgarian culture was finance. According to a quarter of the experts surveyed, this was due to weak government policy and an inadequate strategy for cultural development. A further 22% of the respondents stated during the survey in 2005 that the reason for

[31] Natsionalen tsentar za izuchavane na obshtestvenite naglasi (National centre for research into public opinion). Sofia, 2005, pp. 10–29.

the inauspicious situation that culture found itself in was inappropriate legislation, and it may be assumed that this has not significantly changed up to 2012. It also became very clear that the National Culture Fund was unable acquire third-party funds and was therefore entirely dependent on the state financial budget. The year 2009, in which receipts rose significantly, is an exception in this regard.

Table 45: National Culture Fund, report for 2009[32]

Receipts 2009	BGN
Subsidy from the Ministry of Culture	447 954
Receipts under the Promotion and Development of Culture Act	87 335
Returns from projects	39 760
Total receipts	1 142 064

Table 46: Policy programme within the Ministry of Culture for protecting cultural heritage and creating and distributing art and cultural products and services, "National Culture Fund"[33]

Min. of Culture, National Culture Fund programme, total expenditure in BGN	Under the law	According to plan	Report 31.03.2009	Report 30.06.2009	Report 30.09.2009
	873 163	1 415 749	20 563	512 386	728 624
Dept. expenditure overall	94 863	429 737	21 073	262 067	352 599
Personnel	63 313	94 470	8 754	57 954	72 574
Wages and salaries for employees	28 142	28 213	5 409	11 618	17 027
Other payments to employees	30 000	58 795	2 088	40 700	48 190
Employers' contributions	5 171	7 462	1 257	5 636	7 357
Employers' mandatory contributions	5 171	7 462	1 257	5 636	7 357
Maintenance	31 550	335 267	12 319	204 113	280 025
Administrative costs	778 300	986 012	-510	250 319	376 025

Table 47: National Culture Fund, report for 2010 in BGN thousand[34]

Receipts 2010	BGN
Subsidy from the Ministry of Culture	242 500
Receipts under the Promotion and Development of Culture Act	64 841
Returns from projects	5 104
Interest	0.002
Total receipts	327 447

32 National Culture Fund, 2009 report. [online]. Sofia, p. 5. Available from: http://www.ncf.bg/?page_id=7 (status 11.12.2012).

33 Estimate, based on a source in the Ministry of Culture, 2009.

Table 48: Policy programme within the Ministry of Culture for protecting cultural heritage and creating and distributing art and cultural products and services, National Culture Fund 2010

Min. of Culture, National Culture Fund programme, total expenditure in BGN	Under the law	According to plan	Report 31.03.2010	Report 30.06.2010	Report 30.09.2010	Report 31.12.2010
	563 386	296 989	144 719	187 438	224 502	291 258
	563 386	296 989	144 719	187 438	224 502	291 258
Dept. expenditure overall	63 386	108 265	36 331	50 526	70 992	102 534
Personnel	31 386	50 652	12 149	23 148	33 276	49 869
Wages and salaries for employees	26 802	24 122	5 501	11 050	16 551	23 339
Other payments to employees		20 694	5 182	9 302	12 653	20 694
Employers' mandatory contributions	4 584	5 836	1 466	2 796	4 072	5 836
Maintenance	32 000	55 314	24 182	27 378	37 716	50 366
Capital expenditure	0	2 299	0	0	0	2 299
Acquisition of fixed assets		1 435				1 435
Acquisition of intangible assets		864				864
Administrative costs	500 000	188 724	108 388	136 912	153 510	188 724
Operating costs	500 000	188 724	108 388	136 912	153 510	188 724
Unidentified outlay		118 022		88 780	93 888	118 022
Subsidies NGO		70 702		48 132	59 622	70 702

Table 49: National Culture Fund, report for 2011[35]

Receipts 2010	BGN
Subsidy from the Ministry of Culture	367 166
Receipts under the Promotion and Development of Culture Act	80 731
Returns from projects	10 791
Interest	0.003
OPAC project[36]	124 861
Total receipts	583 552

[34] National Culture Fund, 2010 report. [online]. Sofia, p. 3. Available from: http://www.ncf.bg/?page_id=7 (status 11.12.2012).

[35] National Culture Fund, 2011 report. [online]. Sofia, p. 6. Available from: http://www.ncf.bg/?page_id=7 (status 11.12.2012).

[36] ÅS "OPAK" operativna programa administrativen kapatsitet (Operational Programme Administrative Capacity, EU). [online]. Available from: http://www.opac.government.bg/bg/home, 11.12.2012.

Table 50: Policy programme within the Ministry of Culture for protecting cultural heritage and creating and distributing art and cultural products and services, National Culture Fund 2011

Min. of Culture, National Culture Fund programme, total expenditure in BGN	2011	According to plan 2011	Report 31.03.2011
Total expenditure	309 378	309 378	17 294
Dept. expenditure overall	309 378	309 378	17 294
	59 378	59 378	18 442
Personnel	32 050	32 050	15 149
Wages and salaries for employees	24 122	24 122	5 542
Other payments to employees	3 600	3 600	7 763
Employers' mandatory contributions	4 328	4 328	1 844
Maintenance	27 328	27 328	3 293
Capital expenditure	250 000	250 000	-1 148

4.3 NGOs in the Culture Sector

In 2006, the state developed a programme which could serve as a new basis for the strategic and planned development of the cultural institutions and the free arts scene. Qualitative changes in culture, the education system and the sciences are not to be expected unless those in power start to realize that the culture sector is a strategic field. The results are not immediately obvious, though they can already be observed at the universities. The Protection and Development of Culture Act was passed by parliament in 1998/1999 and has allowed free development in many sectors. At the same time, the state as a provider of funds has the final word, and this means that there is a centralist orientation in the arts. In Article 2.2 of the abovementioned Act, which allows cultural institutions to alter their statutes and register themselves as private entities, the general wish for the promotion of greater individuality was granted.[37]

However, the Act did not stipulate what would happen if an existing theatre wanted to define itself as private. The desire for funds and foundations was acknowledged, but the focus was not on the form of ownership (state, municipal, private), but on the legal framework that the state had to improve in order to support the cultural institutions' aspiration to define themselves as private or state-owned.

In this connection, the new constitution of the republic answered the question of the form of ownership long ago as guaranteed equality. The National Culture

[37] Law Gazette. Zakon za zakrila i razvitie na kulturata (Protection and Development of Culture Act), 28.12.2011.

Fund was founded in 2000 on the basis of the Protection and Development of Culture Act. It supported Bulgarian culture and funded the arts, cultural activities and artists. All cultural institutions could participate in the fund, including NGOs and individual artists. This was at least an indication that more intensive civic activity was beginning and that the state was willing to find solutions and a direct correction of the centralist funding model. The NGO sector, through its activities, is playing an ever greater role in correcting policy. At the same time, society has become more pluralistic. As mentioned above, NGOs in Bulgaria had a clear vision regarding the country's cultural development, but were not strong enough to take on this role. It was not possible to separate Bulgarian cultural policy from the overall context of global economic phenomena and regard it in isolation. From 1996 to 2001, the ratio of state funds to NGOs' funds was 60:1 in Bulgaria. That means that the NGOs in Bulgaria contributed 1.69% of all funds for culture.

"The ratio of state subsidies delivered through the state budget (741 326 254 USD) to funds provided by the third sector (13 567 975 USD) for support to cultural projects between 1996 and 2004 is approximately 50:1, i.e. 2% of all funds invested in cultural projects have been granted by NGOs."[38]

The ideas of von Beyme are also crucial to this discussion. Von Beyme is convinced that the standard bearers of civil society were only able to make a society's self-organization in the political sphere clear for a brief moment of dual hegemony consisting of the old nomenclature and the new power wielded by the people. Just as power fell into its hands with surprisingly little struggle, the idea of the civil society then proceeded to dwindle quite quickly to a helpless power.[39]

The NGOs whose activities were related to culture were many and varied, and the organizational terms they used to describe themselves reflected this diversity: associations, societies, foundations, funds, committees, centres, festivals, *chitalishta*; NGOs in Bulgaria could also register as municipal or corporate organizations.

The support needed to set up an NGO came from abroad. In this way, a blow was struck for decentralization and a counterweight against the one-sided dominance of the state created. As in all the former satellite states of the Soviet Union, George Soros and his Open Society foundations (following Karl Popper's ideas)

---

[38] Council of Europe. *Compendium of Cultural Policies and Trends in Europe, Strasbourg 2010.* [online]. Available from: http://www.culturalpolicies.net/web/bulgaria.php?aid=813&language=de&PHPSESSID=5qcjae3tpa8peann4snvkepg60

[39] von Beyme, K. *Transition to Democracy in Eastern Europe*. Palgrave Macmillan, 1996.

[41] Open Society Foundation. Annual reports for 1996, 1997, 1999, 2000, 2001, 2002, 2003, 2004. Soros Centre for the Arts. Annual reports for 1999, 2000. National Culture Fund. Annual reports 2000, 2001, 2002, 2003, 2004. Fondatsiya badeshte za Balgariya (Future for Bulgaria Foundation). Annual reports 1997, 1998. Alexandrov, A. *Bulgarische Kulturpolitik 1995–2008.* Master's thesis. IKM, Vienna, 2005 (unpublished).

Table 51: Support from the NGO Open Society for cultural funding and other purposes[42]

Organization	1996	1997	1998	1999	2000	2001	2002	2003	2004
Open Society Foundation in USD	1 326 818	1 050 504	2 473 000	1 311 000	785 000	749 401	1 347 479	790 210	265 563
Incl. Soros Arts Centre in USD	924 989	686 344	801 295	714 388	596 769	n/a	n/a	115 210	79 000
Future for Bulgaria in BGN	*	*	427 530	*	*	*	*	*	*
Phare programme in USD	*		1 605 000	*	*	*	*	*	*
13 Centuries of Bulgaria in BGN	*	49 636	*	*	*	*	*	*	*
National Culture Fund	*	*	*	*	19 931	216 764	562 479	507 691	387 141

were the most important patrons of culture. Here, special mention must be made of the diplomatic missions in those countries which provided funds to make many cultural initiatives possible.

Although passed extremely late and hotly disputed, the Sponsorship and Patronage Act made it easier for companies all over the country to participate in supporting the decentralization of culture.[42] In 2007, 3,017,835 people in Bulgaria, 70.3% of the population, had not attended a single cultural event.[43]

In the table, the sum of $1,605,000 is comparatively high. After the Landry report, it is obvious that urgent reforms are necessary in culture. It must be decentralized, administrative costs must be cut and the outdated structures reorganized. New funding instruments and a new legislative framework are needed. The PHARE pilot scheme echoes the Landry report, and the project is known as PHARE BG 96 06. It is conducted from 1998 to 2000. The project report is commissioned by the British Council as technical support for the Bulgarian Culture Ministry. The project consists of five main points:

- Analyses of, reports on and recommendations for cultural policy; the reports on cultural policy in Bulgaria are written and compiled by Richard Pulford. His account, five years after the Landry report on culture, is not as detailed, but nevertheless accurately reflects the situation in the cultural sector.[44]

---

42 Law Gazette. Zakon za metsanatstvoto (Patronage Act) 13.12.2009. Regarding the coming into effect of amendments and additions to the Patronage Act with Law Gazette 34 of 25.04.2006, see § 56 of the transitional and final provisions of the Trade Register Act. Josifova B., 2008. *Dalgo shte chakame balgarskite Medichi (We will wait a long time for the Bulgarian Medicis)*. [online]. In: *Sega*, 05.04.2008. Available from: http://www.sega.bgCOMSSSS (status 12.01.2009).

43 Natsionalen tsentar za izuchavane na obshtestvenite naglasi (National centre for research into public opinion), ed. Sofia, 2005, pp. 10–29.

44 Pulford Richard, PHARE BG 96 06, tehnicheska pomost za ministerstvoto na kulturata, Bal-

- Training of eighty administrators, private producers, gallery managers, people working in the cultural sector and civil servants from the municipalities and the Ministry of Culture in cultural policy
- Workshops in England for civil servants from the Ministry of Culture, organized by the British Council, are very effective
- Deadlines for submitting projects in all genres for funding; the first project of this size, that motivates and teaches cultural institutions to submit applications for project funding; 800 projects are submitted, 170 funded.
- Foundation of the Euro-Bulgarian Culture Centre with a bookshop, exhibition space, cinema and internet café. This centre still exists and has the same structure, but a completely different legal form.

Richard Pulford's work is not so widely read, but is very important. It is the basis of good results of the project funding introduced subsequently, the training of administrative staff and the foundation of the Euro-Bulgarian Culture Centre in 1998.

4.4 Places and Symbols of Cultural Development

4.5 The National Culture Palace

The National Culture Palace can be regarded as a symbol and a metaphor for cultural policy both before the end of communism and during the chaotic transition. It was built by a team of architects led by Alexander Barov and opened in 1981 to mark the celebrations of 1300 years of Bulgaria. The Palace's emblem, a bronze creation seven metres in diameter, is the work of the sculptor Georgi Chapkanov. It is a stylized portrayal of the sun based on the typical decorative elements found on ceilings in old Bulgarian houses. Since then, the Palace has been regarded as a symbol of the People's Republic of Bulgaria and communism. Its name was intended to determine its function in the heart of Bulgaria's capital, but in reality its rooms have chiefly been rented out to commercial enterprises and political organizations.

The Culture Palace was entered in Bulstat, the Bulgarian company register, on 1 February 1990 and was managed by an elected director who headed the Creative-Economic Council made up of creative workers and experts from science and technology. In the 1980s it had over a thousand employees, and even after the end of communism in 1989 the workforce remained over three hundred strong for a long time.[45]

garia, Razvitie na kulturnata politika v Balgaria (technical support of the Ministry of Culture, Bulgaria; Development of Cultural Policy in Bulgaria, final report, 21–30 March, 2000). Ministry of Culture, Sofia.

45 Stankova, M. *Koi ubi balgarskata kultura. Edno kriminalno razsledvane* (*Who killed Bulgarian*

Table 52: Opinion poll: The audience, 2005[43]

Events attended in the last 12 months		Total	1–3		4–6		7–12		More than 12		None	
		Number	Number	%	Number	%	Number	%	Number	%	Number	%
Sex	Total	4 295 030	947 486	22.1	207 809	0.8	64 058	1.5	57 842	1.3	3 017 835	70.3
	Men	2 120 002	427 668	20.2	88 227	0.2	23 856	1.1	24 232	1.1	1 556 019	73.4
	Women	2 175 027	519 818	23.9	119 582	0.5	40 202	1.8	33 609	1.5	1 461 816	67.2
Age	25–34	1 141 616	282 475	24.7	67 079	0.9	19 708	1.7	20 527	1.8	751 826	65.9
	35–54	2 127 408	465 610	21.9	109 081	0.1	34 111	1.6	28 450	1.3	1 490 156	70.0
	55–64	1 026 006	199 401	19.4	31 649	0.1	10 238	1.0	8 865	0.9	775 853	75.6
Education level	Elementary, no schooling	1 039 266	75 759	7.3	2 375	0.2	-		2 733	0.3	958 399	92.2
	Secondary	2 284 298	510 358	22.3	88 304	0.9	16 952	0.7	18 787	0.8	1 649 897	72.2
	Tertiary	971 466	361 369	37.2	117 130	2.1	47 106	4.8	36 322	3.7	409 539	42.2
Employment status	Employed	2 929 552	736 859	25.2	176 445	0.0	54 469	1.9	50 720	1.7	1 911 059	65.2
	Unemployed	604 843	66 697	11.0	10 323	0.7	5 213	0.9	1 385	0.2	521 224	86.2
	Economically inactive	760 635	143 930	18.9	21 041	0.8	4 376	0.6	5 736	0.8	585 552	77.0
Place of residence	Town	3 172 067	777 338	24.5	188 422	0.9	61 188	1.9	53 027	1.7	2 092 092	66.0
	Village	1 122 962	170 149	5.2	19 387	0.7	2 869	0.3	4 814	0.4	925 743	82.4

Despite this, criticism was levelled at the Culture Palace's management, because, although it was public property and financed by the state, no statements of receipts and expenditure were issued for many years and the finances were consequently not inspected by the Audit Office.[46]

The sculpture "1300 Years of Bulgaria", proposed by the then chair of the culture committee Lyudmila Zhivkova and created by Valentin Starchev, stood in

culture? A criminal investigation). [online]. [viewed 19.02.2012]. Available from: http://www.slovo.bg/old/litforum/215/mstankova.htm.

44 Ibid.

45 NSI. [online]. Available from: http://www.nsi.bg/otrasal.php?otr=24 (status 26.09.12).

46 Mihalev, I. *Posledniyat dvorets na sotsialisma. Pazarnata ikonomika vse oshte ne e stignala do NDK*. (*The last bastion of socialism. The market economy did not reach the NDK after all*). [online]. [viewed 21.02.2012]. Available from: http://www.vesti.bg/?tid=40&oid=998970.

Table 53: Analysis of visitors to cultural events: the audience, 2011[46]

Cultural events attended in the last 12 months	Total	1–3		4–6		4–6		More than 12		None	
		Number	%	Number	%	Number	%	Number	%	Number	%
Total	4 081 384	963 975	23.6	245 079	0.0	66 472	1.6	41 203	1.0	2 764 655	67.7
Men	2 044 957	422 273	20.6	92 895	0.5	26 599	1.3	15 770	0.8	1 487 418	72.7
Women	2 036 427	541 702	26.6	152 184	0.5	39 872	2.0	25 433	1.2	1 277 236	62.7
Age											
25–34	996 335	292 145	29.3	82 496	0.3	22 077	2.2	10 492	1.1	589 124	59.1
35–54	2 043 782	493 378	24.1	123 221	0.0	32 480	1.6	22 529	1.1	1 372 175	67.1
55–64	1 041 266	178 452	17.1	39 362	0.8	11 915	1.1	8 182	0.8	803 355	77.2
Level of education											
Elementary	833 740	56 130	6.7	3 337	0.4	-	-	717	0.1	773 555	92.8
Secondary school with qualification for university entrance	2 237 621	496 477	22.2	76 772	0.4	23 035	1.0	10 772	0.5	1 630 566	72.9
Univ. degree or equivalent	1 010 023	411 368	40.7	164 970	6.3	43 437	4.3	29 713	2.9	360 534	35.7
Employment status											
Employed	2 566 066	721 604	28.1	207 654	0.1	55 208	2.2	34 665	1.4	1 546 934	60.3
Unemployed	773 227	119 016	15.4	14 858	0.9	3 257	0.4	2 428	0.3	633 668	82.0
Retired	740 331	122 308	16.5	22 567	0.0	8 006	1.1	4 110	0.6	583 339	78.8
Place of residence											
Town	3 071 397	835 066	27.2	223 279	0.3	60 342	2.0	38 085	1.2	1 914 624	62.3
Country	1 009 987	128 909	12.8	21 800	0.2	6 129	0.6	3 118	0.3	850 031	84.2

front of the Culture Palace for many years, before the ravages of time left their mark and the question was raised of whether it should be dismantled. At first, this appeared to be the solution, but in the wake of the ensuing public debate a committee was formed that was willing to provide the funds necessary for restoring the work of art.

On 9 May 2011, the Council of Ministers passed a resolution to the effect that the Culture Palace should be reorganized by a national art association as a public limited company owned by the state. This resolution applied not only to the Culture Palace, but also to the festival complex in Varna. Accordingly, both cultural institutions were reorganized under the terms of the laws in force at the time. Following this change it became clear from a report published in the trade register that the Palace was operating at a loss. In 2011, the PLC posted a loss of BGN 6.7 million. In 2010 the loss was BGN 7.2 million, in 2009 BGN 4.2 million and in 2008 BGN 6.7 million. Behind the scenes, some shareholders were calling for the company to be privatized, and this debate was still continuing when the present study was concluded. Almost every month, the monument in front of the Palace was turned into an ideological battlefield. In addition to this, it became clear in 2012 that restoration of the Palace would cost BGN 500 million, a sum that at that time was completely out of the question for the municipal budget.

4.6 The Chitalishta

The *chitalishta* were always the foundation of Bulgarian culture, so to speak. They emerged during the Bulgarian National Revival in the nineteenth century. The name is derived from the verb "to read" and a noun meaning "place". Over time, the *chitalishta* evolved into a cultural institution with manifold roles. Because the cultural activities they offer were easily accessible, their long tradition and the institutions themselves played a central role in cultural life in Bulgaria. The crisis in the country also threatened the existence of the numerous cultural venues. Many of them were forced to rent out their premises, for example, and close their libraries. The *chitalishta* were turned into amusement arcades or meeting-places for businessmen. Their property was either sold or lost. Between 1998 and 2005, 287 of these amenities were closed down. However, since 2005 a revival of the *chitalishta* and cultural venues has been in progress which has seen their gradual stabilization and reorganization.

The first of Bulgaria's *chitalishta* were founded in early 1856 in Svishtov. Following the country's liberation from Ottoman rule, the facilities offered by these *chitalishta* were used to resurrect Bulgarian culture, language and spirit. In early 1990, nearly 4,000 of these institutions were still in existence in Bulgaria with their own libraries, groups of amateur artists and educational programmes. As a typical form of Bulgarian community culture, they were in a position to determine the direction that a new cultural policy should take. Regrettably, they were neglected, and it was not until 2005 that efforts were made to reorganize them with a new structure and raise funds. In principle, their transformation into educational and creative multi-purpose venues with imaginative and innovative programmes meets the conditions necessary for local and agricultural-cultural development. Some of the ethnic minorities have developed their own forms of *chitalishte* within their own communities. Examples of these are the E. Shekerdiyskis *chitalishte*, a Jewish house of culture, and the Roma *chitalishte* of the City of Plovdiv in the district of Stolipinovo. Although the cultural and educational policy with regard to ethnic minorities initially remained unclear, various ethnic groups tried to work together and live together.

Table 64: Number of chitalishta, 1995–2012[47]

Art centres	*1995*	*1996*	*1998*	*1999*	*2000*	*2005*	*2007*	*2012*
Number	4 225	4 223	3 125	3 056	3 027	2 838	2 895	3 075
In towns	544	544	514	510	511	539	548	587
In villages	3 681	3 679	2 611	2 546	2 516	2 299	2 347	2 488
Tsd. members	x	203	191	180	170	164	168	238
In towns	x	93	86	81	74	68	67	96
In villages	x	110	105	99	96	96	101	142

Table 54: Activities of chitalishta, 2005[48]

	Total
Language courses	327
Participants	4 827
Music courses	440
Participants	4 624
Ballet courses	149
Participants	3 079
Other courses	428
Participants	5 766
Amateur associations	7 494
Participants	108 294
Performances	43 224
Music societies	1 769
Participants	22 865
Performances	12 936
Dance societies	1 522
Celebrations on important national holidays, book reviews, folklore feasts and others.	

	Total
Participants	28 222
Performances	9 779
Drama societies	520
Participants	6 049
Performances	2 807
(authentic) folklore societies	2 017
Participants	27 305
Performances	10 363
Clubs and circles	941
Participants	14 095
Performances	4 143
Others	727
Participants	9 758
Performances	3 196
Cultural activities	51 010

The foundation "Chitalishta 2001–2004" was a joint project conducted by the Ministry of Culture in Bulgaria and the UN Development Programme. It received funding from the US-American Development Agency and the Dutch government's Matra programme. One of the foundation's long-term goals was the promotion of Bulgaria's *chitalishta* as community centres. Its concept corresponded to the national strategy for these cultural centres. The foundation had six branch offices and was headquartered in Sofia, the capital. Its objective was clearly ex-

47 National Statistics Institute (NSI). *Satisticheski spravochnik 2009 (Statistical guide 2009)*. Sofia, 2009, p. 87. NSI. *Statistical Yearbook for Culture and Art*. Sofia, 1996, p. 440.

48 National Statistics Institute. [online]. Available from: www.nsi.bg (status 29.04.2006). (author's translation).

50 National Statistics Institute. [online]. Available from: www.nsi.bg (status 29.04.2006). (author's translation).

51 National Statistics Institute. [online]. Available from: www.nsi.bg (status 29.04.2006).

Table 55: Receipts and expenditure of *chitalishta* in regions and districts, submitted for planning purposes in 2005, in BGN[51]

Regions for planning purposes, districts	Total receipts		Budget subsidies		Total expenditure	
Northwestern region	2 925 130	2 479 410	103 108	2 810 337	1 297 379	261 473
Vidin	715 641	617 416	21 968	701 223	320 445	74 780
Montana	885 513	701 430	41 118	847 255	369 404	87 127
Vratsa	1 323 976	1 160 564	40 022	1 261 859	607 530	99 566
North central region	6 160 802	4 606 845	323 703	5 974 093	2 571 776	510 274
Pleven	1 768 996	1 189 885	141 797	1 754 041	689 414	105 587
Lovech	987 771	792 285	84 721	951 099	430 062	90 823
Veliko Tarnovo	1 665 598	1 346 708	50 334	1 577 711	751 220	120 767
Gabrovo	895 481	559 629	35 225	867 632	292 578	111 868
Ruse	842 956	718 338	11 629	823 610	408 502	81 229
Northeastern region	6 664 337	5 228 969	291 050	6 497 696	2 508 730	738 468
Varna	1 587 491	1 086 339	172 478	1 587 490	567 981	155 784
Dobrich	1 503 882	1 297 660	28 921	1 471 523	475 568	224 281
Shumen	1 043 902	771 473	40 393	1 012 786	432 402	90 870
Targovishte	740 504	577 174	16 556	728 048	335 207	71 740
Razgrad	959 159	834 038	26 420	896 354	410 128	123 569
Silistra	829 399	662 285	6 282	801 495	287 444	72 224
Southwestern region	9 537 388	6 419 093	1 019 465	9 087 568	3 814 457	729 519
Sofia	4 606 417	2 597 685	798 011	4 276 396	1 850 903	250 822
Sofia region	1 979 695	1 446 104	160 207	1 932 251	748 597	174 548
Blagoevgrad	1 563 433	1 273 199	26 290	1 522 939	644 792	127 899
Pernik	748 701	577 699	19 186	733 714	298 272	99 762
Kyustendil	639 142	544 436	15 771	622 268	251 983	76 488
South-central region	7 402 087	5 425 699	404 492	7 191 047	2 988 909	652 624
Plovdiv	2 122 198	1 526 744	104 260	2 063 329	892 988	133 376
St. Zagora	1 714 500	1 235 101	204 576	1 654 562	695 488	179 830
Haskovo	941 046	727 390	38 417	930 290	350 898	125 307
Pazardzhik	1 202 151	964 672	23 493	1 182 062	524 628	69 565
Smolyan	862 323	519 678	18 879	811 506	313 228	63 231
Kardzhali	559 869	452 084	14 867	549 298	211 679	81 315
Southeast region	3 799 903	2 995 004	188 297	3 588 312	1 470 280	469 148
Burgas	2 145 274	1 701 872	89 548	1 969 326	777 686	329 097
Sliven	907 935	710 303	63 366	890 737	366 325	96 369
Yambol	746 694	582 829	35 383	728 249	327 269	43 682

pressed: To continue stabilizing the *chitalishta* so that they might fulfil their role which is so important for Bulgarian culture as a whole.[52]

[52] Cf. Fondatsiya za razvitie "Chitalishta" (Foundation for the development of *chitalishta*) [online]. [viewed 19.02.2012]. Available from: www.chitalishte.bg (status 26.07.2011).

Table 56 : *Chitalishta* planned in regions and districts, 2005[52]

Regions for planning purposes, districts	*Chitalishta*			Members			Mean no. of members		
	Total	Towns	Villages	Total	Towns	Villages	Total	Towns	Villages
Country-wide total	**2 838**	**539**	**2 299**	**163 630**	**68235**	**95 353**	**58**	**127**	**41**
Northwestern region	**228**	**28**	**200**	**12 181**	**4 139**	**8 042**	**53**	**148**	**40**
Vidin	65	7	58	2931	716	2 215	45	102	38
Montana	86	12	74	3 497	909	2 588	41	76	35
Vratsa	77	9	68	5 753	2 514	3 239	75	279	48
North central region	**495**	**87**	**408**	**28 151**	**9 796**	**18 355**	**57**	**113**	**45**
Pleven	129	25	104	6 505	2 437	4 068	50	97	39
Lovech	97	15	82	5 388	1 462	3 926	56	97	48
Veliko Tarnovo	134	21	113	7 825	2 585	5 240	58	123	46
Gabrovo	55	12	43	3 170	1 346	1824	58	112	42
Ruse	80	14	66	5 263	1 966	3 297	66	140	50
Northeastern region	**607**	**79**	**528**	**30 413**	**9 787**	**20 626**	**50**	**124**	**39**
Varna	129	29	100	8 317	4 136	4 181	64	143	42
Dobrich	90	8	82	3 942	927	3 015	44	116	37
Shumen	115	18	97	6 205	2 084	4 121	54	116	42
Targovishte	103	10	93	3 788	852	2 936	37	85	32
Razgrad	82	7	75	4 211	1 127	3 084	51	161	41
Silistra	88	7	81	3 950	661	3 289	45	94	41
Southwestern region	**499**	**159**	**340**	**35 119**	**20870**	**14 249**	**70**	**131**	**42**
Sofia((capital)	126	96	30	15 245	13580	1 565	120	141	52
Sofia	128	20	108	7 285	2 247	5 038	57	112	47
Blagoevgrad	105	13	92	5 025	1 677	3 348	48	129	36
Pernik	71	15	56	3 141	1 491	1650	44	99	29
Kyustendil	69	15	54	4 523	1 875	2 648	66	125	49
South central region	**679**	**127**	**552**	**41 229**	**17304**	23 925	**61**	**136**	**43**
Plovdiv	196	44	152	14 211	7 214	6 997	73	164	46
St. Zagora	141	16	12 5	8 345	1 717	6 628	59	107	53
Haskovo	98	26	72	6 866	2 904	3 962	70	122	55
Smolyan	73	12	61	3 888	2 082	1 806	53	174	30
Kardzhali	68	9	59	2 235	646	1 589	33	72	27
Southeastern region	**330**	**59**	**271**	**16 537**	**6 339**	**10 198**	**50**	**107**	**38**
Burgas	147	32	115	8 224	3 954	4 270	56	124	37

The general public saw the community art centres as an example of a sustainable national cultural institution that performed the specific task of preserving and developing the nation's traditional values. The *chitalishta* drew their authority and legitimacy in society from their deep-rooted interrelationship with the past, traditions, educational processes, culture and charity.

Over the course of its 150-year history, the institution that is the Bulgarian *chitalishte* had therefore maintained the position it had achieved as a pillar of community activities and continued to enjoy a high degree of trust. It has great potential for promoting and strengthening civil society. Thanks to their unique social prestige and wide geographical spread, the *chitalishta* were better able to meet the population's specific cultural and educational needs, and this in turn meant that more people became involved in their activities. At the same time, they brought their origins as a national, social, cultural, educational and informative organization to bear. It will be interesting to see in future how they perform their task of building a bridge between Bulgaria's past, present and future.

In his report on Bulgaria's cultural policy, Charles Landry describes the *chitalishta* as the most important anchor for both cultural development and the development of civil society since they are an extremely extensive form of institution that was found all over the country.[53]

The *chitalishta* are normatively governed by a special law pertaining to them that was passed in 1945.[54]

In late 1996, the law on these institutions was passed that stayed in force until 2008. Since then they have been classified as non-profit organizations whose priorities are the cultural needs of the population.[55]

With the passing of this law, the idea was put into practice of giving the *chitalishta* the chance to transform themselves from organizations dependent on the budget into robust cultural institutions. To achieve this, they were to raise funds from a variety of sources, and these included not just membership fees or fee-charging public activities, but also renting out, endowments, gifts, bequests, use of farmland and many more besides. Their main source of funds, however, remained state subsidies and subsidies granted out of the budgets of the municipalities they were connected to.

Rescission of Article 7 of the law, which provided for the creation of a fund titled "*Chitalishta* and their activities" within the Ministry of Culture, meant the institutions lost the possibility of raising capital and of directly supporting the art centres as they carried out their cultural projects and programmes. This was reflected in the influence of the state and the way cultural policy was implemented

53 Landry, C. *Bulgaria's Cultural Policy in Transition: From the Art of the State to the State of the Art.* London, 1997.

54 Darzhaven vestnik no. 142 (1945). No. 152 (1945). No. 59 (1996).

55 Zakon za chitalishtata (Art Centres Act), 1996. Publ. in Darzhavenvestnik no. 89, 22 Oct 1996, amend. No. 95, 21 Oct 1997. No. 90, 15 Oct 1999. No 28, 1 Apr 2005, effective from 1 Apr 2005. No. 94, 25 Nov 2005, effective from 25 Nov 2005. No. 108, 29 Dec 2006, effective from 1 Jan 2007, amend. and expanded. No. 42, 5 Jun 2009, amend. No. 74, 15 Sep 2009, effective from 15 Sep 2009. No. 47, 22 Jun 2010. No. 97, 10 Dec 2010, effective from 10 Dec 2010. Law Library – APIS, Vol. 4, Section 3, no. 580.

in rural areas. It was in these areas in particular that the *chitalishta* were often the only community amenity for culture.

Table 57: Supplemental subsidies 2003–2008 for the activities of chitalishta in BGN million[56]

2003	2004	2005	2006	2007	2008
804 640	1 000 000	1 500 000	2 500 000	4 000 000	5 000 000

During this period, the *chitalishta* were integrated into the so-called system of delegated state activities. The funds required from the national budget were calculated on the basis of a subsidized quantity, although the benefits due to each employee were linked to a subsidy standard and included the salary, social security payments and provision of material needs.

Distribution of art centres across the country was very uneven. The same can be said of smaller municipalities and large towns. In some places there was a real danger that the activities would become commercialized to the detriment of their essentially cultural and social functions. The comparative analysis shows that one *chitalishte* caters for nearly 2 500 people. A *chitalishte* consequently becomes an institution with a wide reach and the task of meeting the general public's cultural needs.[57]

The year 2005 can be regarded as a turning point in the number of registered *chitalishta*, since before then their number had been falling steadily. During the transition, their role and their appeal to the contemporary generation had successively diminished. But after 2005, a revival set in.

The continuing process of registering more and more new art centres in many small municipalities where there is no real opportunity for community groups to develop could become a problem, which could perhaps be solved by setting up new branch establishments and agency structures.

For this reason, more and more *chitalishta* tried to conclude new treaties of association or partnership under the existing legal provisions. These agreements were based primarily on the territorial principle. Those of them who were in equal partnerships were in a position to improve their activities, their management and their budgeting themselves. This need for optimization is the basis of the trend observed in these institutions in recent years towards the greatest possible degree of autonomy. The *chitalishta* operated in the region in which they were located. Supraregional networks were not in their interests and were therefore not an aim.

In 2005, construction of regional experts' and information desks in community centres was started as a complement to the *chitalishta*. These desks supported

[56] Ministry of Culture. *Balgarskite chitalishta dnes – analiz* (*Bulgarian* chitalishta*today — an analysis*). Sofia, 2007, p. 16 (author's translation.)

[57] Ibid.

national policy with respect to cultural institutions which was based on the principles of decentralization, preservation of local traditions and an active community.

The chief tasks of these centres were:

- To compile a database of all art centres in the region
- To offer help with procedures and professional advice
- To draft reports on the status and problems of *chitalishta* presented to the Ministry of Culture and to regional and municipal authorities
- To prepare and support the development of projects and participate in them
- To organize and take part in the implementation of educational measures, courses and other training strategies
- To coordinate the art centres' involvement in the regional library information network and to support their modernization as important centres of culture and information in the community
- To organize and conduct regional meetings to discuss issues relating to the art centres

The foundation "Chitalishta 2001–2004" was headquartered in Sofia and had six regional branch offices in Blagoevgrad, Vidin, Kardzhali, Pleven, Sliven and Shumen (former regional centres). This enabled the foundation to operate all over the country. It had a large database of art centres and carried out analyses of practice and experts' reports. Its long-term objective was to strengthen the role of Bulgarian art centres as community centres and valuable players in local development. Its strategic concept corresponded to the national policy on the art centres which was based on the principles of decentralization, preservation of traditions, formation of civil society and espousal of modern global community values.

In general, the *chitalishta* had a sound and extensive infrastructure before 1989, which included buildings and furnishings. However, most of them could not afford either to maintain these or to subscribe to the daily newspapers. This was not least because most of them were built in the middle of the twentieth century, meaning that nearly all needed some form of investment in modernization and maintenance.

Approximately 95% of the buildings housing the art centres were registered as municipal-public property that was placed at the disposal of the art centre foundation boards for their use and activities under the terms of the law on art centres and municipal property. This in turn obliged the management of the centres not merely to maintain, renovate and modernize the structures, but also to make prudent use of the tangible assets.[58]

[58] Darzhaven vestnik. Zakon za korporativnoto podohodno oblagane (SKPO) (Corporation Tax Act). Zakon za danaka varchu dobavenata stoinost (VAT Act, SDDS). Zakon za mestni danatsi i taksi (SMDT) (Local Taxation Act). Darzhaven vestnik no. 89, 22 Oct 1996; Darzhaven vestnik no. 95, 21 Oct 1997; Darzhaven vestnik no. 90, 15 Oct 1999; Darzhaven vestnik no. 8, 1 Apr 2005; Darzhaven vestnik no. 94, 25 Nov 2005; Darzhaven vestnik no. 108, 29 Dec 2006.

Another crucial point is that many art centres had only one possible venue in the town or village where concerts and community gatherings could take place. Accordingly, they had facilities such as their own stage and an auditorium for movies which gave the centre the character of a natural focal point of community life. However, most of the art centre rooms, which could seat as many as five hundred visitors, were in need of modernization and refurbishment of the stage, stage machinery, the library inventory and the substance of the building itself. To this end, the Ministry of Culture has in recent years provided funds on a project basis for the partial renovation of the buildings or the updating of the library stock, digitizing, the purchase and repair of musical instruments, costumes, props for theatre plays etc.

Towards the end of 2006, the previous stipulations governing the *chitalishta* were superseded by specific transitional and final provisions in the law on the state budget of the Republic of Bulgaria for the year 2007.

This change freed the *chitalishta* from all state and municipal taxes and duties on the most important of their activities and related assets.[59] It changed taxation of their activities under the terms of the corporation tax law and the VAT law as well as local taxes and levies. The amending law was accepted by the cabinet and in parliament with discussion and was justified with reference to European norms and regulations.

This very important step in shaping the future of the old institution was nothing short of drastic since it had never been discussed or agreed with any of the associations who represented not just their own interests, but also those of the *chitalishta* and of over 3,000 organizations. This meant that it affected, either directly or indirectly, thousands of people. The question of the role played by the Ministry of Culture and exactly how its function as a visionary for the future of culture was to be defined if no discussion about changes of this kind is held was therefore plain for all to see. One result was, at least, centralization of funding, which possibly returned the art centres to the situation they had originally been in in 1989 when the reforms began.

As cultural organizations, they had previously had the objective of enlightening the population and preserving the Bulgarian spirit and traditions for coming generations. During the transition they found themselves in an economic and social situation that was completely different from what had been before and could not be compared to it. Consequently, the *chitalishta* made virtually no impression at all on the country's cultural map by staging significant cultural events.

[59] Darzhaven vestnik no. 108, 29 December 2006, effective from 1 January 2007, § 6.

4.7 Assessment

The lack of appreciation and understanding of the role of a free market as a whole and of the cultural market in particular, coupled with the state's ignorance of how it could use its prerogatives to contribute to the smooth function of this market, left many people in Bulgaria disappointed in the idea of free enterprise. In some sectors, rash measures were taken such as the sale of the Bulgarian airline or the privatization of the agricultural sector. It is to be noted in this connection that the influence of the state fluctuated between the extremes of total control in certain sectors and a complete lack of regulation in others so that economic and social inconsistency and instability ensued. The fields of action open to cultural policy and measures to protect cultural institutions were activated either very late or not at all. Consequently, this policy limited itself, and from 1995 to 2008 this caused considerable losses, both in general and in the culture sector. One very clear example is the field of publishing and libraries. The figures in the culture sector deserve closer scrutiny:

- The share of funds spent on culture from the national budget was 1.37% of GDP in 1995 and 0.6% in 2008.
- The nominal costs of culture in the national budget rose tenfold from 1990 to 1995, but in real terms their value fell by 80% in 1995. Without including the costs of radio and television, the budget of the Ministry of Culture had nominally increased fivefold in 1995 compared to 1991, but because of the high rate of inflation its real value fell by 58%.
- From 1995 to 2008, the increase in the budget of the Ministry of Culture amounted to 849%.

It can be observed that in the period 1997–2008 subsidies for the media from the central budget were almost twice as high as for all other art categories. Funds for National Radio, for example, rose by 194%, and those of BNTV by 15%.

Although an increase had been promised in the election manifestos of all the parties, the budget for culture in 2008 remained around 0.6% of GDP and even fell by 1.2% compared to 1995. If spending on the media is also deducted, the percentage for the funding of the other art categories is significantly lower, namely 0.4%.

In the period 1988–1993, the average percentage of receipts in the cultural institutions remained relatively stable, even though some institutions, such as the theatres, had significantly increased their percentage of the receipts until 1995. From 2000 to 2008, the level of receipts remained almost unchanged, while the percentage of the subsidies reported in the budget increased.

The ratio of the total costs in the culture sector to be borne by the state and the municipalities under the terms of the Municipal Act, namely 70% to 30%, had not changed significantly since 1989; in 1989 the ratio of distribution was 64% from the state and 36% from the municipalities.

Expenditure within the Ministry of Culture on, for example, theatres, was as follows:

1995: 18%

1991: 20.3%

2000: 55.6%

2008: 24.65%

2011: 24.89% (total for the category of theatres).

Receipts in the last nine years amounted to only 38%, while expenditure increased by 162.3% until 2008. Whereas the marginal income changed in absolute terms, there was also an increase in receipts. This can be attributed to rising admission prices, which also means, however, that there was no significant change in visitor numbers.

98% of the costs of maintaining the opera houses and the Philharmonic Orchestra were borne by the state.

The composition of spending remained almost unchanged from 2000 to 2008. On the one hand, this is ideal, on the other it meant that unprofitable sectors were stimulated, and this did nothing to support the development of those sectors which had hitherto been neglected, such as books, libraries, art centres or the promotion of talented children.

In 1995, spending on art education amounted to 15.8% of the Culture Ministry's budget, compared to 1991 when it was 14.4%. In 2000 it had fallen to only 3.82%. However, it was in this year that inflation was brought under control thanks to the long-term measures taken by the Ivan Kostov government (1997–2001).

A look at how each category developed allows the following conclusions to be drawn:

- In the music and dance categories, the receipts and expenditure produced a positive trend. As with the overall costs, the costs in the individual art institutions increased disproportionately until 2008, while their receipts remained almost unchanged. This means that money alone is insufficient to support this sector and that strategies must be developed to raise more funds by increasing its attractiveness.

- The chief budgetary priorities of the Ministry of Culture in 2000 were theatre, music and dance, and these sectors remained crucial in 2012. However, their percentage share of the falling receipts was to the detriment of other sectors. A negative trend was also observed in the development of the book trade, specifically the *chitalishta* and libraries, as well as of the training of staff in the entire art and culture sector.

- Although preservation of the historical cultural heritage was regulated by several resolutions passed by the Ministry and parliament, it was not until 2007 and 2008 that more funds were made available for this activity, which consequently led to increased receipts.

The conclusion that must be drawn is that the implementation of the strategy and planning was unsatisfactory up to this point. The increase of 5000% in 2008 provided ample evidence that this sector possessed great potential for development which was still a long way from being fully realized.

- Expenditure in the film industry in the period under review, 1995–2012, was higher than its receipts. This is true of all categories. Subsidies for the film industry in 2008 amounted to BGN 11,808,013, while the receipts reached only BGN 552,590. Despite this, the figures clearly show that the 8.53% of the budget allocated to the film sector by the state falls short of the amount stipulated by law, which was 10%. The film industry itself was expected to find an answer to the question of how to raise more money. Privatization in culture took place primarily in cultural industries such as the media, film production and the book trade. From 1995 to 2012, few foundations or funds were set up by private enterprise for the purpose of supporting cultural institutions. The way for funding cultural projects was paved only by the establishment of the National Culture Fund in the year 2000 and by a number of small culture funds in the municipalities. What this did mean, however, was a major step towards decentralizing cultural funding in the country.

From 2008 to 2012, expenditure on the media fell by 30% overall for BNTV and 22% for BN radio. Compared to the year 2008, the Ministry of Culture's budget recorded an increase of 9% in 2012. But when the rate of inflation for this period is taken into account, no significant increase in expenditure is apparent. On the basis of the conclusions drawn from the real economy over the past years, the Ministry of Culture considerably increased subsidies for movable and non-movable cultural heritage. An additional factor in this decision was that cultural tourism is indispensable for the revenue of individual municipalities.

In this discussion, it is essential to recognize that it is the task of the Ministry of Culture to create general parameters, but that the Ministry failed for years to understand that its role was not to produce art, but to promote and support it with appropriate legislation. Twenty-four years after the end of communist rule, this is a fact and it is to be hoped that the negative trends in the development of cultural policy and the detrimental effects of inappropriate funding models are recognized. A further aspect of this discussion is the necessity of gathering statistics on regional support of culture, since this has so far not been done. It is, however, necessary in order to record and have complete figures on total spending on the arts and culture in the country. Another result of examining spending on the arts and culture through all these years is a statistical representation of the cultural policy of every government from 1989 to 2012.

It is to be hoped that a new generation of experts will make the components of culture in society clear and visible.

5. BASIC PRINCIPLES AND PRACTICE OF MUNICIPAL CULTURAL POLICY IN BULGARIA

5.1 The Decentralization Model

On 10 November 1989, Bulgaria embarked on the path to democratization and decentralization. From that point on, the state was to be governed at two levels: by central government, responsible for issues of national importance, and by the local authorities. Within the system of self-administration, so-called local finances emerged which became part of Bulgaria's financial system. These local finances were concerned with local development. This fiscal decentralization, which was based on the European Charter of Local Self-Government adopted on 15 October 1985 in Strasbourg, delegated duties and responsibilities with a view to making local public assets available. The Charter was ratified in Bulgaria by legislation passed on 17 March 1995.[1]

Self-government gave local authorities the right, within the limits of the law, to regulate and manage a substantial share of public affairs under their own responsibility in the interests of the local population. This right was exercised by councils or assemblies whose members were elected by universal suffrage and which had subordinate executive bodies.

Within the limits of the law, these local authorities had the right to manage all issues not explicitly excluded from their jurisdiction or assigned to other bodies. The financial resources of these local authorities came at least partly from municipal taxes and rates, which they fixed themselves in accordance with the law. The financing systems governing administration of the funds were many and varied; they were designed to be flexible so that they could keep pace with the way costs developed as the authorities performed their tasks.

To protect local authorities on a less solid financial footing and counteract the effects of uneven distribution of funds and costs, a procedure for redistribution of funds was introduced. Through the appropriate channels, the municipal authorities were asked how such redistributed funds should be placed at their disposal. The assignment of funds should not curtail the local authorities' fundamental freedom to determine policy within their own jurisdiction. For the funds needed to cover

---

1 Cf. The federal authorities of the Swiss Confederation, European Charter of Local Self-Government, 05.02.2012. [online]. [viewed 19.02.2012]. Available from: http://www.droit-bi lingue.ch/rs/c0_102-d-f.html (status 23.02.2010). NB. The Charter was ratified by parliament on 17 Mar 1995, and not on 17 May 1995 as stated in this docu- ment. Cf. Darzhaven vestnik no. 28, 28 Mar 1995. Ministerstvo na regionalnoto razwitie (Ministry of Reg- ional Development). Publ. in Darzhaven vestnik no. 46, 6 Jun. 2000 r., effective from 1 Sep 1995.

their investment outlay, the local authorities had access to the national capital market.

The distribution of responsibilities for raising and spending funds between the national and local government levels increased economic efficiency and fiscal decentralization. In turn, this led to greater advantages in the use of the limited resources and the production of public goods.[2]

The autonomy of the local authorities was guaranteed by the political freedom cited in the constitution, and financial resources were regarded as the basis for implementing political decisions. The municipalities' receipts were part of national revenue and were directly connected to the funds assigned to local budgets from it.

Individual municipalities' own revenue had to be raised entirely on their own territory. It encompassed levies such as property tax, death duties and inheritance tax, gift tax, motor vehicle taxes and the like. Local fees levied included the tax on the removal of household refuse, trading fees and fees payable for travel services. Municipalities also drew revenue from concessions in areas such as traffic, renting out of property, fines, interest and penalties.

Additionally, the state refunded part of the revenue from projects co-financed by the European Union to the municipalities, which were able to use it to pay for amenities in sectors such as health care, education, culture and social welfare which were their responsibility.

> "In the municipal budget, provision can be made for urgent and unforeseen costs: these reserves can amount to 10% of the budget resources for sectors delegated by the state where these are provided for by the state budget law for the year in question."[3]

Until relevant regulations came into effect in 2008, each municipality drafted its budget individually. This caused enormous difficulties for inspections by the Audit Office and other supervisory bodies.

The subsidies granted by the state guaranteed the minimum of funds necessary for supplying local public goods. The municipalities were able to take out bank loans, interest-free loans from the national budget and debenture loans or could subscribe to issues of municipal securities. Tax revenue was vital for self-government. The higher the subsidies, the greater the municipalities' dependence on the central administration. If they wanted to maintain their independence, the

---

2 Cf. Stanev, H., Spiridonova, J. and Dzhildzhov, A. *Detsentralizatsiata i vliyanieto i varchu vazmozhnostite na obshtinite i oblastite za usvoyavane na sredstva ot fondovete na evropeyskiya sayuz* (*Decentralization and its influence on municipalities' and regions' capacity to absorb EU subsidies tied to funds*). (Open Society Foundation). Sofia, 2006, pp. 14–24.

3 Zakon za obshtinskite byudzheti (Municipal Budgets Act). Darzhaven vestnik no. 33, 24 Mar 1998 ã., last update 01.06.2005. Zakon za obshtinskite byudzheti (Municipal Budgets Act). Darzhaven vestnik no. 33, 24 Mar 1998, last up- date 11.06.2008. Section 14, Item 1 (amend.: Darzhaven vestnik no. 107, 2003).

municipalities were forced to look for their own sources of revenue. The spending sectors were stipulated by the law relating to municipal budgets. These were:

- Health, social services, education, culture, sport, tourism and youth activities
- Management of municipal property and administrative services for the population
- Active protection of the environment
- Upkeep of the local council and municipal administration
- Support of businesses
- Implementation of international programmes on the territory covered by the municipal budget
- Repayment of loans

In an address on 17 October 2003, President Georgi Parvanov stressed the particular importance of local government for cultural policy:

> "Culture emerged as one of the victims of the transition. The state did, in fact, relinquish its responsibility for its protection and maintenance. For years, the budget for culture, science and education was drafted according to the principle of leftovers. Decentralization is not yet a fact. Even our *chitalishta*! These centres of the Bulgarian renaissance and Bulgarian consciousness do not receive the little they need, such as tax relief, a supply of information and additional resources. This is why the discussion of the problems of cultural policy in the general public and in government circles, at national and especially at municipal and regional level, is not only topical, but essential for our country. It is particularly important that this discussion begins by dealing with those sectors of our cultural system that are most at risk — in the little villages, where the inhabitants are in many cases utterly cut off from cultural life and have no possibility of taking part in it. That the driving force behind this discussion is the population itself and civil organizations is extremely important, as is the fact that they are concerning themselves with Bulgarian culture and are making culture and the arts more accessible to the people.
>
> "The national discussion shows that it is time to coordinate all ideas and initiatives and time that the state commits to implementing them. Culture must become our national priority."[4]

In a study conducted in 2007, the rating agency Global Rating and representatives of the National Association of Towns and Municipalities in Bulgaria showed, along with the Foundation for the Reform of Municipal Self-Government, that 188 projects with a combined value of EUR 11 thousand million had been carried out in Bulgaria, with 83% of the funds provided by the ISPA being spent on them. The study examined the situation of municipal budgets and trends in the management of infrastructure projects funded by this EU instrument.

4 Parvanov, G., 2003: Privetstvie na prezidenta do uchastnizite v natsionalnata diskusiya za regionalni kulturni politiki (Svishtov, 17-18 oktomvri 2003) (Welcome address by President G. Parvanov, national discus- sion on regional cultural policy, Svishtov, 17–18 October, 2003). In: President 17.10. 2003. [online]. Avail- able from: http://www.president.bg/news.php?id=1010&st=445 (status 03.08.2007).

For 2006, the funds earmarked for projects in Bulgaria amounted to BGN 19,163,391, of which BGN 19,274,453, or 100.6%, was used; in 2007 the sum set aside was BGN 24,422,702, of which only BGN 13,745,075, or 56.3%, had been used by 30 September 2007.[5]

In 2008, ninety-two projects with a total volume of EUR 13.7 million were carried out under the banner of "Beautiful Bulgaria". Although revenue in the municipal budgets raised from their own sources accounted only for a fraction of the total sum, it was increasing nonetheless.[6]

The rate of direct taxation in Bulgaria was among the lowest in Europe. As a result, a 10% tax on profits and income tax of 10% were introduced. Under the Corporation Tax Act, the tax on dividends was reduced from 7% to 5%. The patents tax was made a local tax.

Because they were dependent on the national budget, the local municipal authorities had no chance of pursuing their own policies, which would have focused on developing the individual regions and assuming full responsibility for developing the municipality.

At this time, representatives of NGOs had the idea of creating a municipal culture fund. Following several conferences with representatives of seven municipalities in Sofia, an agreement on the future of the city's culture fund was reached. The campaign was led by the Open Society foundation in Sofia.

The statutes of the culture fund contained the following principal objectives:

Section 1. The Municipal Culture Fund has the objective of implementing support of priority projects and activities of Sofia City Council.

Section 2. The Municipal Culture Fund will base its activities on the following principles:

- Increased opportunities for all citizens of Sofia to have access to culture in all its forms
- Promoting the development of a competitive cultural product by coordinating various subjects, transparency and competitiveness
- In cooperation with organizations of civil society and professional elites, sup-

5 Smetna Palata (Audit Office). Doklad za posledvasht kontrol na ispalnenieto na preporakite po oditen doklad No 0600003407 za isvarshen odit na deinostta po Proekt "Krasiva Balgariya" v Ministerstvoto na truda i sotsialnata politika za perioda ot 01.01.2006 g. do 30.09.2007, No 0600003407 (Report on the results of the implementation of the recommendations made in Audit Office report no. 0600003407 for examination of the project "Beautiful Bulgaria" in the Ministry of Labour and Social Affairs for the period 01.01.2006 to 30.09.2007, no. 0600003407), p. 6.

6 Cf. Indikativna programa za 2008 na operativna programa "Razvitie" (Indicative Regional Development Programme). [online]. In: Europe.bg, 31.01.2008. Sofia. [viewed 20.02.2012]. Available from: http://www.europe.bg/htmls/page.php?category=329&id=12334 (status 09.03.2009).

porting the development and implementation of the capital city's cultural strategy

- Developing and implementing new, transparent and accessible financial mechanisms to raise and allocate resources to culture
- Creation of conditions necessary for part-time and full-time employment
- Creation of conditions necessary for alignment with the development practice in the capital cities of the European Union's members states[7]

The role of culture as a factor in sustainable regional development has become part of the political agenda in Bulgaria only in the last few years.

In 2007, an amendment to the constitution of the Republic of Bulgaria allowed part of the planned decentralization to be accomplished, namely by increasing the municipalities' own revenue. The municipal councils were given the right to set the rates of taxes and other levies themselves so that the costs of local activities would be covered. This decision was very important for fiscal decentralization in the culture sector. However, most municipal cultural institutions received financing from the Ministry of Culture and not from the municipal budget, which meant that although they had the status of municipal cultural institutions, the meagre resources in the municipal budgets for cultural activities meant that they did not receive sufficient funds to cover their overheads. In 2005, the proportion of funds allocated to the culture sector in Bulgaria from central government was higher than in any other central or eastern European country.[8]

Table 58: Comparison of the share of funds allocated by central government to the culture sector[9]

Romania	44.0%	Slovenia	60.0%
Slovakia	53.5%	Ukraine	23.8%
Poland	19.6%	Moldova	52.3%
Lithuania	42.3%	Latvia	58.4%
Hungary	29.6%	Serbia	45.8%
Croatia	43.0%		

These figures show that the trend towards significant decentralization of expenditure on the culture sector observed in the member states of the European Union has not taken place in Bulgaria. Analysis of the distribution of costs at central and municipal level shows that there was no notable change in the decentralization of cultural funding from 1990 to 2012.

7 Sofia City Council, 2010. Supplement no. 1, ruling no. 38, protocol no. 56 of 28.01.2010, archives of Sofia City Council.

8 Andreeva, D., 2008. Tsentralizirane i detsentralizirane na kulturata v usloviya na evrointegratsiya (Centraliza- tion and decentralization of culture with respect to integration in the EU). [online]. In: *Medii i obshtestveni komunikatsii, No. 1.* [viewed 22.02.2012.] Available from: http://media-journal.info/?p=item&aid=13 (status 04.04.2010).

9 Ibid.

"On the other hand, the figures show that the percentage of state spending in Bulgaria that is regulated by the budget is among the highest in Europe (...) Compared to 1999, the concentration of cultural spending at central level has even increased; at that time it was 63%."[10]

The difficulties involved in self-government indicate that the decentralization process will be a long and arduous one. Against this background, the establishment of workable local management mechanisms remained one of the top priorities of regional development in Bulgaria. The venues available where local and regional projects could be carried out were too small and too weak to form networks with each other.[11]

Table 59: Expenditure on culture at central and municipal level as a percentage, 1990–2001[12]

Year	Central level	Municipal level
1990	68.8 %	31.2 %
1991	61.5 %	38.5 %
1992	62.7 %	37.3 %
1993	61.3 %	38.7 %
1994	62.4 %	37.6 %
1995	64.6 %	35.4 %
1996	62.3 %	37.7 %
1997	60.7 %	39.3 %
1998	58.0 %	42.0 % ´

Year	Central level	Municipal level
1999	63.7 %	36.3 %
2000	67.4 %	32.6 %
2001	61.3 %	38.7 %
2002	56.9 %	43.1 %
2003	74.7 %	25.3 %
2004	79.5 %	20.5 %
2005	65.5 %	34.5 %
2006	67.3 %	32.7 %
2007	67.7 %	32.3 %

In the first part of this period (1990–1998), a falling share of funds spent on culture can be seen. These funds were distributed by central government from the state budget and fell from 68.8% in 1990 to 58.0% in 1998. However, this trend in favour of regional allocation was not maintained: in 2004 spending on culture at local level had dropped to only 20.5%. This was the lowest figure in the period under review.[13] Subsequently, the level returned to that of 1990 (approximately 32%).

For the period investigated, 1990 to 2012, it can therefore be concluded that no clear trend towards decentralization of the allocation of funds for the culture

[10] Dimitrov, G. *Kultur im Transformationsprozess Osteuropas. Zum Wandel kultureller Institutionen am Beispiel Bulgariens nach 1989*. Munich, 2009, p. 165.

[11] Ibid., p. 164.

[12] Cited in: Andreeva, D., 2008. Tsentralizirane i detsentralizirane na kulturata v usloviya na evrointegratsiya (Centralization and decentralization of culture with respect to integration in the EU), No. 1. Council of Europe/ERICarts. *Compendium of Cultural Policies and Trends in Europe*, 9th edition.

[13] Andreeva, D., 2008. Tsentralizirane i detsentralizirane na kulturata v usloviya na evrointegratsiya (Centraliza- tion and decentralization of culture with respect to integration in the EU). [online]. In: *Medii i obshtestveni komunikatsii, No. 1.* [viewed 22.02.2012.] Available from: http://media-journal.info/?p=item&aid=13 (status 04.04.2010).

sector could be observed. There was no distinct, long-term plan for decentralization. To explain the sporadic shifts in the distribution of funds, the lack of a national strategy for the development of Bulgarian culture may be cited. The inability of cultural policy to devise a long-term funding plan meant that there were no alternative market-based sources of funding.

The concept of decentralization of culture, and especially the decentralization of its funding, does not imply reduced support from the state budget. Increases in subsidy and the diversity of creative forms within a country are among the objectives of good cultural policy. The subsidies themselves should not be regarded merely as costs, but as a form of investment in the future and future generations, although during the process of decentralization the municipalities did indeed have the freedom to determine the fate and future of the cultural institutions on their territory themselves.

With regard to cultural development, the 1999 law focused entirely on describing and systematizing the existing system of state and municipal cultural institutions rather than on encouraging the many publicly financed commercial and non-profit organizations to reach a distant goal, namely a consensus and a clear-cut national cultural strategy for the future. In 2006, the Ministry of Culture proposed a change in the law, without consulting the NGOs. The group of experts for effective and transparent cultural policy, which also included representatives of NGOs from the field of culture, responded to the proposed changes and highlighted the following problems that they would entail:

- Lack of equality among state and municipal cultural organizations when it comes to receiving funds for salaries, building maintenance and financing activities.
- The state, municipal and cultural organizations that receive funds for salaries, building maintenance and activities, and other independent cultural organizations that receive funds only on a project basis or for particular activities.
- Contradictions between the Protection and Development of Culture Act and the laws on local self-government and municipal budgets which make it impossible in practice to set up municipal funds for culture.
- Lack of a solution in law to the financial problems of the National Culture Fund that every year receives funds from the dwindling state budget without being in a position to obtain income itself from sources cited in the legislation such as fees, fines, revenue from rent etc.
- No regulation in law of the so-called mixed financing of cultural institutions either from the state or the municipal budget.
- Insufficient opportunity provided to the population to take part in planning, monitoring and implementing cultural policies.
- Insufficient differentiation between principles and priorities of national cultural policy in Article 2 of the law.

The definition of fundamental terms, such as cultural value, is extremely problematic. Bulgarian society has always — i.e. since 1878, and all the more so since 1944 — regarded culture as something that is under the protection of the state. The Bulgarian population has always been in favour of the state's being completely committed to the culture sector, and remains so today.

The crisis at the beginning of parliamentary democracy in Bulgaria in 1989 showed that, with the country in the grip of an economic catastrophe, culture was one sector too many for the state to look after with the budget at its disposal. It withdrew from this sector in order to manage and finance pressing matters such as pensions, civil servants' salaries, the health service and education.

This situation intensified with the introduction of the IMF currency board in 1997 which amounted to Bulgaria's loss of financial sovereignty. In this context, the funds spent on culture by the banks were viewed with no great approbation. Consequently, a situation developed until 2008 in which the state was administered with the assistance of the International Monetary Fund, which adopts a strongly Anglo-Saxon approach nurtured by neoliberal thinking and adhering strictly to the principle of monetarism. The population, however, preferred the French model, just as most EU countries did. Under these circumstances the culture sector could have shown its quality and gained renewed strength, but the sector itself and its administrative machinery still adhered to the state model, i.e. the conviction that the state must be in charge.

With this assumption, the Promotion of Culture Act attempted to circumvent reality and take a step towards creating a social contract between the state, artists and employees in the sector. By doing so, the state called upon the population to assume the cultural responsibility for the burden of developing the nation and the individual that the state carried, and obliged the administration to provide resources for cultural goods at national and local level.

The project "Beautiful Bulgaria", launched in 1997 and originally called "Beautiful Sofia", is emblematic of the decentralization of the municipalities. The latter project was funded by Sofia City Council and the United Nations Development Programme (UNDP) and became the concept of the project "Beautiful Bulgaria".

- In 1998, the concept was launched in five cities with the support of the EU and the UNDP.
- In 1999, the project was extended to cover thirteen towns and cities.
- The period from 1999 to 2001 contributes to Bulgaria's accession to the European Union which offered the prospect of EU funds to promote the development of the capacities of central and local authorities using the pre-accession fund.
- In the year 2000, the project was extended to twenty-one municipalities, and was subsequently implemented in over 120 municipalities all over the country.
- In 2005, a new phase of the "Beautiful Bulgaria" concept began when it became

a separate entity within the Ministry of Labour and Social Policy (MASP), now without the support of the UNDP. The project is financed by the state budget using funds from the Ministry's budget and aims to reduce unemployment, improve the urban environment, promote tourism and support the development of small and medium-sized enterprises.

Section 36:

1. The local council creates a municipal "culture" fund and establishes regulations for its work.
2. Funds are raised by means of
   a) resources provided for carrying out target programmes and projects in the fields of culture
   b) donations, bequests and sponsorship on the part of natural persons or corporate entities in Bulgaria and abroad
   c) interest accrued on accounts held by the fund
   d) other sources defined by the municipal council.
3. The funds are used to
   a) carry out projects and programmes in the field of culture
   b) support the organization of cultural events
   c) co-finance cultural projects involving Bulgarian and international participants in association with natural persons and corporate entities
   d) support amateur arts
   e) obtain scholarships for talented children and adolescents

The principle of subsidiarity stipulated in the law as fundamental to European cultural policy meant that decisions are made at the level closest to the population. The local cultural funds were the perfect embodiment of the idea of ensuring publicity and transparency for cultural projects when providing funds for them.

The idea of creating municipal cultural funds was the basis to involve large parts of the local community in appraising cultural projects, although the decision on approving a project for funding lay not just with the local government, but also depended on a wide range of representatives of local artists and experts. Although the law was passed, its implementation in all 244 municipalities of the country did not start until late 2008; moreover, its effectivity has been hampered since then by the large number of legal norms.[14] Thanks to the project "Beautiful Bulgaria", many municipalities were able to restore their architectural attractions at least partially.

Financial difficulties in the municipalities following the reforms and the transfer of responsibility to the municipal cost plans meant, for example, that a 36% cut was slated in Sofia's projected budget for 2003 which resulted in virtually all

[14] Cf. Zakon za zashtita i razvitie na kulturata (Protection and Development of Culture Act). Darzhaven vestnik no. 50 1. Sofia, 01.06.1999.

the capital's theatres going bankrupt. What was paradoxical in this situation was that the buildings themselves would have been preserved the moment they stopped being used as theatres. Sofia City Council could do no more than pay the monthly salaries of the theatres' employees, and had no money for the venues' overheads, let alone for new productions. The state was forced to pay its share of the costs, taking the money from Sofia's taxpayers.[15]

Preserving the cultural heritage located on a municipality's territory is a big responsibility because the municipalities have a budget which is either minimal or allows them only to maintain a certain level. A list was drawn up containing 39,037 cultural monuments, including approximately 1,000 graves, several hills belonging to towns, over 200 museums with large collections from various eras, and libraries and cultural centres.[16]

The Open Society Foundation's annual report for 2004/2005 on public monitoring of Sofia city council's activities included a comparative analysis of spending on culture as a percentage of the budget of the country's biggest municipality compared to three other large municipalities and regional centres.[17]

Table 60: Comparative analysis as a percentage, 2004–2005[18]

Culture	Council of the capital city	Average in Bulgaria	Regional centres	Plovdiv	Varna	Burgas
%	2.53%	4.43%	4.80%	4.27%	5.27%	4.54%

The percentage of the costs of culture as a budget item was 2.53% for Sofia City Council compared to 4.27% in Plovdiv, 5.27% in the city of Varna and 4.54% in the city of Burgas.

The average share of costs allocated to culture in municipal budgets was 4.43% and 4.80% in the regional centres.

Compared to other cities, Bulgaria's capital spent only 2.53% of its budget on

---

15 *Obshtinskite teatri v Sofia za pred falit* (Municipal theatres in Sofia face bankruptcy). [online]. Available from: http://fakti.bg/imoti/6643-obshtinskite-teatri-v-sofiia-sa-pred-falit-22.01.2003 (status 25.03.2006).

16 Ministry of Culture. *Otchet za ispalnenie na zelite na Ministerstvo na kulturata za 2008* (*Report on the activi- ties of the Ministry of Culture for 2008*). [online]. [viewed 19.02.2012]. Available from: mc.government.bg/files/620_Otchet%20na%20Ministerstvo%20na%20kulturata%20za%202008.doc. (status 14.03.2009).

17 Cf. Open Society Foundation. Grazhdanski Monitoring varchu deinosta na stolichniya obshtinski savet 2004–2005 (Public monitoring of the activities of Sofia City Council 2004–2005). Sofia, 2005. [online]. Available from: http://news.osf.bg/?p=news&in=news&id=85 (status 06.06.2006).

18 Cf. Grupa za prozrachna kulturna politika (Group for transparent cultural policy). [online]. [viewed 22.02.2012]. Available from: www.culturpolicy.dir.bg (status 28.03.2005).

cultural activities. In practice, this amounted to much less since other sectors were also included in this category.[19]

The costs of cultural activities financed from municipal budgets in 2007 amounted to BGN 103,800,000, of which 99.4 million was for overheads and 4.4 million for investment.[20]

5.2 The Municipalities' Budgets

5.2.1 Sofia

The city of Sofia has a rich heritage comprising unique and complex cultural and historical treasures. Among its distinctive features are:

- the great cultural importance of the many historical strata which provide outstanding examples of individual architecture and architectural ensembles that illustrate especially the values of antiquity, the Middle Ages, the period after liberation and the twentieth century.
- a rich historical stratification in the surrounding area, the result of a seminal exchange of influences between the West and the Orient at a European cultural crossroads.
- plurality of the cultural heritage — stylistic, religious and ethnic — symbolizing the harmonious co-existence of different religions, ethnic groups and aesthetic concepts. All in all, approximately 1,400 cultural monuments are to be found in the city of Sofia and the surrounding area, of which approximately 840 are in the centre of Sofia itself. One of these monuments is of global significance and is under the protection of UNESCO: the Boyana Church.

The distinctive characteristics of Sofia's cultural-historical and aesthetic heritage are revealed most clearly in the historic heart of the city centre where its cultural values are embodied in the two most important cultural and historical features, the cultural preservation zone Sredets Serdica with the Sofia Necropolis around the Church of St. Sofia which gave the city its name, and the St. Alexander Nevsky Cathedral. Cultural monuments in Sofia such as the Church of St. Sofia, the Rotunda of St. George and the Church of St. Petka of the Saddlers are of great importance.

An event of great significance for Sofia that raised hopes of a change in the country's cultural policy was the creation of a municipal programme for culture

---

19 Stolichniat byudzhet: golyam ili malak (Budget of the capital city: large or small). [online]. Blog. Available from: www.culturalpolicy.dir.bg (status 28.09.2006).

20 Zakonoproekt za darzhavniya byudzhet na Republika Balgariya za 2007 i stanovishte po proekta na byudzhet na sadebnata vlast za 2007, No 602-01-93, vneseni ot Ministerskiya savet na 31.10.2006 (Parliamentary com- mittee for culture, budget act 2007 (…). [online]. Available from: http://www.parliament.bg/bg/archive/2/3/168/reports/ID/793c (status 11.12.2006).

in 2005. The programme set itself the aim of supporting cultural projects culture which were selected after a public competition had been announced with clearly defined priorities, criteria and assessment procedures. The introduction of transparent mechanisms to support cultural projects in the city was planned. This procedure was put into practice when the city's budget for 2005 was passed and included BGN 1,000,000 for the programme. The culture programme project, as it was called in the council resolution, introduced the principle of transparency as a mark of the quality of democratization. In addition, the first municipal fund for culture was set up in the city of Shumen.

When NGOs demanded transparency during the transition, culture was ignored. The distribution of the Ministry of Culture's budget to the various cultural sectors, institutions and projects remained one of the best-kept state secrets.

Awareness and understanding of what culture is or should be and how it can be defined had undergone a change. For a long time the common view was that culture was to be seen as a product of the cultural institutions; in the meantime it has come to be understood differently: culture is everywhere, is created everywhere, develops in a process.

The following figures and tables show the culture budget of the City of Sofia in the years named and can be seen as a reflection of the policy and the economic crisis that prevailed at the time. The cultural institutions had been financially ruined.

Table 61: Sofia City Council, culture budget 1996[21]

Municipal budget overall	18 961 316
Culture budget overall	11 870

Table 62: Sofia City Council, culture budget 1997[22]

Municipal budget overall	158 104 934
Culture budget overall	2 968 445
Salaries	1 107 220

The general increase in this period compared to the budget planned for 1997 amounted to BGN 302,513, divided among the following areas:

- BGN 20,913,000 for a salary increase of 10%
- BGN 121,000 for refurbishment of the municipal theatres (in accordance with transcript no. 33 of 24 September 1997, resolution no. 27 of Sofia City Council)

21 Stolichen obshtinski savet (Sofia City Council). Transcript no. 9, 25 April 1996. Transcript no. 16, 27 Sep- tember 1996. Transcript no. 19, 6 December 1996.

22 Stolichen obshtinski savet (Sofia City Council). Transcript no. 35, 10 November 1997. cf. Stolichen obshtinski savet, supplement to ruling no. 1, transcript no. 31, 28 July 1997.

Table 63: Culture budget in Sofia, annexe 2: transcript no. 51, 30 Nov. 1998[23]

Municipal budget overall BGN 353 280 255	Annual budget for 1998 in BGN	Statement as of 30.08.1998	Proposed adjustment	Project for adjustment
Culture overall	6 229 457	4 507 827	1 347 671	1 347 091
Including				
Salaries	309 114	194 286	799	799
Social security contributions	114 369	72 392	298	298
No. of subsidized salaries	3 159 700	2 409 355	65 856	65 856
Expenses	2 646 274	1 813 794	1 280 718	1 280 138
Culture	4 103 274	2 794 374	602 135	602 135
Salaries	127 295	78 693	102	102
Social security contributions	47 096	28 487	39	39
Maintenance	3 928 883	2 687 194	601 994	601 994
Zoo	748 850	557 897	717	717
Salaries	136 608	89 000	523	523
Social security contributions	50 545	3 400	194	194
Expenses	561 697	434 897	0	0
Vrana Park Museum	79 976	51 863	12 689	12 239
Bereavement Ritual House	1 203 201	1 016 798	700 000	700 000
Registry Office	94 156	86 895	32 130	32 000

Table 64: Culture budget of the City of Sofia for 1999 in BGN[24]

Municipal budget overall BGN 439 355 382	Annual budget for 1999 in BGN	Statement as of 30.08.1999	Proposed adjustment
Culture overall	7 904 803	7 822 845	9 635 284
Including			
Salaries	348 603	345 842	1 748 862
Social security contributions	128 786	127 190	641 460
Culture and other expenses	4 381 474	4 311 295	5 717 998
Including			
Salaries	141 813	138 362	1 293 694
Social security contributions	52 287	50 684	471 789
Expenses	4 187 374	4 122 249	3 952 515
Zoo	841 429	841 429	948 415
Including			
Salaries	154 854	158 571	179 583
Social security contributions	57 282	58 410	65 491
Expenses	629 293	624 448	703 341
Vrana Park Museum	79 976	51 863	12 689

23 Stolichen obshtinski savet (Sofia City Council). Transcript no. 51, 30 November 1998, Ruling no. 2.

Following a decision taken on 18 November 1999, the budget was increased for both receipts and expenditures by EUR 2,449,918. Following this adjustment, the overall budget of the municipality of Sofia amounted to BGN 444,967,038.

Table 65: Culture budget of the City of Sofia for 2000[25]

Municipal budget overall BGN 416 869 778	Annual budget for 2000 in BGN	Statement as of 30.08.2000	Proposed adjustment
Culture overall	10 541 206	9 384 915	8 468 431
Including			
Salaries	1 745 006	1 644 949	1 763 722
Social security contributions	640 137	616 248	506 203
Culture and other expenses	5 692 023	5 213 376	5 794 400
Including			
Salaries	1 289 838	1 203 463	1 304 976
Social security contributions	467 716	452 071	374 528
Expenses	3 934 469	3 557 842	4 114 896
Zoo	948 415	814 421	936 513
Including			
Salaries	179 583	179 540	181 440
Social security contributions	65 991	65 921	52 073
Expenses	702 841	568 960	703 000
Vrana Park Museum	116 245	113 347	111 938
Bereavement Ritual House	2 959 996	2 530 027	740 000
Registry Office	219 720	198 446	292 437

The council of the capital city reduced its own funds for investment, specifically in the budget item General Repairs, by BGN 3,000,000 and transferred them to social activities such as:

- health care, prevention and treatment for children
- maintenance and social welfare
- free medicines
- maintenance of educational institutions, cultural and religious activities (the budget was increased by BGN 500,000).

Table 66: Culture budget of the City of Sofia for 2001[26]

Municipal budget overall BGN 382 076 172	Annual budget for 2001	Statement as of 30.08.2001	Proposed adjustment
Culture overall	7 762 127	7 435 245	8 157 745
Including			
Salaries	1 703 361	1 673 963	2 017 153
Social security contributions	541 557	529 978	530 512

24 Stolichen obshtinski savet (Sofia City Council). Supplement no. 1 of transcript no. 55 of 8 March 1999 (au- thor's translation)

25 Stolichen obshtinski savet (Sofia City Council). Transcript no. 9, 22 March 2000.

Table 66: Culture budget of the City of Sofia for 2001[26]

Culture and other expenses	5 282 670	5 139 962	5 532 896
Salaries	1 008 264	984 212	1 213 693
Social security contributions	3 944 241	319 337	319 203
Expenses	3 944 241	3 836 613	4 000 000
Library of the capital city	652 459	650 660	699 457
Salaries	287 712	287 356	332 112
Social security contributions	88 177	88 177	87 345
Expenses	276 570	275 127	280 000
Zoo	943 722	907 245	981 209
Including			
Salaries	185 976	184 252	214 704
Social security contributions	55 001	55 001	56 467
Expenses	702 745	667 992	710 038
Vrana Park Museum	n/a		
Registry Office	295 463	245 989	262 376

For the first time, funds were allocated in the budget for the preservation of cultural and historical monuments. The financing of theatres and cultural centres was not yet listed as a separate item.

Table 67: Culture budget of the City of Sofia for 2002[27]

Municipal budget overall BGN 378 758 190	Annual budget for 2002 in BGN	Statement as of 30.08.2002	Proposed adjustment
Culture overall	7 690 379	5 539 239	7 023 776
Including			
Salaries	1 859 891	1 314 420	2 057 983
Social security contributions	523 200	383 215	509 793
Expenses	5 307 288	3 841 604	4 456 000
Culture and other expenses	5 727 337	4 133 989	5 158 694
Including			
Salaries	1 211 473	844 859	1 340 194
Social security contributions	346 099	252 674	332 500
Expenses	4 169 765	3 036 456	3 486 00
Library of the capital city	699 457	534 915	706 222
Salaries	330 115	235 647	365 856
Social security contributions	89 573	66 810	90 366
Expenses	279 769	232 458	250 000
Zoo	946 209	643 602	794 914
Vrana Park Museum	n/a		
Registry Office	277 376	203 231	273 946

26 Stolichen obshtinski savet (Sofia City Council). Transcript no. 22, 1 March 2001.

27 Sofia City Council. Transcript no. 34, 14 February 2002.

For the year 2002, no further increases were planned for the budget item Culture as compared to 2001. In addition, the overall municipal budget was decreased, with this trend continuing for 2003 with consequences for both spending on culture and the funding of the municipal cultural institutions.

Table 68: Culture budget of the City of Sofia for 2003[28]

Municipal budget overall BGN 353 292 928	Annual budget for 2003 in BGN	Statement as of 30.08.2003	Proposed adjustment
Culture overall	7 528 921	7 524 222	8 041 642
Including			
Salaries	2 018 975	2 015 530	2 219 705
Social security contributions	688 265	687 984	723 835
Expenses	4 821 681	4 820 708	5 098 102
Culture and other expenses	3 413 420	3 409 273	3 270 661
Including			
Salaries	2 018 975	2 015 530	2 219 705
Social security contributions	688 265	687 974	723 835
Expenses	4 821 681	4 820 708	5 098 102
Arts Centres	1 983 626	1 983 613	2 495 430
Library of the capital city	803 985	803 487	915 514
Galleries	130 414	130 414	118 699
Zoo	847 216	847 186	892 477
Vrana Park Museum	n/a		
Registry Office	320 530	320 519	313 861

Because the division of responsibilities was not clearly defined, and owing to the distinction made between municipal and state cultural institutions, Sofia City Council defined its additional responsibilities itself. As in the previous year, the overall budget for culture fell significantly. On 21 January 2003, the directors of the four municipal theatres in Sofia organized a press conference on the 36% reduction in the funding of cultural institutions.

The directors described this cut as inexplicable in view of the general economic growth of 4.5% that the country was experiencing at the time. Despite this, the municipal budget was reduced. In the previous year, Sofia's authorities had promised, according to the directors, that the theatres would be able to keep the receipts from their performances. An announcement was made to the effect that this promise had been honoured. At the press conference, the directors stated that the overheads of the building housing the Sofia Theatre alone amounted to BGN 300,000, whereas receipts from the successful season had reached only BGN 120,000. The theatres could not make any savings in their ensembles or staff since they were already operating with the bare minimum.

[28] Sofia City Council. Transcript no. 48, 17 February 2003.

In Article 8(2) of the Development of Culture Act, the allocation of subsidies for municipal theatres was clearly defined:

"Municipal cultural institutions are financed from the municipal budget."

"(3) The level of subsidy allotted to each municipal cultural institution when drafting the budget for a subsequent year cannot be lower than it was in the previous year, irrespective of the receipts accrued from its activity."

"(4) The level of subsidy as defined in Art. 3 will be determined according to a sum of costs which is not lower than the amount provided for the same purpose in the previous year's budget."[29]

The situation represented a breach of the law on the part of the municipality; it could, however, also be regarded as an attempt to use the protests of the cultural institutions in Sofia as a way of increasing pressure for an increase in the overall municipal budget even though the national budget had already passed parliament and the vote on the municipal budget was not due to be taken until the city council met. The differences between the municipal and the state theatres, apart from the differences in financing, lay in the theatre reform implemented in 1998/1999.

With the Development of Culture Act, an attempt was made to overcome the preconception that both the municipal and regional theatres were on an insecure footing and barely able to survive owing to insufficient funding. Bearing this in mind, the efforts of many municipal theatres to become nationalized is understandable.

Table 69: Culture budget of the City of Sofia 2004[30]

Municipal budget overall BGN 386 346 265	Annual budget for 2004	Statement as of 30.08.2004	Proposed adjustment
Culture overall (municipal activities)	5 084 669	5 048 929	4 801 491
Including			
Salaries	1 723 306	1 703 666	1 864 872
Social security contributions	610 290	602 679	610 495
Expenses	2 751 073	2 742 584	2 326 124
Culture and other expenses	3 583 913	3 097 772	3 512 405
Including			
Salaries	1 334 366	986 562	1 468 437
Social security contributions	474 850	342 371	482 844
Expenses	1 774 697	1 768 839	
Cultural centres (co-financing with municipal receipts)	2 551 570	2 538 447	2 590 245

[29] Zakon za zashtita i razvitie na kulturata (Protection and Development of Culture Act). Publ. in Darzhaven vestnik no. 50, 1 Jun 1999, amend. Darzhaven vestnik no. 28 (2005), amend. Darzhaven vestnik no. 93 (2005). [online]. Available from: http://lex.bg/laws/ldoc/2134664704 (status 28.12.2011).

Table 69: Culture budget of the City of Sofia 2004[30]

Library of the capital city	2 551 570	2 538 447	2 590 245
Galleries (state activity)	109 838	109 837	168 201
Zoo	1 142 769	1 142 444	932 186
Vrana Park Museum	n/a		
Registry Office	319 937	312 781	321 900

Table 70: Culture budget of the City of Sofia 2005[31]

Municipal budget overall BGN 467 805 536	Annual budget for 2005 in BGN	Statement as of 31.12.2005	Projected budget for 2006
Culture overall (municipal activities)	8 541.332	9 680 051	9 925 973

With the approval of the minutes, the funds in the culture budget were increased by BGN one million to carry out the culture programme, and the funds for leisure activities, culture and religious activities were increased by BGN 200,000.

The figures in the category of Culture in the municipal budget show the changes in the city's level of financial commitment to culture and the institutions that implemented its cultural policy on its territory with the aim of developing culture, arts and the cultural heritage.

When Simeon Saxe-Coburg-Gotha came to power in 2001, the prime minister's residence became his private house, but funds from the meagre culture budget, with which the zoo, the registry office and the bereavement ritual house also had to be financed, were assigned to its restoration and maintenance. It remains inexplicable why the cultural centres did not appear as an item in this budget until 2004. The capital's galleries and libraries, for their part, were not included at all before the year 2000. This was due not least to the inflationary stagnation that plagued the whole country from 1996 to 1998 and doomed all the capital's cultural institutions to destruction since the funds allocated to them were used primarily to pay salaries. The chaos that reigned in the national administration had devastating effects on the municipalities' culture budgets and their management.

On 29 January 2001, Simeon II handed the Vrana park residence over to the local council. His Majesty's solicitor, Asen Oshanov, and the Lord Mayor of Sofia, Stefan Sofiyansky, signed the deed of gift. The donation was agreed between the former Tsar Simeon, Princess Maria Louisa and the mayor on 6 November 1999. The plan was then to open Vrana Park to the public. The museum that was planned was to house all the former Tsar's possessions which were at that time still scattered all over the country.

30 Sofia City Council. Transcript no. 12, 15 March 2004.
31 Sofia City Council. Resolution no. 107, 24 February 2005.

Table 71: Culture budget of the City of Sofia 2006[32]

Municipal budget overall BGN 479 490 361	Initial budget	Budget as of 31.12.06	Statement as of 31.12.06	Projected budget for 2007
Culture overall 11 525 339				
Culture (state responsibility)	4 103 797	4 306 786	4 281 188	4 625 457
Salaries	523 953	520 931	520 437	678 153
Social security contributions	148 269	135 511	135 511	191 905
Expenses	3 431 575	3 650 344	3 625 240	3 755 399
Co-financing with municipal receipts incl. maintenance	31 716	129 014	108 094	30 920
Insurance premiums				0
Including	31 716	129 014	108 094	30 920
Chitalishta	2 886 832	3 013 722	2 988 896	3 188 924
Co-financing with municipal receipts incl. maintenance	0	39 900	39 900	0
Library of the capital city	1 051 623	1 116 302	1 116 024	1 251 210
Salaries	475 736	472 714	472 714	616 127
Insurance premiums	126 102	123 412	123 412	163 874
Expenses	449 785	520 176	519 898	471 209
Co-financing with municipal receipts incl. maintenance	9 038	9 038	9 038	0
Galleries	165 342	176 762	176 268	185 323
Salaries	48 217	48 217	47 723	62 026
Insurance premiums	22 167	12 099	12 099	28 031
Expenses	94 958	116 446	116 446	95 266
Co-financing with municipal receipts incl. maintenance	22 678	80 076	59 156	30 920
Culture (municipal responsibility), overall	7 194 292	7 359 660	7 136 057	8 737 375
Salaries	2 546 446	2 520 116	2 510 960	2 969 570
Insurance premiums	620 844	618 007	616 227	713 467
Expenses	4 027 002	4 221 537	4 008 870	5 074 338
Including				
Cultural administration. Theatres and regions / municipal responsibility	5 613 288	5 509 953	5 301 728	6 815 947
Salaries	2 098 114	2 075 268	2 066 112	2 485 192
Insurance premiums	515 172	509 981	508 201	599 817
Expenses	3 000 000	2 924 704	2 727 415	3 730 938
Zoo	1 175 681	1 442 824	1 442 824	1 445 145
Salaries	295 930	294 761	294 761	319 774
Social security contributions	69 751	70 919	70 919	75 371
Expenses	810 000	1 077 144	1 077 144	1 050 000
Registry Office	368 323	369 883	369 883	459 283

[32] Sofia City Council. Resolutions 131 and 96, 22 February 2007

Table 72: Culture budget of the City of Sofia 2007[33]

Municipal budget overall BGN 892 902 156	Initial budget	Budget as of 31.12.07	Statement as of 31.12.07	Projected budget for 2008
Culture overall 15 189 468				
Culture (state responsibility)	4 625 457	4 902 955	4 871 456	5 442 361
Salaries	678 153	665 483	665 483	773 364
Social security contributions	191 905	169 047	169 047	185 901
Expenses	3 755 399	1 008 025	4 036 926	4 483 096
Co-financing with municipal receipts, overall	30 920	608 990	595 838	184 940
Social security contributions	0	3 160	3 160	7 880
Incl. Expenses	30 920	593 511	580 359	138 050
Salaries		12 319	12 319	39 010
Cultural centres	3 188 924	3 363 054	3 336 452	3 817 995
Co-financing with municipal receipts incl. maintenance		312 615	312 113	0
Library of the capital city	1 251 210	1 268 476	1 268 476	1 378 385
Salaries	616 127	591 980	591 980	677 831
Social security contributions	163 874	151 280	151 280	154 484
Expenses	471 209	525 216	525 216	546 070
Co-financing with municipal receipts incl. maintenance	0	8 470	8 470	0
Galleries	153 323	211 025	211 025	245 981
Salaries	62 026	73 503	73 503	95 533
Social security contributions	28 031	17 767	17 767	31 417
Expenses	95 266	119 755	119 755	119 031
Co-financing with municipal receipts incl. maintenance	30 920	287 905	275 255	184 940
Culture (municipal responsi-bility)	8 757 375	9 677 523	9 225 827	10 174 848
Salaries	2 969 570	2 855 786	2 866 171	3 341 311
Social security contributions	713 467	719 172	706 540	569 057
Expenses	5 074 338	6 102 565	5 653 116	6 133 755
Including				
Cultural administration. Theatres and regions / mu-nicipal responsibility	6 815 947	7 627 286 455	7 224 455	7 758 498
Salaries	2 485 192	1 314 760	2 325 145	2 685 686
Social security contributions	599 817	590 895	578 263	569 057
Expenses	3 730 938	4 721 631	4 321 047	4 503 755

33 Sofia City Council. Resolution no. 114, projected budget for 2008, 6 March 2008.

5.2.2 Varna

Varna is a port with a population of 353,000 (2009). Its municipal archaeological museum contains the world's oldest hoard of gold treasure which was found in the prehistoric necropolis near the city. In total, 294 tombs were explored during the dig.[34]

Prior to 1981, the records of the National Institute for Cultural Monuments listed 1,200 structures as culturally or historically significant. As of 2008, five hundred structures had been preserved as cultural monuments. However, the costs of restoring these buildings, most of which were restituted in 1992, were now to be borne by the owners, most of whom could not afford it. The "Beautiful Bulgaria" programme was likewise unable to meet the country's restoration requirements. Interest-free loans to those owners with a demonstrably low income and the support of the local council would have given them the chance of restoring these monuments.

Table 73: Culture budget of the City of Varna, 2000 and 2001[35]

Cultural institution	Budget for 2000 in BGN	Statement of accounts in BGN	Budget for 2001 in BGN
Library, salaries, social security contributions	172 240	182 382	197 310
Library, maintenance	61 000	93 709	89 190
Total	233 240	276 091	289 700
Opera	280 000	34 000	60 000
Orchestras and ensembles, salaries and social security contributions	14 490	15 596	16 440
Orchestras and ensembles, maintenance	20 000	14 885	12 000
Total	34 490	30 481	28 440
Cultural centres, maintenance	130 000	130 000	100 000
Salaries and social security contributions	340 110	371 443	384 545
Museums, galleries, maintenance	160 000	171 135	130 000
Museums and galleries overall under §50 Investment expenditure	500 110 44 000 544 110	542 578 65 212 607 790	514 800 30 000 544 800
Other cultural activities	517 750	491 794	432 560

[34] Tchobanov, T. and, Stanilov, S. *Kulturen turizam i regionalno razvitie* (*Cultural tourism and regional development*). [online]. National Culture Fund. [viewed 29.01.2012.] Available from: http://ncf.bg/wp-content/kulturenturizam.pdf, p. 79.

[35] Varna City Council, budget item Leisure and Culture, budget for 2000, draft budget for 2001, budget for 2002.

Table 74: Culture budget of the City of Varna, 2002, draft budget 2003[36]

Cultural institution	Budget for 2002 in BGN	Statement of accounts in BGN	Budget for 2003 in BGN
Library, salaries, social security contributions	204 510	215 009	217 800
Library, maintenance	90 000	166 663	207 963
Total	294 600	381 672 19 159 400 831	289 700
Opera	95 000	106 272	100 000
Orchestras and ensembles, salaries and social security contributions	21 260	17 818	18 100
Orchestras and ensembles, maintenance	17 090	14 852	17 000
Total	38 350	32 670	35 100
Cultural centres, maintenance	170 000	170 000	301 036
Salaries and social security contributions	396 700	435 414	415 110
Museums and galleries, maintenance	120 300	253 371	239 926
Museums and galleries overall under §50 Investment expenditure	517 110 60 000 577 000	542 578 65 212 751 464	514 800 30 000 655 036
Other cultural activities	556 950	754 633	1 096 678

Table 75: Culture budget of the City of Varna, 2004, projected budget for 2005[37]

Cultural institution	Budget 2004 in BGN	Statement of accounts in BGN	Budget for 2005 in BGN
Total: libraries with regional character	570 460	533 214	470 659
Total: municipal libraries	0	0	30 000
Opera, maintenance	115 000	112 048	150 000
Total: orchestras and ensembles	91 100	77 446	59 100
Cultural centres, maintenance	342 522	342 404	324 810
Total: museums and galleries with regional character	1 097 735	1 097 480	887 900
Total: museums and galleries with local character	0	0	82 531
Other cultural activities	1 496 600	1 446 088	1 256 000

36 Varna City Council, budget item Leisure and Culture, 2002 budget, draft budget for 2003.

37 Varna City Council, budget item Leisure and Culture, budget for 2004, draft budget 2005.

Table 76: Culture budget of the City of Varna for 2005, projected budget for 2006[38]

Cultural institution	Statement of accounts 2005 in BGN	Budget for 2006 in BGN
Total: libraries with regional character	497 980	512 003
Total: municipal libraries	98 255	50 000
Total: orchestras and ensembles	34 168	130 000
Chitalishta, maintenance	515 498	360 824
Total: museums and galleries with regional character	925 470	824 674
Total: museums and galleries with local character	281 377	279 200
Other cultural activities	1 590 958	1 601 874

Table 77: Culture budget of the City of Varna for 2007, projected budget for 2008[39]

Cultural institution	Statement of accounts in BGN, 2007	Budget for 2008 in BGN
Total: libraries with regional character	540 111	655 564
Total: municipal libraries	183 567	75 000
Total: orchestras and ensembles	326 260	294 000
Chitalishta	762 769	715 413
Total: museums and galleries with regional character	1 159 020	1 076 366
Total: museums and galleries with local character	552 744	650 000
Other cultural activities	2 832 620	3 541 657

Cultural institutions supported by the local council:

- Opera and philharmonic society
- Stoyan Bachvarov dramatic theatre
- State Puppet Theatre
- Festival and Congress Centre
- Palace of Culture and Sport
- Artists' groups and associations
- Association of Freelance Writers
- Union of Bulgarian Authors
- Authors' Association
- Painters' Association, Varna
- Municipal Children's Complex

The City of Varna continued to finance the Museum of History, the Regional Library, the Municipal Art Gallery, the choirmasters, Varna Boys' Choir and the following international cultural activities in the city:

- International choir competition in May
- Varna International Summer Drama Festival

[38] Varna City Council, budget item Leisure and Culture, budget for 2005, draft budget 2006

[39] Varna City Council, budget item Leisure and Culture, budget for 2006, draft budget 2007

- Varna International Summer Music Festival
- International Summer Science Seminars
- International ballet competition
- International jazz festival
- International folklore festival[40]

Careful tracking of the budgets over the years reveals that the share of funds allotted to other cultural activities is impressive. The state institutions received funds for salaries, while expenditure for investment remains the responsibility of the municipality. This policy was detrimental to the creative process, or rather to its quality. The private cultural institutions financed their activities entirely independently, but were able to participate in projects if funds were available for them.

From 1996 to 2008, no study of the private culture sector and the economic and social indicators such as turnover, taxes and staff qualifications existed in the country. Such a study would have been able to provide information on how interaction with the private sector can be brought about and how support could have been provided for this sector's initiatives. Varna hosted numerous festivals.

If there was a tendency in 1991 to ignore the festivals that took place all over the country, their number had increased to over four hundred per year by 2008. The festivals themselves became increasingly inflationary since despite their number they did not bring forth festival communities or did not survive for very long. In general, these festivals appeared as a phenomenon in Bulgaria over a ten-year period and most depended for their existence either completely or partially on subsidies from the city authorities and the municipalities' culture budget.

5.2.3 Veliko Tarnovo

Table 78: Culture budget of the city of Veliko Tarnovo 1999–2008[41]

	Total receipts	Spending on culture in BGN
1999	20 940 285	1 999 694
2000	23 375 417	1 233 117
2001	20 012 398	1 383 175
2002	23 436 576	1 256 333
2003	25 815 033	1 855 145
2004	30 119 471	2 302 200
2005	35 434 651	2 632 737
2006	37 315 440	3 219 054
2007	46 897 081	5 228 473
2008	58 857 195	6 227 073

40 Varna City Council. [online]. Available from: www.varna.bg (status 22.10.2009).

In a resolution on preservation of cultural monuments passed by parliament, the city of Veliko Tarnovo was declared a historic place of national importance. There are approximately 3,000 artefacts and 620 individual cultural monuments in the city's actively populated zones.

Because of the economic crises, the cabinet of the three-party coalition government (2005) froze more than BGN 500,000 that was earmarked for the restoration of the fortification wall. Despite this, the Trapezitsa hill was named a priority for the state by Culture Minister Prof. Danailov.

5.2.4 Ruse

With its 169,000 inhabitants, Ruse is Bulgaria's fifth-largest city and the biggest city in the north of the country. The city owns a theatre, a state opera house, a puppet theatre and a symphony orchestra. It also has a History Museum, a Museum of Natural History, the National Transport Museum and a municipal art gallery. The Regional History Museum has nine permanent exhibitions including the Kaliopa House, the Pantheon, the open-air exhibition at the Roman castle of Sexaginta Prista, the Rock-hewn Churches of Ivanovo, the mediaeval city of Cherven, the Basarbovo cave monastery, the Prince Battenberg III Museum in the town of Byala etc.

Construction of a museum complex was planned which was to house the various archaeological, ethnographical and historical exhibitions linked to the history of the city and the region, as well as an ecological museum.

Table 79: Culture budget of the city of Ruse, 2006–2008[42]

Ruse	2008 in BGN	2007 in BGN	2006 in BGN
Activities	Budget spending	Budget spending	Budget spending
Culture: state activities	1 046 74 9	883 260	773 928
Culture: municipal activities	1 322 34 3	1 111 214	923 375
Culture Co-financing	104 441	216 219	58 951
Culture overall	2 473 533	2 210 693	1 756 254
History Museum state activities	333 444	304 672	259 196
History museum Co-financing	128 792	158 548	100 649
History museum overall	462 236	463 220	359 845

41 Obshtina Veliko Tarnovo (Municipality of Veliko Tarnovo). *Otchet za funktsiya VII, Pochivno delo, kultura i religiozni deinosti po godini za perioda 1999–2008* (*Report on budget item VII, Leisure, Culture and Reli- gious Activities by year for the period 1999–2008*). Veliko Tarnovo, 2008. Source: Financial report of the municipality, 1999–2008.

Table 80: Culture budget of the city of Ruse, 2003–2005[43]

Ruse	2005 in BGN	2004 in BGN	2003 in BGN
Activities	Budget spending	Budget spending	Budget spending
State activities	955 119	907 810	838 091
Municipal activities	874 968	661 494	625 268
Co-financing	113 954	70 150	n/a
Total	1 944 041	1 639 454	n/a

The fate of local cultural policy in Ruse is exactly reflected by the budget, which for a long time was not produced systematically or clearly. The municipality failed to supply the data requested for the period from 1996 to 2002.

The director of the Ruse Philharmonic Society, Nayden Todorov, had repeatedly informed the Ministry of Culture of this. One consequence was that in 2008, Ruse's opera house was incorporated into a regional development project conducted by the Ministry of Culture, with restoration of the building planned for BGN 1.5 million.

In the city of Ruse, the oldest international music festival for symphonic, oratorio and cantata has been held for over fifty years: the March Music Days festival was founded in 1961. In addition, jazz music and the Ruse Jazz Festival have been establishing themselves for over thirty years. Other festivals that traditionally enjoy a high profile include the Golden Fiddle International Folklore Festival for authentic and arranged folk music, the International Theatre Festival and the Elias Canetti literature competition. The Canetti House, once the Canetti family shop, is also in the city. The International Elias Canetti Society is named after the author.

5.3 Assessment

Over the years, decentralization progressed only slowly. In more recent years, city authorities gradually began to see culture as a central element of subsidies allocated to activities. They took on the task of maintaining cultural institutions as stipulated by the law. The country's gradual recovery from the global economic crisis allowed them to invest, and steps were taken to redress the complete breakdown of culture. In this process, which lasted until 2008, the existence of certain

42 Obshtina Ruse, Obshtinski Savet Ruse (Budget of the municipality of Ruse). Naredbata za sastavaneto, ispal nenieto i otchitaneto na obshtinskiya byudzhet prepis izvlechenie (Decree for the justification, implementa- tion and reporting on the municipal budget). Ruling no. 323, passed in transcript no. 36-27.04.2001. Ruling no. 83, passed in transcript of 28.02.2008. Ruling no. 488, passed in transcript no. 24-05.03.2009. Ruling no. 863, passed in transcript no. 42-10.02.2006. Ruling no. 1207, passed in transcript no. 56- 09.02.2007. Ruling no. 112, passed in transcript no. 9-12.03.2004. Ruling no. 487, passed in transcript no. 25-14.02.2005. Ruling no. 528, passed in transcript no. 50-01.03.2002. Ruling no. 890, passed in transcript no. 67- 05.03.2003.

43 Source: Budget of the municipality of Ruse

cities and municipalities would have been unthinkable without the revenue generated by cultural tourism. This stabilization, based primarily on the economy and defined as the necessity for measures in the culture sector, underwent a change two years later, in 2010, when the culture budget was reduced by 10%–15%.

A more complete picture of the lines of communication at the time is provided by two important letters exchanged between the Ministry of Culture and the municipalities. The Culture Minister noted with concern that in 2011 most local councils had reduced the funds for theatre and opera two- or threefold compared to the subsidies allocated to cultural activities in previous years.[44]

> "Against the background of the serious economic situation, and especially during the current reform in the performing arts, the introduction of a new financing model gives cause for great concern."[45]

Contrary to the Culture Minister's assertion that there was a trend towards reducing funds, nearly all municipalities increased the gross amounts or kept them at the same level as 2010. It is worth noting that in some municipalities the increase in gross funds was 50%. On the other hand, there was a noticeable shift in the form of support given: the municipalities were allocating more funds to the state cultural institutions for material support and orders placed with companies. The reason for the increased adoption of this procedure in recent years was that the resources for cultural institutions were often to be found, in reduced form, in the budget for the theatres and opera houses owing to contracts entered into with the Culture Ministry. This means that the funds granted to state cultural institutions actually increased considerably compared to 2010.

> "There has been a considerable increase in the funds for municipal cultural institutions, and, accordingly, the inequality between the funding of state structures and municipal structures has also increased. These facts provide decisive proof of the responsible approach taken by municipal authorities to the fate of their theatres and music institutions which generate cultural life for the Bulgarian citizens of the municipalities. By no means do they indicate a unilateral decision on the part of local councils to withhold financial support, and nor do they imply a transfer of all responsibility for the material support and the existence of cultural institutions in the country's larger cities. (...) it is up to us to find the right decisions together to guarantee the preservation of Bulgarian culture and intellectual values."[46]

---

44 Ministry of Culture, 2011. Ministarat na kulturata Vezhdi Rashidov isprati pismo do natsionalnoto sdruzhenie na obshtinite (the culture minister Vezhdi Rashidov sent a letter to the National Association of Towns and Municipalities expressing his concern at the cut in funds for the country's cultural institutions). [online]. Publ. 21.03.2011. [viewed 19.02.2012]. Available from: http://mc.government.bg/newsn.php?n=2503&l=1

45 Ibid.

46 Jankova, D. Natsionalno sdruzhenie na obshtinite v Balgariya (NAMRB, National Association of Towns and Municipalities in the Republic of Bulgaria). Letter to the Minister of Culture

Although this is undoubtedly the right approach to take, it is also likely that the situation of the cultural institutions will remain unchanged, or even worsen, until the right solution is found. This will mean that more investment will be needed in future to ensure their continued operation.

Table 81 : Report on financial support given to cultural institutions (theatres) by municipalities in 2010 and 2011

According to the contract with the Ministry of Culture		Additional subsidy		Total		
Municipality	2010	2011	2010	2011	2010	2011
Blagoevgrad	20 000	300 000	188 191	380 000	208 191	680 000
Burgas	390 000	250 000	0	261 000	390 000	411 000
Varna	90 000	210 000	170 793	135 100	260 793	345 100
Veliko Tarnovo	86 400	86 400	0	0	86 400	86 400
Vidin	11 214	65 000	0	0	11 214	65 000
Vratsa	150 000	150 000	0	0	150 000	150 000
Gabrovo	120 000	120 000	108 000	120 000	228 000	240 000
Dobrich	40 000	100 000	0	0	40 000	100 000
Kardzhali	85 000	50 000	0	0	85 000	50 000
Lovech	82 100	82 100	0	0	82 100	82 100
Montana	28 000	60 000	79 686	107 590	107 686	167 590
Pazardzhik	94 000	50 000	0	50 000	94 000	100 000
Pleven	232 500	415 000	0	0	232 500	415 000
Plovdiv	190 000	211 000	0	0	190 000	211 000
Razgrad	0	0	100 000	100 000	100 000	100 000
Ruse	196 160	172 000	210 000	236 000	406 160	408 000
Silistra	11 600	50 000	0	0	11 600	50 000
Sliven	175 000	110 000	0	0	175 000	110 000
Smolyan	0	0	50 000	50 000	50 000	50 000
Stara Zagora	367 500	180 000	168 000	429 310	535 500	609 310
Targovishte	60 000	60 000	10 000	10 000	70 000	70 000
Haskovo	65 000	72 000	65 000	72 000	130 000	144 000
Yambol	177 650	182 000	0	0	177 650	182 000

Vezhdi Rashidov. [online]. [viewed 19.02.2012]. Available from: www.namrb.org/doc11/VRa6idovRE.doc

6. SUMMARY AND OUTLOOK

Bulgaria's development after the end of communist rule in 1989 has generally been perceived as a change from a planned economy to a free market economy with legal, administrative, crime-related and psychological problems. Only rarely has it been regarded as an intellectual transition.

It is for this reason that cultural policy was unable to define new objectives and demonstrate new perspectives for the future. The frequent administrative reforms never brought the main problem to light, which was to make the intellectual basis of culture and consequently the intellectual wellbeing of the nation a priority.

In 2010, Culture Minister Vezhdi Rashidov announced that Bulgarian culture, and especially the theatre, opera and operetta, were to be reformed by a process of "natural selection". Since the dramatic economic crisis of 1995 in Bulgaria, theatres and musical theatres should only be given enough money to ensure their survival. There would be virtually no funds for new productions.

According to the new reform of 2010, theatre ensembles are now supposed to fund their monthly salaries from ticket sales, while the state bears the administrative costs and otherwise finances projects only. However, this system applies only to state theatres. This "natural selection" will probably mean that municipal theatres will have to close because the municipalities are unable to maintain them and because there is no concept for a cultural policy covering the cultural scene in its entirety.

The revolution of 1989 had unprecedented demographic consequences, namely a dramatic decrease in the population. However, from the point of view of cultural policy these drawbacks of the revolution have not yet been dealt with. The culture reform of 2010/2011 is contingent on the new demographic situation, but does not offer any solutions to these problems.

The Minister's idea of pushing the reform through without attracting too much attention and within the space of twelve months was detrimental to theatres and musical theatres: venues that had previously presented over one hundred performances a year are now often able to stage only one performance a month. The idea behind this was to consolidate the Ministry of Culture's budget. In an attempt to justify the dramatic cutbacks and restructuring of theatres and musical theatres, the Culture Minister cited the opera at Stara Zagora that had managed only fifty performances in 2010. What he failed to realize, however, was that this is the oldest opera house in the country which, exactly twenty years previously (so before the economic crisis and population decrease), had enjoyed a very different status with approximately two hundred performances a year. The aim of this reform, therefore, was not to close venues, but to destroy long-standing traditions and values. Furthermore, the discussions never touched upon the question of how new sections of the population could be won as audience members. Instead, they were dominated by quarrels over the budget and possible savings.

In defence of his plans, the Minister said: "Greece, with its twelve million inhabitants, has one opera, three national theatres, ten municipal theatres and 185 private theatres. Italy, with a population of sixty million, has five operas. Bulgaria, with 7.5 million people has seven operas, eight philharmonic orchestras and fifty-four state theatres that play once a year."[1]

According to him, maintenance of theatres, operas and orchestras consumes 60% of the Ministry's budget, and only between ten and fifteen of the currently existing venues are capable of maintaining themselves. Consequently, between ten and twelve of the existing theatres should close down because they have no income.

Another reason for the cuts in theatre funds was that the majority of the Ministry of Culture's budget was spent on the media. In 2003, this spending was 2.39 times higher than for all the other culture categories put together. This share was subsequently reduced, but in 2011 it was still 1.38 times higher, and in 2012 0.9 times higher.[2]

In 1999, selling off of the sites of the Bulgarian musical institutions began, and its continuation was also part of the Ministry's new draft in 2010. No regulations or legislation pertaining to the continuation of these changes in the culture sector followed, and decentralization of cultural funding and administration did not take place at all. Closure of the arts centres by the Ministry of Culture meant a return to a centralized cultural policy.

The changes in the culture sector took place in three stages:

- 1995–1998: Decline and collapse of the culture sector
- 1999–2004: Reform and partial stabilization
- 2005–2008: Improved financing and launch of the municipalities' culture funds and the National Culture Fund.

In his examination of Bulgarian culture following the end of communism, the Austrian Bulgaria expert Peter Bachmaier reaches the following conclusion:

> "The liberal reforms after 1989, and especially after 1997, have had lasting consequences for Bulgarian culture. The state largely relinquished its responsibility for culture. Many cultural institutions were closed and the employees laid off. The remaining cultural institutions can only pay meagre salaries and cannot carry out any new projects or productions. [...] A cultural renaissance is required to reappraise the past and shape the future, but the

---

1 Zhelev, V. and Rashidov, V., 2010. *10–12 trupi otsega izglezhdat obrecheni* (*10–12 companies not yet doomed*). [online]. Culture Minister V. Rashidov in an interview for the magazine *24 Chasa*, 11.05.2010. [viewed 22.02.2012]. Available from: http://www.24chasa.bg/Article.asp?ArticleId=475495 (status 17.05.2010).

2 See chapter: Budget of the Ministry of Culture and Funding by Category, p. 131.

question is whether the 'global cultural values', which are in reality the values of consumer society, are the right foundation for this. For this reason, Bulgaria should not — faced with the crisis of society — rashly throw its own cultural traditions from the time of the National Revival in the 19th century overboard as unnecessary ballast, but should retain those essential elements of them that were moulded by the Enlightenment and humanist education and find a synthesis with which the tasks of the present day and the 21st century can be mastered."[3]

The global economic crisis of 2008 led to a further 15% reduction of the Ministry of Culture's budget. The larger municipalities found themselves in a similar situation, since they had to support the state budget, but at the same time they were expecting funds for contracts from the Ministry and looking for resources for the cultural institutions on their territory. The demographic upheaval, also a result of the political transition and the continuing crisis, has since become the main criterion.

The constant dwindling of the population has become a significant factor for cultural policy and will naturally have consequences in the foreseeable future on the number of visitors at existing cultural institutions and for decisions on how much to invest in old and new institutions.

Another unsolved problem is the Cultural Heritage Act of 2009 that has been criticized by public figures because it helps justify the private collections that were put together during the transition and are of dubious provenance. Over time, the collections have become a matter of national pride and even of national identity.

The principal objective of this investigation is to provide the basis for further discussions in the field of cultural policy. If politicians claim that culture is important for Bulgaria, this study set out to scrutinize the reality of this "cultural industry" and how it is reflected in legislation and life. The information on this, which was previously unavailable, was gathered in the course of this study and can serve as the basis for further research.

---

3 Bachmaier P., 2010. Kulturnaya politika i kulturnoe razvitie Balgarii pod vlianiem zapada, 1989–2009 (Bul- garia's Cultural Policy and Cultural Development under the Influence of the West, 1989–2009). (Conference: *Revolutions and Reforms in the Countries of Central and Southeast Europe: Twenty Years Later. Moscow, Institut slavyanovedeniya 2010.* Also publ. in: *Ponedelnik*, No. 11/12, 2010.

7. BIBLIOGRAPHY

References

Agentsiya za ikonomicheski analizi i prognozi (Agency for economic analyses and forecasts). Natsionalen plan za razvitie na Republika Balgariya za perioda 2007–2013 (National development plan of the Republic of Bulgaria for the period 2009–2013). Sofia, 2005, pp. 111–115.

Atanasov, P. *Jakov Kraikov: knizhnovnik, izdatel, grafik XV v.* (*Jakov Kraikov, scholar, publisher, illustrator, 15th century*). Sofia: Nauka i Izkustvo, 1980.

Chervenkov, Valko. Speech before the party meeting of the Association of Bulgarian Authors on 28.01.1949, p. 38. In: Central State Archive.

Darzhaven vestnik (State Gazette) (May 1991). Konventsiya za zashtita na architekturnoto nasledstvo na Evropa (Convention on the Protection of the Architectural Heritage in Europe), No. 42.

Darzhaven vestnik (State Gazette), budget 1995–2012.

Darzhaven vestnik (State Gazette). Zakon za korporativnoto podohodno oblagane (Corporation Tax Act), Zakon za danaka varchu dobavenata stoinost (VAT Act), Zakon za mestni danatsi i taksi (Local Taxation Act). No. 89, October 1996. No. 95, October 1997. No. 90, October 1999. No. 28, April 2005. No. 94, November 2005. No. 108, December 2006.

Delors, J. *Learning the treasure within* [online]. Report to UNESCO of the International Commission on Education for the Twenty-first Century. Paris: Unesco Publishing, 2009, pp. 15–16. [viewed 19.02.2012]. Available from: http://www.unesco.org/delors/utopia.htm (status: 07.12.2009).

European Audiovisual Observatory. *Yearbook 2007. Film, Television and Video in Europe No. 1. Television in 36 European Countries*. Strasbourg, 2007.

Fondatsiya Badeshte za Balgariya (Future for Bulgaria Foundation). Annual reports 1997, 1998. Sofia.

Fondatsiya Otvoreno Obshtestvo (Open Society Foundation). Tsentar po izkustva (Centre for the Arts). Annual reports for 1996, 1997, 1999, 2000, 2001, 2002, 2003, 2004.

Karmen Moissi, P. In Wien gedruckte Bulgarica des 19. Jahrhunderts im Bestand der Österreichischen Nationalbibliothek (ÖNB). In: *Wiener Slavistisches Jahrbuch*, Vol. 55/2009. Vienna: Austrian Academy of Sciences, 2009, pp. 67–94

Ministerstvo na kulturata (Ministry of Culture). *Balgarskite chitalishta dnes – analiz* (*Bulgarian art centres today — an analysis*). Sofia, 2007, p. 16

Ministerstvo na kulturata (Ministry of Culture). Natsionalna programa 2004. Zaetost v podkrepa na balgarskiya teatar (National programme 2004. Employment at Bulgarian theatres). Sofia, 2004, p. 1.

National Statistics Institute. Census of the population of the Republic of Bulgaria. Sofia, 2011, pp. 2–5.

National Statistics Institute. Statistical Yearbooks for 1995, 2000, 2001, 2002, 2003, 2004, 2005, 2006, 2007, 2008, 2010. Sofia.

Natsionalno Dvizhenie Simeon Vtori (National Movement Simeon II for Stability and Progress). Pravitelstvena programa (programme of the government of the Republic of Bulgaria). Sofia, 2001, p. 50

Natsionalno Sdruzhenie na Obshtinite (National Association of Municipalities in the Republic of Bulgaria) Letter to the Minister of Culture Vezhdi Rashidov from Dora Jankova. [online]. [viewed 19.02.2012]. Available from: www.namrb.org/doc11/VR a6idovRE.doc

Natsionalen tsentar za izuchavane na obshtestvenite naglasi (National centre for research into public opinion). Anketa, Sofia, 2005, pp. 10–29

Obshtina Ruse Byudzhet (budget of the municipality of Ruse). Obshtinki savet Ruse (Ruse City Council). Naredbata za sastavaneto, ispalnenieto i otchitaneto na obshtinskiya byudzhet prepis izvlechenie (Decree for the justification, implementation and reporting on the municipal budget), text extract, 2001–2008.

Obshtina Slatina Byudzhet (budget of the municpality of Slatina), Obshtinski savet Slatina (Slatina Town Council), text extract, 2000–2008.

Obshtina Varna Byudzhet (budget of the municipality of Varna). Budget item Leisure and Culture, 2000–2008.

Obshtina Veliko Tarnovo Byudzhet (budget of the municipality of Veliko Tarnovo). Otchet za funktsiya VII, Pochivnodelo, kultura i religiozni deinosti po godini za perioda 1999-2008 (Report on budget item VII, Leisure, Culture and Religious Activities by year for the period 1999–2008). Veliko Tarnovo, 2008.

Smetna Palata (Audit Office). Doklad za rezultatite ot izvarsheniya odit na finansovoto upravlenie na byudzheta, isvanbyudzhetnite smetki i fondove na ministerstvoto na kulturata za perioda ot 1.01.2003 do 30.09.2003 (Report on the findings of the examination of the financial management of budget funds and accounts of the Ministry of Culture for the period 01.01.2003 to 30.09.2003). Sofia, 2000–2008.

Tsentralen darzhaven archiv (Central State Archive). *Firmite na BKP v chuzhbina* (*The companies of the Bulgarian Communist Party abroad*). CDA Index no. 117, pp. 970–972.

UNESCO. *Our Creative Diversity. Report of the World Commission on Culture and Development*, 1995.

World Bank. World Development Indicators database, 2006. [online]. Available from: http://www.euro.who.int/Document/E90023.pdf. (status: 03.01.09.) National Institute of Statistics. Sofia, p. 30.

Zakon za chitalishtata (Law on the *chitalishta*). No. 89, publ. 22.10.1996.

Zakon za filmovata industriya (Law on the film industry). No. 105, publ. 02.12.2003.

Zakon za obshtinskite byudzheti (Law on municipal budgets). No. 33, publ. 24.03.1998.

Zakon za radio i televiziyata (Law on radio and television). No. 138, publ. 24.11.2003.

Zakon za zakrila i razvitie na kulturata (Protection and Development of Culture Act). No. 106, 2006.

Secondary Sources

Adorno, T. W. Kultur und Verwaltung. In: *Merkur, Deutsche Zeitschrift für europäisches Denken*, No. 2, 1960.

7. BIBLIOGRAPHY

Afman R. and Knoop R, eds. *Moving Heritage, Managing Movable Heritage in the EU, Bulgarian-Dutch Experiences 2005–2008.* Publishers: AO Consultants for Development, Driebergen, Netherlands, 2008, in cooperation with the Ferdinandeum Association for Bulgarian National Heritage with the financial support of the Matra Programme of the Dutch Ministry of Foreign Affairs. Driebergen-Sofia, 2008, p. 159

Alexander, T., and Stumpf, S. Aspekte Interkulturellen Führungsverhaltens. In: Niels, Sourisseaux and L. J. Andreas, eds. *Interkulturelles Management.* 3rd edition. Berlin inter alia, 2003, pp. 69–104.

Alexandrov A. *Bulgarische Kulturpolitik 1995–2008.* Master's thesis. IKM, Vienna, 2005. (unpublished).

Andreeva, D. Tsentralizirane i detsentralizirane na kulturata v usloviya na evrointegratsiya (Centralization and decentralization of culture with respect to integration in the EU). [online]. In: *Medii i obshtestveni komunikatsii, No. 1*, 2008. [viewed 22.02.2012.] Available from: http://media-journal.info/?p=item&aid=13 (status 04.04.2010.)

Angelski S. *Bulgaria — an Economic Overview (Univ. of Economics Bratislava, Price Decision Making, Working Paper)*, Bratislava, 2009.

Asotsiatsiya ArHea. *Strategiya za opazvaneto i ustoychivo razvitie na kulturno-istoricheskoto nasledstvo v Balgariya* (*Strategy for the preservation and sustainable development of cultural heritage*). Sofia: Sfera IK, 2003.

Ataka. *Ustroystvo i printsipi na organizatsiyata Ataka* (*Rules and principles of the Ataka organization*). Sofia, 2005.

Bachmaier, P. Bulgarien und der Westen. In: Bulgarisches Forschungsinstitut in Österreich / P. Bachmaier, ed. *Der Transformationsprozess in Bulgarien und der Weg in die EU* (Miscellanea Bulgarica, No. 18). Vienna, 2006, pp. 23–32.

Bachmaier, P. Der Wertewandel in Ostmitteleuropa. In: P. Bachmaier, ed. *Der kulturelle Umbruch in Ostmitteleuropa: Der Transformationsprozess und die Bildungs- und Kulturpolitik Tschechiens, der Slowakei, Polens und Ungarns im Kontext der internationalen Beziehungen.* Frankfurt am Main, 2005.

Bachmaier, P. Die Bildungspolitik Bulgariens vom Staatssozialismus zum neoliberalen Modell. In: I. Schwarcz and A. Suppan, eds. *Quo vadis EU? Osteuropa und die EU-Erweiterung* (Series Europa Orientalis, Vol. 5). Vienna/Berlin, 2008, pp. 309–324.

Bachmaier, P. Die Rolle der Kulturpolitik in den österreichisch-bulgarischen Beziehungen, 1962–2008. In: P. Bachmaier, A. Schwarcz and A. Cholakova, eds. *Österreich und Bulgarien. Geschichte und Gegenwart* (Miscellanea Bulgarica, No. 19). Vienna, 2008, pp. 156–175.

Bachmaier, P. Österreichisch-Bulgarische kulturelle Beziehungen. In: A. Suppan and W. Mueller, eds. *Friedliche Koexistenz oder Eiserner Vorhang? Österreich, Neutralität und Osteuropa während des Kalten Krieges und Détente, 1955–1989* (Europa Orientalis, Vol. 7). Vienna/Berlin, 2009, pp. 487–508.

Bachmaier, P. Ot vtoriya kam tretiya svyat: Prechodat na Balgariya ot darzhaven sotsializam kam neoliberalizam 1989–2008 (From the second world to the third: Bulgaria's transition from a socialist state structure to neoliberalism) (*Ponedelnik*, year 10, No. 7/8). Sofia, 2009, pp. 21–33.

Bachmaier, P. Von der zweiten zur dritten Welt: Der Übergang Bulgariens vom sozialistischen Staatsgefüge zum Neoliberalismus. In: *Current Concern*, No. 3-4). Zurich, 2008.

Bell, D. *The Cultural Contradictions of Capitalism*. New York, 1976. *Die kulturellen Wiedersprüche des Kapitalismus*. Frankfurt am Main, 1991.

Beron, P. Rolyata na carskoto semeystvo za sazdavane i razvitie na prirodnonauchnite institutsii (The role of the families of the tsars in the foundation and development of scientific institutions). In: Z. Kyoseva. *Tsarskite kolektsii v balgarskite muzei, arhivi i biblioteki (The tsars' collections in Bulgarian museums, archives and libraries)*. Sofia: Balgarski bestselar. Natsionalen muzei na balgarskata kniga i poligrafiya, 2004, pp. 54–63.

Beshevliev, V. *Prabalgarite. Istoriya, bit i kultura* (Protobulgaria. History, tradition and culture). Issue 1. Plovdiv: Fondatsiya Balgarsko istorichesko nasledstvo, 2008.

Bielka, E. Österreich und seine volksdemokratischen Nachbarn. In: E. Bielka, P. Jankowitsch and H. Thalberg, eds. *Die Ära Kreisky. Schwerpunkte der österreichischen Außenpolitik*. Vienna, 1983.

Biks, R., Yaneva A. and Karakostova, R. In: M. Drinov, ed. *Balgarski muzikalen teatar* 1890–2001 (Bulgarian musical theatre 1890–2001: Opera, Ballet, Operetta, Musicals. Theatres, Companies, Performances). Sofia, 2005, pp. 223–245.

Bourdieu, P. *La distinction. Critique sociale du jugement.* Paris: Les Éditions de Minuit, 1979. *Distinction: a Social Critique of the Judgement of Taste*, Cambridge, Mass.: Harvard University Press, 1984.

Bourdieu, P. *Schwierige Interdisziplinarität. Zum Verhältnis von Soziologie und Geschichtswissenschaft*. Münster, 2004.

Bozhilov, I. and Gyuselev, V. *Istoria na srednovekovna Balgariya VII-XV vek* (*The history of mediaeval Bulgaria, 7th–15th centuries*). Vol. 1, Sofia: Anubis, 1999.

Brix, E. Die sogenannten "weißen Flecken" in der Geschichte Mitteleuropas im 20. Jahrhundert. In: P. Gerlich and K. Glass, eds. *Der schwierige Selbstfindungsprozeß. Regionalismen – Nationalismen – Reideologisierung*, Vienna: Toruń, 1995.

Brix, E. Volk begnadet für das Schöne — Anmerkungen zur österreichischen Kulturpolitik. In: K. Csúri and M. Kóth. *Österreichische Identität und Kultur*. Szeged/Vienna, 2007.

Burger, R. *Im Namen der Geschichte: Vom Missbrauch der historischen Vernunft*. Vienna, 2007.

Burka, A. Was blieb vom Fenster in den Westen? Zur Auslandskulturpolitik Österreichs in Ostmitteleuropa seit 1945 am Beispiel Polens und der Tschechoslowakei/Tschechiens. In: H. Kramer and E. Kreisky, eds. *Politik und Demokratie*. Vol. 23. Vienna, 2011.

Busek, E. *Mitteleuropa. Eine Spurensicherung*. Vienna, 1997.

Busek, E. *Offenes Tor nach Osten. Europas große Chance*. Vienna, 2003.

Busek, E. and Brix, E. *Projekt Mitteleuropa*. Vienna, 1986.

Cholakov, I., Borisova, V. and Keskinova, D. *Ikonomicheski prinos na avtorskopravnite industrii v Balgariya, Varchu danni za perioda 2003–2005* (*Contribution to the economy of the copyright industries in Bulgaria, data for the period 2003–2005*). Sofia: Univ. Izd Stopanstvo, 2007, p. 7.

Chomsky, N. *Language and Mind*. San Diego: Harcourt Brace Jovanovich, Inc., 1968.

Chomsky, N. The Responsibility of Intellectuals. In: *The New York Review of Books*, 1967.

Christova, A., Stanchev, V. and Angelov, G. Anatomiya na prechoda (The Anatomy of the

Transition), Stopanskata ikonomika na Balgariya 1988–2004 (The Bulgarian Economy 1988–2004). Sofia: Institute of Economic Research, 2004.

Christova, N. *Balgarskiyat skandal Solzhenitysn* (*Solzhenitysn: The Bulgarian Scandal*). Sofia: Atelie, 2000, pp. 39–41.

Csáky, M. Ambivalenz des kulturellen Erbes: Zentraleuropa. In: M. Csáky, K. Zyringer, eds. *Ambivalenz des kulturellen Erbes. Vielfachcodierung des kulturellen Gedächtnisses*. Innsbruck/Vienna/Munich, 2000.

de Tocqueville, A. *Democracy in America*. Trans. and eds. Harvey C. Mansfield and Delba Winthrop. University of Chicago Press, 2000

de Tocqueville, A. Discours prononcé à l'assemblée constituante le 12 septembre 1848 sur la question du droit au travail (Discourse on the right to work, held at the constituent assembly on 12 September 1848). In: G. de Beaumont, ed. *Oeuvres Complètes d'Alexis de Tocqueville* (*The Complete Works of Alexis de Tocqueville*). No. 9: Mélanges Académiques, Economiques et Politiques (Academic, economic and political anthologies). Paris, 1866.

Deleva M. *Technological Culture Park (Policies for Culture)*. Sofia, 2004, pp. 25–27.

Dimitrov G. P. *Kultur im Transformationsprozess Osteuropas. Zum Wandel kultureller Institutionen am Beispiel Bulgariens nach 1989*. Munich, 2009.

Dorosiev, R. and Ganev, G. Eine Nation im Transit. Die Demokratisierung von Zentraleuropa nach Asien. In: Freedom House. Budapest, 2007, pp. 185–211.

Doynov P. Knigi bez tirashi (Books with no circulation). In: *Knigite dnes*, No. 4. Sofia, 2005, p. 17.

Dworkin, R. What is equality? Equality of resources. In: *Philosophy and Public Affairs*, Vol. 10, No. 4, 1981, pp. 283–345.

Eliade, M. *Das Heilige und das Profane, Vom Wesen der Religiösen*. Frankfurt am Main, 1984.

Euripedes, A. Umweltschutz macht reich, Global Viewpoint. In: *Modern Times, Das Magazin der besten Geschichten*. Linz, 2006, p. 67.

Fisher, R. *A Cultural Dimension of the EU's External Policies - from Policy Statements to Practice and Potential*. Amsterdam: Bookmanstudies, 2007.

Florida, R. *The Rise of the Creative Class ... and how it's transforming work, leisure, community & everyday life*. New York, 2002.

Foucault, M. *Surveiller et punir: Naissance de la prison*. Paris: Éditions Gallimard, 1975. *Discipline and Punish: The Birth of the Prison*. New York: Pantheon Books, 1977.

Gadamer, H-G. Hermeneutik II. Wahrheit und Methode. In: *Gesammelte Werke*, Vol. 2. Addenda, index. Tübingen, 1993.

Garton Ash, T. Was bleibt von 1989? Eine Debatte zwischen Václav Havel, Viktor Klima, Adam Michnik und Viktor Orbán. In: *Transit*, No. 18. Vienna, 2000.

Gavrilova, D. Teatralnoto izkustvo v Balgariya: politika, praktika i promyana (The art of the theatre in Bulgaria: policy, practice and transformation). Tsentar za kultura i debat Chervenata kashta (The Red House Centre for Culture and Debate). Sofia, 2000.

Geertz, C. The Impact of the Concept of Culture on the Concept of Man. In: J. Platt, ed. *New Views of the Nature of Man*. Chicago: University of Chicago Press, 1965, pp. 93–118.

Geertz, C. The Interpretative Theory of Thick Description: Toward an Imperative Theory of Culture. In: *The Interpretation of Cultures*. New York, 1973.

Gehler, M. *Der lange Weg nach Europa. Österreich vom Ende der Monarchie bis zur EU*, Vol. 1. Vienna, 2002.

Genchev, N. *Balgarsko Vazrazhdane* (*Bulgarian Revival*). Sofia, 1986.

Grossberg, L. The Victory of Culture, Part 1: Against the Logic of Mediation. In: Angelaki. *Journal of the Theoretical Humanities* 3 (3), pp. 3-29.

Grozev, A. *Praveneto na kino u nas vse oshte ne e industriya* (*Filmmaking is not yet an industry in our country*). [online]. [viewed 19.02.2012]. Available from: http://news.ibox.bg/news/id_271135103 (status: 25.07.2008).

Harstup, K., ed. *Human Rights on Common Grounds. The Quest for Universality*. The Hague: Kluwer Law International, 2001.

Hobsbawm, E. *Mitteleuropa, Politik und Kultur*. Opening address at the 1989 International Brucknerfest, Linz. Publ. 1990.

Hofecker, F. O. Introduction. Quo vadis Kulturstatistik? Einige Anmerkungen zum Verhältnis von Kulturstatistik, Kulturwissenschaft und Kulturpolitik. In: F. O. Hofecker and P. Tschmuck, eds. *Kulturpolitk, Kulturforschung und Kulturstatistik: Zur Abklärung einer spannungsreichen Textur*. Innsbruck, 2003, pp. 9–16.

Hofecker, F. O., Tschmuck, P., and Plaschg, W. *Bericht zur Kulturfinanzierung des Bundes*. Vienna, 2002–2008.

Hofecker, F. O. and Tschmuck, P. *Kulturpolitik, Kulturforschung und Kulturstatistik*. Innsbruck, 2003.

Hofstede, G. Cultures and Consequences: Comparing Values, Behaviors, Institutions and Organizations Across Nations. Beverly Hills, 2001, pp. 9–10.

Höll, O. and Kramer, H. Österreich – ein Peripherieland? In: H. Kramer. *Österreich im internationalen System*. Vienna, 1983.

Holland, D. and Quinn, N., eds. Cultural Models in Language and Thought. New York: Cambridge University Press, 1987.

Huntington, S. P. *The Clash of Civilizations*. New York, 1996.

Ivanov, I. Ò. Za nachaloto na godinata v prabalgarskiya kalendar. (On the beginning of the year according to the protobulgarian calendar). In: *Hemus*, No. 2. Sofia, 2006, pp. 51–58.

Janeva A. and Arnaudova M. *Ne moga da otdeliya baleta ot sebe si* (*I cannot detach myself from ballet*). Sofia, 2011.

Johnston, W. M. *The Austrian Mind: an Intellectual and Social History, 1848-1938*. Berkeley: University of California Press, 1972

Jonchev, V. and Joncheva, O. *Dreven i savremenen balgarski shrift* (*Ancient and contemporary Bulgarian script*). Sofia: Balgarski Hudoynik, 1982, p. 2.

Kampits, P. *Die Auslandskulturpolitik Österreichs: Konzepte, Strukturen, Perspektiven*. Vienna, 1990.

Kandinsky W. *Concerning the Spiritual in Art*. New York City, 1946.

Kanitz, F. P. *Donau-Bulgarien und der Balkan, Historisch-geographisch-ethnographische Reisestudien aus den Jahren 1860–1879*. 2nd edition, Vol. 1. Leipzig, 1882, pp 7–65.

Karasek, F. Österreichs kulturelle Beziehungen mit dem Ausland. In: O. Staininger, ed. *Kulturlandschaft Österreich. Analysen und kritische Beiträge*. Vienna, 1977.

Kavrakova, A. Television across Europe: Follow-up reports 2008: Bulgaria. In: *Television across Europe. More channels less independence*. Monitoring Report of the

OSI/EU Monitoring and Advocacy Program. Budapest/New York: Open Society Institute, 2008, pp. 110–149.

Klein, A. *Der exzellente Kulturbetrieb*. Wiesbaden, 2008.

Knapp, M. Österreichische Kulturpolitik und das Bild der Kulturnation. Kontinuität und Diskontinuität in der Kulturpolitik des Bundes seit 1945. In: H. Kramer and E. Kreisky, eds. *Politik und Demokratie*, Vol. 4. Frankfurt am Main, 2005.

Knoop, R. Heritage policies in Europe. In: R. Afman and R. Knoop, eds. *Moving Heritage, Managing Movable Heritage in the EU, Bulgarian-Dutch Experiences 2005–2008*. Publishers: AO Consultants for Development, Driebergen, Netherlands, 2008, in cooperation with the Ferdinandeum Association for Bulgarian National Heritage with the financial support of the Matra Programme of the Dutch Ministry of Foreign Affairs. Driebergen-Sofia, 2008, pp. 193–202.

Koch, R. G. Vergruftungsgefahr. Im etablierten Kulturbetrieb dominieren immer mehr die Alten. In: *Frankfurter Allgemeine Zeitung* (feature section), No. 240, 16.10.2002, p. 33.

Koprinarov, L. *Balgarskata kulturna politika 1990–1995 (Bulgarian Cultural Policy, 1990–1995)*. Sofia: Institute of Culturology, 1997.

Köthke, R. Das Stockholm-Syndrom: Eine besondere Betrachtung des Verhältnisses von Geiselnehmer und Geisel. In: *Praxis der Rechtspsychologie* 9/1999, pp. 78–85.

Kraus, W. *Der fünfte Stand. Aufbruch der Intellektuellen in Ost und West*. Bern/Munich/Vienna, 1966.

Kulturkontakt Austria. EU cooperative programmes with Central and Eastern Europe 1995. In: *KulturKontakt Austria*. Vienna, 1995.

Kyosev, A. Soros George Stiftung – Otvoreno Obshtestvo (Soros Open Society Foundation), Politiki (Politics) 6/2006. [online]. Available from: http://politiki.bg/?cy=44&lang=1&a0i=222739&a0m=readInternal&a0p_id=87 (status 8.11.2009).

Landry, C. *The Cultural Policy of Bulgaria*. Council of Europe, 1997.

Lasky, J. Melvin. *Utopia and Revolution: On the Origins of a Metaphor*. Chicago/London: The University of Chicago Press, 1976

Le Bon, G. *Psychologie des Foules*. France, 1895. *The Crowd: A Study of the Popular Mind*. 1896.

Le Rider, J. *La Mitteleuropa*. Series*Que sais-je ?* No. 2846. Presses Universitaires de France, 1994.

Malek, M. *Drehscheibe Österreich. Österreichische Aktivitäten in Mittel- und Osteuropäischen Ländern*. Vienna: Bundespressedienst, 1998.

Marboe, P. Die Auslandskultur als dritte Dimension der österreichischen Außenpolitik. Kulturförderung in den Alpenländern. In: C. A. Andreas and C. Smekal, eds. Innsbruck, 1992.

Maryanovic, V. Die Mitteleuropa-Idee und die Mitteleuropa-Politik Österreichs 1945-1995. European University Studies, series 31, Political Science, Vol. 360. Frankfurt am Main/Berlin/Bern/New York/Paris/Vienna, 1998.

Mayer-Tasch, P. C. *Über Prophetie und Politik*. Munich: Gerling Akademie Verlag, 2000, p. 67.

Obuljen, N. Why we need European cultural policies: The impact of EU enlargement on cultural policies in transition countries. Amsterdam: European Cultural Foundation, 2005.

Ognyanov, L. *Darzhavno-politicheskata sistema na Balgariya 1944–1948* (*The state political system in Bulgaria 1944–1948*). Sofia, 1993.

Open Society Institute (Soros Foundation). Sofia. [online]. [viewed 29.01.2012]. Available from: http://www.osf.bg/?cy=99 (status 27.11.2011).

Ortega y Gasset, J. *La rebelión de las masas*. Madrid, 1929. *The Revolt of the Masses*. 1930.

Partiya GERB (GERB party). Politicheska programa na partiya GERB za evropeysko razvitie (manifesto of GERB, the Party for the European Development of Bulgaria). Sofia, 01.06.2009, pp. 63–64.

Pavlov, B. The cultural goods market in Bulgaria from illicit trade to cultural industries. In: R. Afman and R. Knoop, eds. *Moving Heritage, Managing Movable Heritage in the EU, Bulgarian-Dutch Experiences 2005–2008*. Publishers: AO Consultants for Development, Driebergen, Netherlands, 2008, in cooperation with the Ferdinandeum Association for Bulgarian National Heritage with the financial support of the Matra Programme of the Dutch Ministry of Foreign Affairs. Driebergen-Sofia, 2008, p. 159.

Plaschka, R., Stourzh, G. and Niederkorn, J. P. *Was heißt Österreich? Inhalt und Umfang des Österreichbegriffs vom 10. Jahrhundert bis heute*. Vienna: Verlag der österreichischen Akademie der Wissenschaften, 1995.

Pribersky, A. *Europa und Mitteleuropa? Eine Umschreibung Mitteleuropas*. Vienna: Sonderzahl, 1991.

Raffler, M. *Museum – Spiegel der Nation? Zugänge zur Historischen Museologie am Beispiel von Landes- und Nationalmuseen in der Habsburgermonarchie*. Vienna: Böhlau, 2008.

Rahn, R. and Utt, R. Bulgarian Economic Growth and Transition Project. Washington, 1990.

Rathkolb, O. Austriakischer Kulturexport. In: G. Kerchbaumer and K. Müller. *Begnadet für das Schöne. Der rot-weiß-rote Kulturkampf gegen die Moderne*. Vienna, 1992.

Rathkolb, O. Zentrale Trends in der Außenpolitik Österreichs nach 1945. In: G. Heiss, A. Mishková, J. Peshek and O. Rathkolb, eds. *An der Bruchlinie. Österreich und die Tschechoslowakei nach 1945 / Na Rozhraní Svètu. Rakousko a Ceskoslovensko po 1945*. Brno/Innsbruck, 1998.

Rousseau, J. J. *Sozialphilosophische und politische Schriften*. 2nd edition. Düsseldorf-Zurich, 1996, pp. 311–312.

Ruskite medii v shok: Boyadisvaneto na pametnika e tsinisam, prokuraturata obrazuva dosadebno proisvodstvo za huliganstvo (Russian media in shock: the picture of the monument is cynical and a result of vandalism). In: *Duma*, No. 139, 21.06.2011.

Said, E. *Kultur, Identität und Geschichte*, cited in Educult. *Kulturelle Bildung für bildungsferne Schichten*. Study for the Wiener Volksbildung society. Vienna, 2004.

Sajdik, M. and Schwarzinger, M., eds. *Die EU-Erweiterung. Hintergrund, Entwicklung, Fakten*. Vienna, 2003.

Schindler, B. *Tanzplan vor Ort. Zahlen und Fakten 2005–2009*. Berlin, 2009.

Schodde, G. H. *The Book of Enoch: Translated from the Ethiopic with introduction and notes*. Andover: Warren F. Draper, 1882.

Schulze, G. *Die Erlebnisgesellschaft. Kultursoziologie der Gegenwart*. Frankfurt am Main 2005, pp. 502–506.

Sofia History Museum. *Austrian Architectural Influences in Sofia at the Turn of the Century*. Sofia, 1998, p. 23.

Solzhenitsyn, A. *One Day in the Life of Ivan Denisovich*. New York: Dutton, 1963.

Solzhenitsyn, A. *The Gulag Archipelago*. New York/Evanston/San Francisco/London: Harper & Row, 1974.

Stanev, H., Spiridonova, J. and Dzhildzhov, A. *Detsentralizatsiata i vliyanieto i varchu vazmozhnostite na obshtinite i oblastite za usvoyavane na sredstva ot fondovete na evropeyskiya sayuz* (*Decentralization and its influence on municipalities' and regions' capacity to absorb EU subsidies tied to funds*). Sofia, 2006, pp. 14–24.

Stillfried, B. Österreichs Rolle in Ostmittel- und Osteuropa. In: A. Khol, ed. *Neue Außenpolitik in einer neuen Welt. Ergebnisse des Symposions der Politischen Akademie in Zusammenarbeit mit der Vereinigung österreichischer Industrieller vom 19. Oktober 1992*. Vienna, 1999.

Stoichev, K. BN-TV. *Denyat zapochva* (*The day begins*), 25.03.2010.

Suppan, A. Die Rolle der nichtstaatlichen Organisationen im Vorfeld der Außenpolitik am Beispiel des Österreichischen Ost- und Südosteuropa-Instituts. In: *Der Donauraum*, 3/1998.

Thomas, A. Psychologie interkulturellen Lernens und Handelns. In: A. Thomas, ed. *Kulturvergleichende Psychologie*. Göttingen, 1993, pp. 380–381.

Tilly, C. *European Revolutions 1492–1992*. Oxford, 1992.

Todorova, H. *Chalcolithic Settlements in Northeast Bulgaria*. (*Kupferzeitliche Siedlungen in Nordostbulgarien*), Vol. 13 of *Materialien zur allgemeinen und vergleichenden Archäologie*. Original from University of Michigan. Munich, 1982.

Tomova, B. Gledaneto na televiziya e nai-masovoto natsionalno zanimanie (Television is the most popular leisure activity). In: *Informatsionen Byuletin Kultura* N1. Sofia, 2005, pp. 5–8.

Tomova, B. and Andreeva, D. *Balgarskata filmova industriya v usloviata na transformatsia* (*The Bulgarian film industry during the transformation process*). Sofia: Observatoriya po ikonomika na kulturata (Observatory of Cultural Economics), 2007, p. 2.

Venediktov, I. *Mednoto gumno na prabalgarite* (Copper field of the Bulgars). Book 1, Sofia, 1983.

von Beyme, K. *Die Kunst der Macht und die Gegenmacht der Kunst. Studien zum Spannungsverhältnis von Kunst und Politik*. Frankfurt am Main, 1998.

von Beyme, K. *Kulturpolitik und nationale Identität: Studien zur Kulturpolitik zwischen staatlicher Steuerung und gesellschaftlicher Autonomie*. Opladen, 1998.

von Beyme, K. *Systemwechsel in Osteuropa*. Frankfurt am Main, 1994.*Transition to Democracy in Eastern Europe*. Palgrave Macmillan, 1996.

Wagner, G. Zum Verhältnis von EU – Bildung und Kultur – Osteuropa. Reflexionen aus österreichischer Sicht. In: Kulturkontakt Austria. EU cooperative programmes with Central and Eastern Europe 1995. Vienna, 1996.

Waidacher, F. *Handbuch der Allgemeinen Museologie*. Vienna, 1999.

Waidacher, F. *Museologie knapp gefasst*. Vienna, 2005.

Wermuth, J., Todor Z. and Geljo G. In: P. Rehder, ed. *Das Neue Osteuropa von A-Z: Staaten, Völker, Minderheiten, Religionen, Literaturen, Geschichte, Politik, Wirtschaft, neueste Entwicklungen in Ost-u. Südosteuropa*. Munich, 1992, pp. 596–597.

Wimmer, M. *Kulturpolitik in Österreich: Darstellung und Analyse 1970–1990*. Innsbruck/Wien, 1995.

Zacharieva, J. Litsenzirane i registratsiya na radio i televizionnite operatori (Licensing and registration of radio and television networks), Balgarska mediina koalitsiya (Bulgarian media coalition). Sofia, 2006, p. 28.

Zembylas, T. *Kulturbetriebslehre, Grundlagen einer Interdisziplin*. Vienna, 2004.

Zhekov, S. Seminar "Pregled na natsionalnata politika za knigata" s uchastieto na ekspertite na saveta na Evropa, Prof. Dr. Hartmut Walravens i David Kingam, predstaviteli na ispalnitelnata vlast, parlamenta i knizhnata obshtnost, Chisar. (Seminar *Appraisal of the national book policy* attended by experts from the Council of Europe Prof. Hartmut Walravens and David Kingam, representatives of the executive, parliament and the literary community). Sofia, 1999.

Zlatarski, V. *Istoriya na balgarskata darzhava prez srednite vekove* (*The story of the Bulgarian state in the Middle Ages*). Sofia: Akademichno izdatelstvo Ìarin Drinov, 1994, p. 212.

Internet references:

Agentsiya po zaetostta (National Employment Agency, Ministry of Labour and Social Policy). [online]. Available from: http://www.az.government.bg/eng/index_en.asp (status 12.07.2009)

Andreeva, D. Tsentralizirane i Detsentralizirane na kulturata v usloviya na evrointegratsiya (Centralization and decentralization of culture with respect to integration in the EU). [online]. In: *Medii i obshtestveni komunikatsii, No. 1, 2008*. [viewed 22.02.2012.] Available from: http://media-journal.info/?p=item&aid=13 (status 04.04.2010).

Asotsiatsiya ArHea. *Ekspertna grupa Antra, Sobstvenostta na kulturnite tsennosti sled 1989* (*Strategy for the preservation and sustainable development of cultural heritage after 1989)*. [online]. Press release. [viewed 22.02.2012]. Available from: http://archaeology.zonebg.com/buletin.pdf (status 30.09.2008).

Asotsiatsiya ArHea. *Strategiya za opazvaneto i ustoychivo razvitie na kulturno-istoricheskoto nasledstvo v Balgariya, osnovni nasoki* (*Strategy for the preservation and sustainable development of cultural heritage — guidelines*). [online]. Sofia: Sfera IK, 2003, p. 31. Available from: http://archaeology.zonebg.com/strategy.pdf (status 29.12.2006).

Baleva, M. and Drumev C., director general of the National Palace of Culture (NDK). *Sala 1 na NDK shte e nai-hubava na Balkanite* (*Hall 1 of the NDK will be the most splendid in the Balkans*). [online]. In: *Trud* 22.08.07. Available from: http://old.kab.bg/press/August_2007/22_08_07.doc (status 7.09.2007).

Balgariya: Varchu danni za perioda 2003–2005 (Bulgaria: Data for the period 2003–2005). [online]. [viewed 22.02.2012]. Available from: http://mc.government.bg/images/NEWS/bro6ura_wipo_02%2007%202007bg.pdf (status5.01.2006).

Balgarska Narodna Banka (BNB) (Bulgarian National Bank, statistics). [online]. [viewed 18.02. 2012]. Available from: www.bnb.bg/bnb/home.nsf/fsWebIndexbul?openframeset (status 14.02.2007).

7. BIBLIOGRAPHY

Balgarska Patriarshia (Bulgarian Orthodox Church). Transcript No. 41, 13 December 2011. [online]. Available from: http://bgpatriarshia.bg/news.php?id=57234 (status 14.12.2011).

Balgarski Praven Portal – Lex.BG (Bulgarian Law Portal). Bulletin No. 80, 6 July 2006. Parlamentat ostavi DDS varchu knigite (Parliament introduces VAT on books). [online]. [viewed 18.02.2012]. Available from: http://lex.bg/bulletin/?isu=80&tp=n&id=103 (status 10.07.2006).

Ballet Arabesque [online]. Available from: http://www.arabesque.bg/ (status 21.02.2008).

Basille, O., 2009. *Resignation or resistance, Bulgaria's embattled press hesitates*. [online]. Reporters Without Borders, For Press Freedom, Bulgaria. Available from: http://www.rsf.org/IMG/pdf/rsf_rep_bulgaria_en.pdf (status 05.02.2009)

Bodakov, M and Vandov, N. *Vsichki sme chast ot svetostta. Razgovor s choreografkata Mila Iskrenova* (We are all part of sanctity. A conversation with choreographer Mila Iskrenova). [online]. In: *Kultura*, Nr. 35, 8.09.2000. [viewed 18.02.2012]. Available from: http://www.kultura.bg/media/my_html/2146/mila.htm, (status 24.09.2006).

Bonina, K. Arhitekturno byuro (Provokad architects' studio). [online]. Sofia, 2008. Available from: http://provocad.com/?p=29 (status 10.01.2008).

Boubnova, I., 2000. *From defects to effect. Self-colonization as an alternative concept to isolationism* [online]. [viewed 28.10.2015]. Available from: http://eipcp.net/transversal/1100/boubnova/en (status 03.12.2011).

Bulgaria Newsletter, 1st quarter, 2009. [online]. Available from: www.austiantrade.at (status 22.05.2009).

Celli, P. L. La Lettera Il direttore generale della Luiss avremmo voluto che l'Italia fosse diversa e abbiamo fallito" Figlio mio, lascia questo Paese" (Letter from the director general of Luiss: "We wished Italy was different, but we failed. My dear son, leave this country.") [online]. In: *La Republicca*, 30. 11. 2009. [viewed 18.02.2012]. Available from: http://www.repubblica.it/2009/11/sezioni/scuola_e_universita/servizi/celli-lettera/celli-lettera/celli-lettera.html (status 2.12.2009).

Chervenata kashta (The Red House). (Europalia-Bulgaria 2002). [online]. Available from: http://www.redhouse-sofia.org/index_b.htm (status 06.03.2005).

Cholakov, I., Borisova, V., Keskinova, D. et al. *Ikonomicheski prinos na avtorskopravnite industrii v Balgariya, Varchu danni za perioda 2003-2005* (*Contribution to the economy of the copyright industries in Bulgaria, data for the period 2003–2005*). [online]. Sofia: Univ. Izd., 2007. [viewed 22.02.2012.] Available from: http://mc.government.bg/images/NEWS/bro6ura_wipo_02%2007%202007bg.pdf (status 14.12.2007).

Constitution of the Republic of Bulgaria. [online]. [viewed 21.02.2012]. Available from: http://www.verfassungen.eu/bg/verf91.htm (status 05.11.2010).

Council of Europe. *European Landscape Convention*, No. 176, Florence 01.03.2004. [online]: Available from: http://conventions.coe.int/Treaty/Commun/QueVoulezVous.asp?NT=176&CL=ENG (status 26.06.2008).

Council of Europe. *Compendium of Cultural Policies and Trends in Europe*, 11th edition, 2010. [online]. Organizational structure, organizational chart. [viewed 19.02.2012]. Available from: http://www.culturalpolicies.net/web/bulgaria.php?aid=31 (status 23.01.2011).

Council of Europe/Committee of Ministers, Second Summit of Heads of State and Government, Final Declaration and Action Plan. [online]. Strasbourg, 10–11 October

1997. [viewed 19.02.2012]. Available from: https://wcd.coe.int/ViewDoc.jsp?id=593437&Site=CM (status12.02.2008).

Council of Europe/ERICarts. *Compendium of Cultural Policies and Trends in Europe.* [online]. [viewed 18.02.2012]. Available from: http://www.culturalpolicies.net/web/index.php (status 27.11.2011).

Council of Europe/ERICarts. *Compendium of Cultural Policies and Trends in Europe,* 11th edition. [online]. Strasbourg 2010, p. 58. [viewed 27.11.2011]. Available from: http://www.culturalpolicies.net/web/index.php (status 28.09.2011).

Council of Europe/ERICarts. *Compendium of Cultural Policies and Trends in Europe,* 6th Edition. [online]. Strasbourg 2005. Available from: http://www.culturalpolicies.net/web/index.php (status 27.11.2011).

Council of Europe/ERICarts. *Compendium of Cultural Policies and Trends in Europe,* 12th edition, 2011. [online]. Chapter updated 19.05.2011: Bulgaria. 6.2 Public cultural expenditure. [viewed 19.02.2012]. Available from: http://www.culturalpolicies.net/web/bulgaria.php?aid=622 (status 5.07.2011).

Daisaku, I. *2005 Peace Proposal. Toward a New Era of Dialogue: Humanism Explored.* [online]. [viewed 18.02.2012]. Available from: http://www.daisakuikeda.org/assets/files/pp2005.pdf, p. 7. (status 05.10.2010).

Danailov, S., 2008. Otgovor na ministara na kulturata na vapros na narodniya predstavitel Nikolay Michailov, otnosno politikata na Ministerstvoto na kulturata po opazvaneto na pametnizite na kulturata (answer given by the Culture Minister to a question asked by Nikolai Michailov relating to the preservation of cultural monuments). [online]. Available from: http://mc.government.bg/page.php?p=1&s=11&sp=407&t=409&z=0 (status 28.11.2008).

Darzhaven vestnik (State Gazette). [online]. Available from: http://dv.parliament.bg/DVWeb/broeveList.faces (status 18.02. 2012).

Darzhaven vestnik (State Gazette). Strategiya za razvitie na radio- i televisionnata deinost chrez naszemno radiorazpraskvane (Resolution of the National Assembly of the Republic of Bulgaria of 28 September 2005 relating to television and radio). [online]. State Gazette 82, 14 October 2005. Effective from 1 January 2006. Available from: http://www.cem.bg/r.php?sitemap_id=100 (status14.08.2010).

Darzhavna Agentsiya za turizma (State Agency for Tourism, Dept. of Statistics and Analysis). Internatsionalen turizam Balgariya januari-dekemvri 2008 (*International tourism in Bulgaria January–December 2008*). [online]. Sofia, p. 1. [viewed 19.02.2012]. Available from: www.tourism.government.bg/.../file_64_bg.doc, (status 15.01.2010).

Deliyska, A. *Koristta izyade glavite na jurnalistite agenti* (*The minds of the journalist agents were consumed by self-interest*). [online]. Interview with Metodi Andreev. *Novinar* magazine, 03.12.2008. [viewed 22.02.2012]. Available from: http://novinar.bg/news/metodi-andreev-koristta-iziade-glavite-na-zhurnalistite-agenti_MjgxNzs0MQ==.html (status 19.09.2008).

Delors, J. *Learning the treasure within* [online]. Report to UNESCO of the International Commission on Education for the Twenty-first Century. Unesco Publishing, Paris, 2009. pp. 15–16. [viewed 19.02.2012]. Available from: http://www.unesco.org/delors/utopia.htm (status: 07.12.2009).

Dimitrov, D., Grigorova, V. and Decheva, J. Grazhdanski doklad za izpalnenieto na natsionalnata strategiya za integratsiya na romite i plana za izpalnenie na desetiletie na romskoto vklyuchvane v Balgariya 2012 (Citizens' report, implementation of the national integration strategy for Roma and implementation plan for the decade of integration of Roma in Bulgaria, 2012). [online]. Open Society Institute, Sofia, indie Roma97 social foundation, Roma Health foundation, Roma Academy of the Arts, Education and Culture, Inegro association, Amalipe Centre for Interethnic Dialogue and Tolerance, World Without Borders. Sofia, 2012. [viewed 29.07.2014]. Available from: http://osi.bg/downloads/File/2013/BG_civilsocietymonitoringreport_BG.pdf (status 23.06.2010).

Dimitrova, B. *Dalchev prenaregda bratskata mogila v Plovdiv* (*Dalchev restructures the monument in Plovdiv*). [online]. In: *Trud*, 30.09.2009. [viewed 18.02.2011]. Available from: http://www.trud.bg/Article.asp?ArticleId=240599 (status 13.11.2011).

Dimitrova, G. *Boyana veche ne e Studioto na Balkanite. Razgovor s Evgeni Mihaylov (Boyana is no longer the studio of the Balkans*). [online]. In: *Kultur*, 6, 18.02.2005. [viewed 20.02.2012]. Available from: http://www.kultura.bg/bg/article/view/10660 (status 26.04.2005).

Dimitrova, G. Muzeiat na Sofia ostava v tsentralnata mineralna banya (The Museum of Sofia stays in the central mineral baths). [online]. In: *Stroitelsivo Gradat* 4, February 2008. [viewed 20.02.2012]. Available from: http://stroitelstvo.info/show.php?storyid=454580 (status 23.02.2008).

Dimitrova, N. and Topalova, V. *Gara Podujane se prevarna za chas v art-instalatsiya* (Podujane railway station was transformed into an art installation for an hour). [online]. In: *Sega*, 28.04.2005. Available from: http://www.segabg.com/online/new/articlenew.asp?issueid=430&sectionid=8&id=00001 (status 29.4.2005].

Dogan, A. *Doklad na predsedatelya na Dvigenie za Prava i Svobodi (DPS) – Achmed Dogan pred VII-ta Natsionalna konferentsiya na DPS, 12.12.2009 (Report of the president of the Movement for Rights and Freedoms, Ahmed Dogan, at the 7th national conference (DPS) 12.12.2009*). [online]. Sofia, p. 4. [viewed 29.01.2012]. Available from: http://old.dps.bg/cgi-bin/e-cms/vis/vis.pl?s=001&p=0037&n=000018& (status 21.01.2010).

Dorosiev, R. and Ganev, G. *Nation in Transit 2008. Democratization from Central Europe to Eurasia: Bulgaria*. [online]. [viewed 21.02.2012]. Available from: http://www.cls-sofia.org/uploads/files/NT-Bulgaria-final.pdf (status 17.05, 2009).

Efektivni politiki za protivodeistvie na sivata ikonomika v Balgariya (An effective strategy for combating the informal economy in Bulgaria). [online]. Brochure. Univ. Izd., Sofia, 2007. Available from: http://mc.government.bg/images/NEWS/bro6ura_wipo_02072007bg.pdf (status 14.12.2007).

European Audiovisual Observatory. [online]. Press release, Strasbourg, 09.02.2006. [viewed 19.02.2012]. Available from: http://www.obs.coe.int/about/oea/pr/berlin2006_pdf.pdf.de (status 05.10.2007).

European Commission / Communication from the Commission of the European Parliament, European Economic and Social Committee and the Committee of the Regions. *Progress Report on the Single European Electronic Communications Markets 2008* (14th Report on the Implementation of the Telecommunications Regulatory Package 2008). [online]. Brussels, 2009, p. 141. [viewed 19.02.2012]. Available from: http://ec.europa.eu/information_society/policy/ecomm/library/communications_reports/annualreports/14th/index_en.htm (status 16.10.2009).

Fakti.bg. *Obshtinskite teatri v Sofia za pred falit* (Municipal theatres in Sofia face bankruptcy). [online]. Available from: http://fakti.bg/imoti/6643-obshtinskite-teatri-v-sofiia-sa-pred-falit-22.01.2003 (status 25.03.2006).

Familia NPO za izkustvo i kultura (Family NGO for Art and Culture. *Resolution on acceptance of the provisions made by the Ministry of Culture regarding the organization and closure of the National Centres for the arts and cultural activities.* [online]: In: http://familia.cult.bg/?page_id=3 (status 14.09.2006).

Federal authorities of the Swiss Confederation. European Charter of Local Self-Government, 05.02.2012. [online]. [viewed 19.02.2012]. Available from: http://www.droit-bilingue.ch/rs/c0_102-d-f.html (status 23.02.2010).

Fondatsiya za razvitie "Chitalishta" (Foundation for the development of the reading rooms [chitalishta]) [online]. [viewed 19.02.2012]. Available from: www.chitalishte.bg (status 26.07.2011).

Food and Agriculture Organization of the United Nations (FAOSTAT). *Population in Bulgaria.* [online]. Available from: http://faostat.fao.org/faostat/help-copyright/copyright-e.htm (last updated 21 September 2009) (status 17.08.2010).

Foucault, M. Lecture, 17.03.1976. *In Verteidigung der Gesellschaft. Vorlesungen am Collège de France (1975–76)* [online]. Frankfurt am Main, 1999, pp. 276–305. Available from: http://www.momoberlin.de/Foucault_Vorlesung_17_03_76.html (status 20.04.2008).

Ganchev, R. Sastoyanie, problemi i perspektivi pred balgarskite Musei i Galerii. Doklad na Rumyan Ganchev – direktor na NZMGII, predstaven na Natsionalnata rabotna sreshta na direktorite na muzeite i galeriite v Balgariya (Status, problems and perspectives of Bulgarian museums and galleries. Report by R. Ganchev, Director of the National Centre for Museums and Galleries in the Ministry of Culture. [online]. *National conference of curators of museums and galleries in Bulgaria, Sofia, 20 June 2006*). Available from: *mc.government.bg/... /Nacsreshta-dokladG(3).do (status 30.06.2006).*

Ganev, P. Minimalnite pragove i sivata ikonomika (Minimum values and the informal economy). [online]. In: *Dnevnik*, 22.09.2008. [viewed 19.02. 2012]. Available from: http://www.dnevnik.bg/show/?storyid=553161

Georgieva, A. Rashidov, V. Talantat e siguren v sebe si a posredstvenostta vdiga samo shum. (Talents are self-assured and the mediocre merely noisy). [online]. *Novinar* online daily newspaper, p. 2. Available from: http://mc.government.bg/files/1634_892_Novinar-20.10.10.pdf [03.02.2014].

Grozev, A. *Praveneto na kino u nas vse oshte ne e industriya* (*Filmmaking is not yet an industry in our country*). [online]. In: News.bg, 25.07.2008. [viewed 19.02.2012]. Available from: http://news.ibox.bg/news/id_271135103 (status 25.07.2008).

Grupa za prozrachna kulturna politika (Group for transparent cultural policy). [online]. [viewed 22.02.2012]. Available from: www.culturpolicy.dir.bg (status 28.03.2005).

Heritage Foundation, The. Index of economic freedom; a product of the Heritage Foundation and *The Wall Street Journal.* [online]. [viewed 22.02.2012]. Available from: www.heritage.org/index/Country/Bulgaria;2009 (status 14.01.09).

Ilieva, S. and Kolev, P. We talked with Prof. Alexander Grozev, Executive Director of the National Film Centre, Picture Europe. In: *Bulgarian Diplomatic Review* [online]. Available from: http://www.diplomatic-bg.com/c2/content/view/1402/47/ (status 27.10.2009).

Indikativna programa za 2008 na operativna programa "Razvitie" (Indicative Regional Development Programme). [online]. In: Europe.bg, 31.01.2008. [viewed 20.02.2012]. Available from: http://www.europe.bg/htmls/page.php?category=329&id=12334 (status 9.03.2009).

Indzhev, I. In: *Zapochva li jurnalisticheski bunt sreshtu tiraniyata v mediite? (Are journalists starting to oppose the tyranny in the media*?). [online]. Publ. 02.11.2009. Available from: www.ivo.bg (status 19.11.2009).

Institut Otvoreno Obshtestvo (Soros Open Society) ed. Grazhdanski Monitoring varchu deinosta na stolichniya obshtinski savet 2004 – 2005 (Public monitoring of the activities of Sofia City Council 2004–2005). Sofia, 2005. [online]. Sofia, 2005. Available from: http://news.osf.bg/?p=news&in=news&id=85 (status 6.06.2006).

Institut za pazarna ikonomika (Institut of Market Economy). *Uspekhite i provalite na balgarskite pravitelstva 1998-2007. Pregled na oditnite dokladi na Smetnata Palata (The successes and failures of the Bulgarian governments 1997–2007. Examination of the economic reports of the Audit Office*). [online]. Trust for Civil Society in Central and Eastern Europe, 2008. [viewed 19.02.2012]. Available from: http://ime.bg/uploads/b205d6_FullReport.pdf (status 26.12.2008).

Internet Society Bulgaria (ISOC Bulgaria). Palna statistika za Internet potreblenieto v Balgariya (Full statistics on internet use in Bulgaria). Posted by ISOC.BG News, 16.10.2009. Cited in the blog by V. Markovski, chair of ISOC Bulgaria. [online]. Available from: http://isocbg.wordpress.com/2009/ (status 16.10.2009).

Ivanov, Y. *Bogomilski knigi i legendi* (*Books and Legends of the Bogomils*). [online]. [viewed 19.02.2012]. Available from: http://www.kroraina.com/knigi/ji/ji_1b_1.htm #2 (status 07.08.2009).

Josifova, B. *Dalgo shte chakame balgarskite Medichi* (*We will wait a long time for the Bulgarian Medicis*). [online]. In: *Sega*, 5.04.2008. Available from: http://www.sega.b gCOMSSSS (status 12.01.2009).

Kavrakova, A. Monitoring Report of the OSI/EU Monitoring and Advocacy Program. Overview. Country reports: Albania, Bulgaria, Czech Republic, Italy, Lithuania, Poland, Republic of Macedonia, Romania, Slovakia. In: *Television across Europe. More channels less independence*. Budapest/New York: Open Society Institute, 2008, pp. 25–39. Here: p. 39. [online]. Available from:www.soros.org/.../television.../1fullpublication_20080429.pdf (status 17.02.2009).

Klein, A. Nachhaltigkeit als Ziel von Kulturpolitik und Kulturmanagement – ein Diskussionsvorschlag. [online]. [viewed 19.02.2012]. Available from: http://www.theaterportal.de/portal/downloads/Nachhaltigkeit_als_Ziel_Prof_Klein.pdf (status 14.05.2009).

Knigi News. *Nikomu ne e izgodno da zashtiti knigata u nas* (*It is to no one's advantage to protect books in Bulgaria*). [online]. [viewed 10.06. 2012]. Available from: http: //knigi-news.com/?in=pod&stat=650&section=12&cur=315.

Koi e v krak s vremeto (Who is in step with the times?) [online]. In: *Edno* magazine, 17, 14.09. 2011. Sofia. [viewed 19.09.2011]. Available from: http://edno.bg/en/edno_magazine/koy-e-v-krak-s-vremeto/ (status 19.09.2011).

Konstitutsiya na Republika Balgariya (Constitution of the Republic of Bulgaria),

Darzhaven vestnik no. 56, 12 Jul 1991 (author's translation) published 13 Jul 1991, effective from 13 Jul 1991, amend. No. 85, 26 Sep 2003, amend. No. 18, 25 Feb 2005. No. 27, 31 Mar 2006. No.78, 26 Sep 2006. Ruling no. 7 of the Constitutional Court 2006, 12, 02.2007 Available from: http://www.parliament.bg/bg/const (status 06.06.2008).

Krastev, T. Proektozakonat za kulturnoto nasledstsho krie riskove (*The cultural heritage bill involves risks*). [online]. [viewed 19.02.2012]. Available from: http://www.icomos-bg.org/filebank/att_28.pdf (status 02.07.2008).

Krasteva, K. *Vrana stava tsarski dvorets* (*Vrana becomes the palace of the tsars*). [online]. In: *24 Chasa*, 24.01.2010. [viewed 19.02.2012]. Available from: http://www.24chasa.bg/Article.asp?ArticleId=354814 (status 5.03.2010).

Kraus, R. Die deutschen und österreichischen Grabungen in Bulgarien. In: *Bulgarien-Jahrbuch 2008*. Munich, 2009. [online]. http://www.ufg-db.uni-tuebingen.de/fileadmin/Juengere/Mitarbeiter/Krauss/deutsche_Grabungen_1.pdf (status 23.9.2009).

Krifta, A. *Der Zusammenhang von Freiheit und Bildung bei Adorno*. [online]. [viewed 19.02.2012]. Available from: http://www.bikrit.org/thesen/Freiheit_und_Bildung_bei_Adorno.pdf (status 05.08.2010).

Kronsteiner, O. Bikulturalität als Medizin gegen NationalFilologie. [online]. In: *Trans: Internet journal for cultural studies,* No. 13, 6/2002, Salzburg. [viewed 19.02.2012]. Available from: http://www.inst.at/trans/13Nr/kronsteiner13.htm (status 17.02.2011).

Krupp, C. Transparenz in der Kulturförderung. [online]. In: KM, No.18, 2008, pp. 35–37. [viewed 22.02.2012]. Available from: http://www.kulturberatung.at/AABgqk2006/downloads/km0804_S35-37.pdf (status 18.04.2008).

Kulturpolitische Gesellschaft e.V. Declaration at the 15th ordinary general meeting, 14.11.2009 in Bonn. [online]. [viewed 18.02.2012]. Available from: www.kupoge.de/presse/2009-11-14_kulturpolitik-erklaerung.pdf (status 17.12.2009).

Kyosev, A. Soros George Stiftung – Otvoreno Obshtestvo (Soros Open Society Foundation), Politiki (Politics) 6/2006. [online]. Available from: http://politiki.bg/?cy=44&lang=1&a0i=222739&a0m=readInternal&a0p_id=87 (status 8.11.2009).

Lazarova, J. Muzeiat na stara Sofia, Golyamata snimka (The Museum of Old Sofia, The Big Picture: 33 Photographs). [online]. In: *Dnevnik*, 2.09.2009. [viewed 20.02.2012]. Available from: http://www.dnevnik.bg/bigpicture/2009/09/02/778130_muzeiat_na_stara_sofiia/ (status 12.09. 2009).

Lenin, V. I. *The Collapse of the Second International*. [online]. [viewed 06.01.16]. Available from: https://www.marxists.org/archive/lenin/works/1915/csi/index.htm

Lepenies, W. Widersprüche des Kapitalismus. [online]. In: *Welt Online*, 9.05.2009. [viewed 19.02.2012]. Available from: http://www.welt.de/die-welt/article3705807/Widersprueche-des-Kapitalismus.html (status 09.05.2009).

Marcus, D. *Bulgarische Symptome: Auf Gastspielreise in Stadt Rousse mit dem Theater Osnabrück. Zwischen menschlich und möglich.* [online]. [viewed 19.02.2012]. Available from: http://www.nachtkritik.de/index.php?option=com_content&view=article&id=1076:bulgarische-symptome-auf-gastspielreise-in-russe-mit-dem-theater-osnabrueck&catid=419:theaterbrief-aus-bulgarien&Itemid=100060 (status 2008).

Mihalev, I. *Posledniyat dvorets na sotsialisma. Pazarnata ikonomika vse oshte ne e stignala do NDK. (The last bastion of socialism. The market economy did not reach the*

NDK after all). [online]. In: Vesti.bg, 03.02.2007. [viewed 21.02.2012]. Available from: http://www.vesti.bg/?tid=40&oid=998970 (status 03.02.2007).

Ministerstvo na finansite (Ministry of Finance). Darzhaven vestnik. Spravka po godini s broeve na darzhaven vestnik v koito e obnarodvan zakonat za darzhavnya byudzhet na Republika Balgariya 1945–2010. (State Gazette, 1945–2010. State Budget). [online]. Available from: http://www.minfin.bg/bg/page/247 (status 13.11.2010).

Minsisterstvo na finansite (Ministry of Finance). *Doklad po zakona za darzhavniya byudzhet, byudzhet na ustoichivost i razvitie, 2008* (*Report on the implementation of the state budget of the Republic of Bulgaria, 2008*). [online]. [viewed 22.02.2012]. Available from: http://www.minfin.bg/bg/page/516) (status 05.02.2011).

Minsisterstvo na finansite (Ministry of Finance). *Doklad za ispalnenieto na darzhavniya byudzhet na republika Balgariya, Sofia, 1997, 1998, 1999* (*Report on the implementation of the national budget of the Republic of Bulgaria for 1997, 1998, 1999*). [online]. Budget Archive. [viewed 19.02.2012]. Available from: http://www.minfin.bg/bg/pag e/247 (status 25.11.2010).

Ministerstvo na kulturata (Ministry of Culture). *Islozhbata Workshop "Kirilskata Azbuka – novata azbuka na EU"* (*The Cyrillic alphabet is the new alphabet of the European Union*). [online]. [viewed 22.02.2012]. Available from: http://www.mc.gov ernment.bg/sredecs.php?s=16&cc=1 (status 06.03.2007).

Ministerstvo na kulturata (Ministry of Culture). *Istoriya* (*History*). [online]. [viewed 19.02.2012]. Available from: http://mc.government.bg/page.php?p=1&s=11&sp=0&t =0&z=0 (status 07.03.2009).

Ministerstvo na kulturata (Ministry of Culture). *Konzeptsiya za vodeshti stolichni musei, Visualisatsii* (*Concept for Sofia's leading museums, visualizations*). [online]. [viewed 19.02.2012]. Available from: http://mc.government.bg/files/749_Koncepcia_part2.p df (status 14.05.2010).

Ministerstvo na kulturata (Ministry of Culture). Ministarat na kulturata Vezhdi Rashidov isprati pismo do natsionalnoto sdruzhenie na obshtinite (the culture minister Vezhdi Rashidov sent a letter to the National Association of Towns and Municipalities expressing his concern at the cut in funds for the country's cultural institutions). [online]. Publ. 21.03.2011. [viewed 19.02.2012]. Available from: http://mc.government. bg/newsn.php?n=2503&l=1

Ministerstvo na kulturata (Ministry of Culture). *Otchet za ispalnenie na zelite na Ministerstvo na kulturata za 2008* (*Report on the activities of the Ministry of Culture for 2008*). [online]. [viewed 19.02.2012]. Available from: mc.government.bg/files/620_Otchet% 20na%20Ministerstvo%20na%20kulturata%20za%202008.doc (status 14.03.2009).

Mitov, M. Predstavyane na konzeptsiya za razvitie na balgarskata kultura (Presentation of the concept for developing Bulgarian culture). In: *Slovoto* 2005 (10.06.2005). [online]. Available from: http://www.slovesa.net/index.php?id=615 (status 07.12.2005).

National Assembly of the Republic of Bulgaria. Constitution of the Republic of Bulgaria. [online]. Prom. State Gazette (SG) No. 13 Jul 1991, amend. SG No.85, 26 Sep 2003. SG No. 18, 25 Feb 2005. SG No. 27, 31 Mar 2006. SG No. 78, 26 Sep 2006 – Constitutional Court Judgment No.7 (2006). SG No. 12, 6 Feb 2007. [viewed 19.02.2012]. Available from: http://www.parliament.bg/en/const.

Natsionalen Fond Kultura (National Culture Fund). Godishen otchet na natsionalen Fond

Kultura, Sofia. National Culture Fund, Annual Report 2005, 2006, 2007, 2008. [online]. Sofia. Archive. Available from: http://ncf.bg/?page_id=7 (status 5.12.2011).

Natsionalen Statisticheski Institut (National Statistics Institute). Naselenie po godini na preproyavaniya za perioda 1990–2011 (*The population in the years 1990–2011*). [online]. [viewed 22.02.2012]. Available from: http://www.nsi.bg/census2011/index.php (status 23.12.2011).

Natsionalno sdruzhenie na obshtinite v Balgariya (NAMRB) (National Association of Towns and Municipalities in the Republic of Bulgaria). [online]. [viewed 19.02.2012]. Available from: http://www.namrb.org/?act=cms&id=175 (status 27.09.2010).

Natsionalno sdruzhenie na obshtinite v Balgariya (NAMRB) (National Association of Towns and Municipalities in the Republic of Bulgaria. Letter from D. Jankova to the Minister of Culture Vezhdi Rashidov. [online]. [viewed *19.02.2012*]. Available from: www.namrb.org/doc11/VRa6idovRE.doc

Novy, L. Eliteunis in der Krise. [online]. In: *Tagespiegel*, 15.04.2009. [viewed 19.02.2012]. Available from: http://www.tagesspiegel.de/wissen/usa-eliteunis-in-der-krise/1496582.html (status 15.04.2009).

Obendörfer, D. Sprache und Nation. [online]. In: *Zeitschrift für Ausländerrecht und Ausländerpolitik* (ZAR), 2/2006, pp. 41–49. [viewed 19.02.2012]. Available from: http://www.zar.nomos.de/fileadmin/zar/doc/Aufsatz_zar_06_02.pdf (status 17.02.2008).

Observatory of Cultural Economics, Sofia. [online]. [viewed 19.02.2012]. Available from: http://www.culturaleconomics.bg/ (status 27.11.2011).

Open Society Institute (Soros Foundation), Sofia. [online]. [viewed 29.01.2012]. Available from: http://www.osf.bg/?cy=99 (status 27.11.2011).

Parliament. Da vdignem zavesata (Commission for the records of former employees of the Bulgarian People's Army's secret service and intelligence service). [online]. [viewed 26.01.2012]. Available from: http://www.comdos.bg (status 14.02.2007).

Parvanov, G. *Kulturata e nai-golemiyat ni argument za chlenstvo v EU* (*Culture is our greatest argument for EU membership*). [online]: In: News bg. [viewed 19.02.2012]. Available from: http://news.ibox.bg/news/id_1923069832 (status 15.07.2006).

Parvanov, G. Privetstvie na prezidenta do uchastnizite v natsionalnata diskusiya za regionalni kulturni politiki (Svishtov, 17-18 oktomvri 2003) (Welcome address by President G. Parvanov, national discussion on regional cultural policy, Svishtov, 17–18 October, 2003). In: President 17.10. 2003. [online]. Available from: http://www.president.bg/news.php?id=1010&st=445 (status 3.08.2007).

Parvanov, G. Slovo na prezidenta Georgi Parvanov na tarzhestvenoto zasedanie na Narodnoto Sabranie po povod priemaneto na Balgariya za palnopraven chlen na Evropeiskiya sayuz (address by Georgi Parvanov, President of Republic of Bulgaria, on the occasion of Bulgaria's accession to the EU). Parliament, 11.01.2007. [online]: Available from: http://www.president.bg/news.php?id=2763 (status 17.01.2007).

Petkova, S. *Zhivot sled euforiyata* (*Life after euphoria*). Interview with I. Moudov. [online]. In: *Kultur, no* 8 (2447), 28.02.2008. [viewed 22.02.2012]. Available from: http://sitekreator.bg/svetlapetkova/ivan_moudov.html (status 29.02.2007).

Petkova, V. Balgariya. 16- a republika na SSSR. Tova e mit! (Bulgaria as the 16th republic of the USSR. That is a myth). [online]. In: *Trud*, 29.10.2010. Available from: http://www.trud.bg/Article.asp?ArticleId=657129 (status 12.07.2011).

PIA, Pressclub. Tvorcheski sayuzi i organisatsii za priyatelstvo s Rusiya izlyazoha s deklaratsiya za oskvernyavaneto na Pametnika na Savetskata armiya v Sofia (Unions and organizations of friends of Russia in a statement on the desecration of the monument to the Soviet Army). [online]. Available from: http://pressclub.bg/society/organizations/20110620/news-43346 (status 20.06.2011).

Ploebst, H. Wolken über Wien. [online]. In:*Texte zur Zukunft der Kulturpolitik*. [viewed 19.02.2012]. Available from: http://kulturpolitik.t0.or.at/txt?tid=a526738a55a53a853fc41a529225f5b7 (status 02.01.2011).

Plovdiv TV-Trakiya. *Kak se zakleymyavat abstraktsionisti – opitat na Khrushchev i Todor Zhivkov* (*How can one condemn abstractionists: the experience of Khrushchev and Todor Zhivkov*). [online]. Available from: http://potv.eu/113259.html?poll=pollresults (status 07.12.2009).

Pravitelstvo na evropeiskata integratsiya (Government of European Integration). Programa na pravitelstvoto na evropeiskata integratsiya ikonomicheskiya rastezh i sotsialnata otgovornost (Programme of the Government of European Integration, Economical Growth and Social Responsibility). [online]. Available from: http://www.europe.bg/upload/docs/GovernmentalProgramme-final-bg.pdf (status 2.05.2006).

Preobrasuvat natsionalnite tsentrove po izkustvata v direktsii (The national arts centres will be converted into directorates). [online]. In: Vesti.bg. [viewed 19.02.2012]. Available from: http://www.vesti.bg/index.phtml?tid=40&oid=874589 (status 17.04.2006).

RNCOS, Bulgaria Banking Sector Analysis, indicators for 2008. Feb 2008. [online]. [viewed 20.02.2012]. Available from: http://www.rncos.com/Report/IM587.htm (status 04.01.2009).

Ruseva, L. Edin den na bezdarnoto statukvo (A day of persisting talentlessness). [online]. In: *Reduta* BG, 26.06.2011. [viewed 19.02.2012]. Available from: http://www.reduta.bg/?p=1014 (status 26.06. 2011).

Sabev, D. *Sreshtu deflatsiyata valutniyat bord v Balgariya e bezsilen (There is no recourse against the deflation of the currency board in Bulgaria*). [online]. In: money.bg, 05.12.2008. [viewed 19.02.2012]. Available from: http://money.ibox.bg/comment/id_570998032 (status 05.12.2008).

Sayuz na Balgarskite Pisateli (Union of Bulgarian Writers). Deklaratsiya na SBP po povod "Archipelag Gulag" na Aleksandr Solzhenitsyn (Declaration of the Union of Bulgarian Writers following publication of *The Gulag Archipelago* by Aleksandr Solzhenitsyn). [online]. In: *Glasove*, 12.07.2010. [viewed 22.02.2012]. Available from: http://www.glasove.com/deklaratsiya-na-sbp-po-povod-arhipelag-gulag-na-aleksandur-solzhenitsin-9025 (status 12.07.2010).

Sayuz na biblioteknite i informatsionnite rabotnitsi (Union of Librarians and Information Sector Employees). *Za neobchodimostta ot neotlozhni merki za reshavane na osnovnite problemi na bibliotekite v Balgariya* (*On the necessity of solving the problems of libraries in Bulgaria*), publ. 21.04.2004. [online]. [viewed 21.02.2012]. Available from: http://www.lib.bg/za_neob.htm (status 11.06.2007).

Sidorov, M. and Kelevedzhiev, E. *An approach to dating the Pliska rosette* (preprint: working paper 4-1998 of The Institute of Mathematics and Informatics at Bulgarian Academy of Sciences, Sofia. [online]. [viewed 19.02.2012]. Available from: http://www.math.bas.bg/~keleved/dplisros/ (status 03.03.2010).

Smetna Palata (Audit Office). Archive. [online. Available from: http://www.bulnao.government.bg/index.php?lang=&p=archive&y=2005&id=18 (status 17.02.2009).

Smetna Palata (Audit Office). Doklad za rezultatite ot izvarsheniya odit na finansovoto upravlenie na byudzheta na Naroden Teatar "Ivan Vasov". (Report on examination of the financial management of the budget of the Ivan Vazov National Theatre 01.01.2004–30.09.2004. Sofia, p. 2. [online]. Available from: http://www.bulnao.government.bg/index.php?lang=&p=archive&y=2006&id=18 (status 17.02.2009).

Sofia University St. Kliment Ohridski. *Konventsiya za zashtita na architekturnoto nasledstvo na Evropa* (*Convention for the protection of the architectural heritage of Europe*). [online]. [viewed 19.02.2012]. Available from: http://www.phls.uni-sofia.bg/cult/suvetnaevropa/SE_konvencii_03.html (status 21.06.2006).

Solzhenitsyn, A. *The Gulag Archipelago*. [online]. New York, Evanston, San Francisco, London: Harper & Row, 1974. Vol. 1, p. 2. Available from: https://archive.org/details/TheGulagArchipelago-Threevolumes

Solzhenitsyn, A. Жить не по лжи! (Do not live with the lie!), Российская газета", nr. 4724, 7.08.2008. Available from: http://www.rg.ru/2008/08/07/solzhenicyn-statya.html (status 3.12.2011).

Spasov, O. Vreme e za pogled otvad Web 2.0 (It is time to look outside Web 2.0). [online]. In: *Kultur* 1., 11.01.2008. [viewed 19.02.2012]. Available from: http://www.kultura.bg/bg/article/view/13688 (status 24.01.2008).

Stankova, M. Koi ubi balgarskata kultura. Edno kriminalno razsledvane (Who killed Bulgarian culture? A criminal investigation). [online]. In: *Lit. Forum*, No. 14, 15 (502), 07.05.2002–13.05.2002, 16.04.02–22.04.2002. [viewed 19.02.2012]. Available from: http://www.slovo.bg/old/litforum/215/mstankova.htm (status 5.02.2006).

Stolichniat byudzhet: golyam ili malak (Budget of the capital city: large or small). [online]. Blog. Available from: www.culturalpolicy.dir.bg (ed). (status 28.09.2006).

Stoyanov ,V. *Minderheiten in Bulgarien aus historischer Sicht und in der Gegenwart* (*Minorities in Bulgaria from a historical perspective and in the present*). [online]. Lecture for the Dept. of Political Science at Klagenfurt University. Sofia, 1 September 2009. [viewed 09.06.2014]. Available from: http://www.ihist.bas.bg/sekcii/CV/_private/Valery_Stoyanov/VS_Minderheiten.htm

Tchobanov, T. and Stanilov, S. *Kulturen turizam i regionalno razvitie* (*Cultural tourism and regional development*). [online]. National Culture Fund. [viewed 29.01.2012.] Available from: http://ncf.bg/wp-content/kulturenturizam.pdf pp. 79–88.

Text of the memorandum "*chetyashta Balgariya*" ("Reading Bulgaria"). [online]. Available from: http://www.lib.bg/kampanii/4bulgaria/memorandum_4B.htm (status 18.04.2006).

Tomova, B. *Finansirane na izkustvata i kulturata v Balgariya – mezhdu darzhavata i pazara* (*Financing the arts and culture in Bulgaria — between the city and the market*). [online.] Ikonomicheski doklad po proekt "Technologichen Park Kultura" po programata "Politiki za kultura" (Economics essay on the "Technological Culture Park"). Sofia, 2001, Available from: http://www.tpc.cult.bg/doc/TPK1 Finansirane na izkustvata.doc (status 24.02.2005).

Tomova, B. and Andreeva, D. Balgarskata filmova industriya v usloviyata na pazarna ikonomika. Sofia, 2010; (*The Bulgarian film industry under the conditions of the market economy*). [online]. Observatoriya po ikonomika na kulturata (Observatory of Cultural Economics). Sofia 2010. Available from: http://ncf.bg/wp-content/film_industry_observatory.pdf (status 07.02.2010).

Tsentar za izledvane na demokratsiyata (Centre for Democratic Research). Policy paper. *Za ednakvi pravila i pochtena konkurentsiya politiki za protivodeistvie na sivata ikonomika i koruptsiyata v Balgariya (For the same rules and fair competition, strategies for fighting the black economy and corruption in Bulgaria, supported by the MATRA programme and the Dutch embassy)*. [online]. Sofia, May 2008, No. 15. [viewed 22.02.2012]. Available from http://www.econ.bg/content/fileSrc.pdf (status 5.01.09).

Tüpper-Fotiadis, R. A. Nicht mit der Lüge leben. [online]. In: *Die Politische Meinung*, KAS International, No. 466, 9/2008, pp. 64–68. [viewed 21.02.2012]. Available from: http://www.kas.de/wf/de/33.14507/, (status 23.11.2011).

TV 7: Otvaryat dosietata na duchovnitsite na Svetiya Sinod (Personal files of priests of the Holy Synod were opened). [online]. TV 7, news bulletin, 13:49. [retrieved 19.02.2012]. Available from: http://tv7.bg/news/society/3123632.html (status 16.12.2011).

Vandov, N. I obshtinskite teatri – kato drugite? (And the municipal theatres — like the others?) [online]. In: kultura.bg., No. 6, 7.02.2003. [viewed 21.02.2012]. Available from: http://www.kultura.bg/media/my_html/2261/teanv.htm (status 05.03.2005).

Vandov, N. Palno e s martvi zakoni (It is full of dead letter laws). [online]. Interview with Prof. Danailov in: *kultura.bg*, no. 14, 05.04.2002. [viewed 21.02.2012]. Available from: http://www.kultura.bg/media/my_html/2222/cpb-lambo.htm (status 2.07.2006).

Varna City Council. Website: www.varna.bg (status 22.10.2009).

Varna Museum of Archaeology. [online]. [viewed 21.02.2012]. Available from: http://www.amvarna.com/eindex.php?lang=2&lid=2&slid=&slid=1 (status 14.09.2010).

Walcker-Mayer, G. Über Bulgaren, ein Orgel Präludium und einer Hand voll Balkanschnee oder über das reine Glück von einer Rose geliebt zu werden. Die Menschen in der bulgarischen Stadt Russe (Rustschuk an der Donau), Bozhidar Abrashev, Prelude for Organ. [online]. In: Walcker, 31.10.2003. [viewed 26.01.2012]. Available from: http://www.walckerorgel.de/gewalcker.de/rousse_rose.htm (status 14.02.2007).

Webcounter. [online]. [viewed 20.08.2006]. Available from: http://bfcounter.com/?vcat,year,,,,,8 (status 20.08.06, 00:07)

World Bank. World Development Indicators database, 2006 (4).Note: a 2004 data. [online]. Available from: http://www.euro.who.int/Document/E90023.pdf, p. 30 (status 03.01.09).

Zakon za kulturnoto nasledstvo (Cultural Heritage Act). [online]. Available from http://www.lex.bg/bg/laws/ldoc/2135623662 (status 18.08.2011).

Zakon za metsanatstvoto (Patronage Act). [online]. Available from: www.lex.bg/bg/laws/ldoc/2135514206 (status 13.12.2009).

Zakon za obshtestvenite biblioteki (Public Libraries Act). Darzhaven vestnik (State Gazette) no. 42, 5 Jun 2009. [online]. [viewed 19.01.2016]. Available from: http://www.lex.bg/laws/ldoc/2135636021 (status 23.12.2010).

Zakon za obshtinskite byudzheti (Law on the municipal budget). Darzhaven Vestnik. [online]. [viewed 22.02.2012]. Available from: http://lex.bg/laws/ldoc/2134393857 (status 11.06.2008).

Zakon za pametnizite na kulturata i muzeite (Law on Monuments and Museums) (repealed). [online]. Available from: mc.government.bg/files/75_10.1.ZAKON_3.doc (status 05.12.2011).

Zakon za zakrila i razvitie na kulturata (Protection and Development of Culture Act). [online]. Available from: http://lex.bg/laws/ldoc/2134664704 (status 28.12.2011).

Zakonoproekt za darzhavniya byudzhet na Republika Balgariya za 2007 i stanovishte po proekta na byudzhet na sadebnata vlast za 2007, No 602-01-93, vneseni ot Ministerskiya savet na 31.10.2006 (Parliamentary committee for culture, budget act 2007 (...). [online]. Available from: http://www.parliament.bg/bg/archive/2/3/168/reports /ID/793 (status 11.12.2006).

Zhelev, V. and Rashidov, V. *10-12 trupi otsega izglezhdat obrecheni* (*10–12 companies not yet doomed*). [online]. Culture Minister V. Rashidov in an interview for the magazine *24 Chasa*, 11.05.2010. [viewed 22.02.2012]. Available from: http://www.24chasa.bg /Article.asp?ArticleId=475495 (status 17.05.2010)

Zones de Protection du Patrimoine Architectural Urbain et Paysager *(Architectural, Urban* and Landscape Heritage Protection *Zones).* [online]. Available from: http://www.vie-publique.fr/documents-vp/zppaup.pdf (status 02.07.2008).

II. International Congress of Architects and Technicians. The Venice Charter for the Conservation and Restoration of Monuments and Sites, 1964. [online]. [viewed 18.02.2012]. Available from: http://www.bda.at/documents/455306654.pdf, (status 7.03 2008).

8. LIST OF TABLES AND FIGURES

8.1 List of tables:

8.1 List of tables:

8.2 List of figures

8.3 List of abbreviations

BNR	Bulgarian National Radio
BNTV	Bulgarian National Television
CI	Copyright industry
ERICArts	European Institute for Comparative Cultural Research
EU	European Union
GDP	Gross domestic product
GNP	Gross national product
ICT	Information and communications technology
IT	Information technology
IKM	Institute for Culture Management
MK	Ministry of Culture
NSI	National Statistics Institute
NGOs	Non-government organizations
WAZ	*Westdeutsche Allgemeine Zeitung*

8.4 Legislation relating to culture prior to 2012

Translated from a German translation of the Bulgarian original

LAW on Public Libraries

Published in Darzhaven vestnik (State Gazette) no. 42, 5 Jun 2009, effective from 6 Jul. 2009, amend. No. 74, 15 Sep 2009, effective from 15 Sep 2009. No. 38, 21 May 2010.

Chapter I
GENERAL PROVISIONS

Art. 1. This Law regulates the foundation, the types, the functions, the management and the financing of public libraries.

AMENDMENT to the Law on Folk Culture Centres (published in Darzhaven vestnik [State Gazette] no. 89 [1996]; amend. No. 95 [1997]. No. 90 [1999]. No. 28 and 94 [2005]. No. 108 [2006]).

Published in Darzhaven vestnik (State Gazette) no. 42, 5 Jun 2009

§ 1. In Art. 1 the word “development” is added after the word “foundation”.

§ 2. In Art. 3 the following amendments and additions are made:

LAW on the Protection and Development of Culture

Published in Darzhaven vestnik (State Gazette) no. 50, 1 Jun 1999, amend. No. 1, 4 Jan 2000, corrected. No. 34, 6 Apr 2001, amend. No. 75, 2 Aug 2002, effective from 2 Aug 2002. No. 55, 25 Jun 2004, effective from 1 Jan 2005. No. 28, 1 Apr 2005, effective from 1 Apr 2005, expanded. No. 74, 13 Sep 2005, effective from 14 Oct 2005, amend. and expanded. No. 93, 22 Nov 2005, amend. No. 99, 9 Dec 2005, effective from 10 Jan 2006. No. 103, 23 Dec 2005. No. 21, 10 Mar 2006. No. 41, 19 May 2006, amend. and expanded. No. 106, 27 Dec 2006, amend. No. 84, 19 Oct 2007. No. 19, 13 Mar 2009, effective from 10 Apr 2009, expanded. No. 42, 5 Jun 2009, amend. No. 74, 15 Sep 2009, effective from 15 Sep 2009, expanded. No. 13, 16 Feb 2010.

Chapter I
GENERAL PROVISIONS

Art. 1. This Law defines the main principles and priorities of national cultural policy, cultural organizations and bodies for the protection of culture as well as bodies for the protection of the national cultural identity and the means of supporting and financing cultural activity and artists.

LAW on Patronage

Published in Darzhaven vestnik (State Gazette) no. 103, 23 Dec 2005, effective from 23 Dec 2005, amend. No. 30, 11 Apr 2006, effective from 12 Jul 2006, amend. and expanded. No. 34, 25 Apr 2006, effective from 1 Jan 2008*, amend. No. 63, 4 Aug 2006, effective from 4 Aug 2006*. No. 80, 3 Oct 2006, effective from 3 Oct 2006*. No. 53, 30 Jun 2007, effective from 30 Jun 2007. No. 109, 20 Dec 2007, effective from 1 Jan 2008. No. 42, 5 Jun 2009, effective from 6 Jul 2009.

* Editor's note: Regarding the coming into effect of amendments and additions to the Patronage Act with Darzhaven vestnik (State Gazette) no. 34 of 25 Apr 2006, see § 56 of the transitional and final provisions of the Trade Register Act.

Chapter I
GENERAL PROVISIONS

Art. 1. This Law regulates relationships within society in connection with the provision of gratuitous aid on the part of natural persons and corporate entities, hereinafter referred to as "patrons", for the creation, preservation and popularization of works of art.

LAW on Cultural Monuments and Museums Repealed

Taking into account redenomination, 5 Jul 1999.

Published in Darzhaven vestnik (State Gazette) no. 29, 11. April 1969, amend. in Darzhaven vestnik (State Gazette) no. 29, 10. April 1973, amend. in Darzhaven vestnik (State Gazette) no. 36, 8 May 1979, amend. in Darzhaven vestnik (State Gazette) no. 87, 11 Nov 1980, amend. in Darzhaven vestnik (State Gazette) no. 102, 29 Dec 1981, amend. in Darzhaven vestnik (State Gazette) no. 45, 8 Jun 1984, amend. in Darzhaven vestnik (State Gazette) no. 45, 13 Jun 1989, amend. in Darzhaven vestnik (State Gazette) no. 10, 2 Feb 1990, amend. in Darzhaven vestnik (State Gazette) no. 14, 16 Feb 1990, amend. in Darzhaven vestnik (State Gazette) no. 112, 27 December 1995, amend. in Darzhaven vestnik (State Gazette) no. 31, 12 Apr 1996, amend. in Darzhaven vestnik (State Gazette) no. 44, 21 May 1996, amend. in Darzhaven vestnik (State Gazette) no. 117, 10 Dec 1997, amend. in Darzhaven vestnik (State Gazette) no. 153, 23 Dec 1998, amend. in Darzhaven vestnik (State Gazette) no. 50, 1 Jun 1999, amend. in Darzhaven vestnik (State Gazette) no. 55, 25 Jun 2004, amend. in Darzhaven vestnik (State Gazette) no. 28, 1 Apr 2005, amend. in Darzhaven vestnik (State Gazette) no. 94, 25 Nov 2005.

Chapter I
GENERAL PROVISIONS

Art. 1. (Amend. – Darzhaven vestnik [State Gazette] no. 112 [1995]). This Law regulates museums, the identification, research, protection and popularization of cultural monuments on the territory of the Republic of Bulgaria for the purposes of supporting the education of the population in a spirit of patriotism and international openness and adding to the cultural heritage.

LAW on the National Donation Fund "13 Centuries of Bulgaria"

Published in Darzhaven vestnik (State Gazette) no. 12, 9 Feb 2001, amend. and expanded. No. 32, 12 Apr 2005, amend. No. 94, 25 Nov 2005, effective from 25 Nov 2005, amend. and expanded. No. 113, 28 Dec 2007, effective from 1 Jan 2008, expanded. No. 42, 5 Jun 2009, amend. No. 74, 15 Sep 2009, effective from 15 Sep 2009. No. 97, 10 Dec 2010, effective from 10 Dec 2010.

Digest – APIS, Book no. 3/2001, p. 7; Book no. 5/2005, p. 81
Law Library – APIS, Vol. 4, Section 3, no. 650

Chapter I
GENERAL PROVISIONS

Art. 1. The National Donation Fund "13 Centuries of Bulgaria", hereinafter referred to as "the Fund", is a legal entity with its offices in Sofia.

LAW on the Film Industry

Published in Darzhaven vestnik (State Gazette) no. 105, 2 Dec 2003, amend. No. 28, 1 Apr 2005, effective from 1 Apr 2005. No. 94, 25 Nov 2005, effective from 25 Nov 2005. No. 105, 29 Dec 2005, effective from 1 Jan 2006. No. 30, 11 Apr 2006, effective from 12 Jul 2006. No. 34, 25 Apr 2006, effective from 1 Jan 2008*, amend. No. 80, 3 Oct 2006, effective from 3 Oct 2006*. No. 53, 30 Jun 2007, effective from 30 Jun 2007, amend. and expanded. No. 98, 27 Nov 2007, effective from 1 Jan 2008. No. 42, 5 Jun 2009, amend. No. 74, 15 Sep 2009, effective from 15 Sep 2009. No. 99, 17 Dec 2010, effective from 1 Jan 2011; Resolution no. 1 of the Constitutional Court of the Republic of Bulgaria, 31 Mar 2011 – No. 31, 15 Apr 2011

Digest – APIS, Book no. 1 /2004, p. 513

Law Library – APIS, Vol. 4, Section 3, no. 635

* Editor's note: Regarding the coming into effect of amendments and additions to the Film Industry Act with Darzhaven vestnik (State Gazette) no. 34 of 25 Apr 2006, see § 56 of the transitional and final provisions of the Trade Register Act.

LAW on the Folk Culture Centres

Published in Darzhaven vestnik (State Gazette) no. 89, 22 Oct 1996, amend. No. 95, 21 Oct 1997. No. 90, 15 Oct 1999. No. 28, 1 Apr 2005, effective from 1 Apr 2005. No. 94, 25 Nov 2005, effective from 25 Nov 2005. No. 108, 29 Dec 2006, effective from 1 Jan 2007, amend. and expanded. No. 42, 5 Jun 2009, amend. No. 74, 15 Sep 2009, effective from 15 Sep 2009. No. 47, 22 Jun 2010. No. 97, 10 Dec 2010, effective from 10 Dec 2010.

Law Library – APIS, Vol. 4, Section 3, no. 580

Chapter I
GENERAL PROVISIONS

Art. 1. (Expanded – Darzhaven vestnik [State Gazette] no. 42 [2009]). This Law regulates the foundation, development, management, activities, assets, financing, maintenance and closure of Folk Culture Centres.

LAW on the Artists' Fund

Published in Darzhaven vestnik (State Gazette) no. 27, 3 Apr 1973, effective from 1 May 1973, amend. No. 101, 27 Dec 1977. No. 20, 9 Mar 1979. No. 153, 23 Dec 1998, effective from 1 Jan 1999.

Art. 1. This Law regulates the affairs of the Artists' Fund which has the objective of supporting the development of artistic activity it its manifold aspects and of implementing policy in the fields of culture, the arts and science in the People's Republic of Bulgaria.

LAW on Copyright and Related Property Rights

Published in Darzhaven vestnik (State Gazette) no. 56, 29 Jun 1993, effective from 1 Aug 1993, amend. No. 63, 5 Aug 1994, amend. and expanded. No. 10, 27 Jan 1998. No. 28, 4 Apr 2000, effective from 5 May 2000, expanded. No. 107, 28 Dec 2000, amend. and expanded. No. 77, 9 Aug 2002, effective from 1 Jan 2003, amend. No. 28, 1 Apr 2005, effective from 1 Apr 2005. No. 43, 20 May 2005, effective from 1 Sep 2005. No. 74, 13 Sep 2005, effective from 14 Oct 2005, amend. and expanded. No. 99, 9 Dec 2005, effective from 10 Jan 2006, amend. No. 105, 29 Dec 2005, effective from 1 Jan 2006, expanded. No. 29, 7 Apr 2006, amend. No. 30, 11 Apr 2006, effective from 12 Jul 2006, expanded. No. 73, 5 Sep 2006, effective from 6 Oct 2006, amend. No. 59, 20 Jul 2007, effective from 1 Mar 2008. No. 12, 13 Feb 2009, effective from 1 Jan 2010, amend. No. 32, 28 Apr 2009, amend. and expanded. No. 25, 25 Mar 2011, effective from 25 Mar 2011.

Digest – APIS, Book no. 7/93, p. 7; Book no. 2/98, p. 7; Book no. 5/2000, p. 15; Book no. 1/2001, p. 7; Book no. 9/2002, p. 7; Book no. 5/2005, p. 11; Book no. 10/2005, p. 16

Art. 1. This Law regulates relationships in connection with the creation and dissemination of literary, artistic and scientific works.

LAW on the Lodging of Printed Works and Others as Stipulated by Law (Title amend. Darzhaven vestnik [State Gazette] no. 42 [2009], effective from 6 Jul 2009)

Published in Darzhaven vestnik (State Gazette) no. 108, 29 Dec 2000, effective from 1 Jan 2001, amend. No. 28, 1 Apr 2005, effective from 1 Apr 2005. No. 88, 4 Nov 2005. No. 94, 25 Nov 2005, effective from 25 Nov 2005, expanded. No. 57, 13 Jul 2007, effective from 13 Jul 2007, amend. and expanded. No. 42, 5 Jun 2009, effective from 6 Jul 2009, amend. No. 82, 16 Oct 2009, effective from 16 Oct 2009, amend. and expanded. No. 87, 5 Nov 2010, amend. No. 101, 28 Dec 2010.

Digest – APIS, Book no. 1/2001, p. 129

Law Library – APIS, Vol. 4, Section 4, no. 67

Chapter I
GENERAL PROVISIONS

Object

Art. 1. (Amend. Darzhaven vestnik [State Gazette] no. 42 [2009], effective from 6 Jul 2009). This Law defines the principles and procedures for lodging printed works or other works created and published in Bulgaria or having a connection with Bulgaria for the purpose of preserving them as part of the national cultural heritage.

LAW on the Administrative Regulation of the Production of and Trade in Optical Storage Media, Matrices and other Data Carriers that Contain Material Protected by Copyright or Related Property Rights

Published in Darzhaven vestnik (State Gazette) no. 74, 13 Sep 2005, effective from 14 Oct 2005, amend. No. 105, 29 Dec 2005, effective from 1 Jan 2006. No. 30, 11 Apr 2006, effective from 12 Jul 2006, amend. and expanded. No. 34, 25 Apr 2006, effective from 1 Jan 2008*, amend. No. 80, 3 Oct 2006, effective from 3 Oct 2006*. No. 53, 30 Jun 2007, effective from 30 Jun 2007, amend. and expanded. No. 84, 19 Oct 2007, amend. No. 82, 16 Oct 2009, effective from 16 Oct 2009. No. 25, 25 Mar 2011, effective from 25 Mar 2011, amend. and expanded. No. 77, 4 Oct 2011.

* Editor's note: Regarding the coming into effect of amendments and additions to the Law on the Administrative Regulation of the Production of and Trade in Optical Storage Media, Matrices and other Data Carriers that Contain Material Protected by Copyright or Related Property Rights with Darzhaven vestnik (State Gazette) no. 34 of 25 Apr 2006, see § 56 of the transitional and final provisions of the Trade Register Act.

Chapter I
GENERAL PROVISIONS

Object of the Law

Art. 1. (1) This law regulates the administrative regulation and monitoring of the production, including reproduction, dissemination, import and export of optical storage media, matrices and other data carriers that contain material protected by copyright or related property rights.

LAW ON RADIO AND TELEVISION

Published in Darzhaven vestnik (State Gazette) no. 138, 24 Nov 1998; Resolution no. 10 of the Constitutional Court of the Republic of Bulgaria, 25 Jun 1999 – No. 60, 2 Jul 1999; amend. No. 81, 14 Sep 1999, effective from 15 Dec 1999, amend. and expanded. No. 79, 29 Sep 2000. No. 96, 9 Nov 2001, amend. No. 112, 29 Dec 2001, effective from 5 Feb 2002, amend. and expanded. No. 77, 9 Aug 2002, amend. No. 120, 29 Dec 2002, expanded. No. 99, 11 Nov 2003, amend. No. 114, 30 Dec 2003, expanded. No. 99, 9 Nov 2004, amend. No. 115, 30 Dec

2004, effective from 1 Jan 2005. No. 88, 4 Nov 2005, amend. and expanded. No. 93, 22 Nov 2005, amend. No. 105, 29 Dec 2005, effective from 1 Jan 2006 No. 21, 10 Mar 2006. No. 34, 25 Apr 2006, effective from 1 Jan 2008*. No. 70, 29 Aug 2006*. No. 80, 3 Oct 2006, effective from 3 Oct 2006, amend. and expanded. No. 105, 22 Dec 2006, effective from 1 Jan 2007, amend. No. 108, 29 Dec 2006, effective from 1 Jan 2007, amend. and expanded. No. 10, 30 Jan 2007, effective from 1 Jan 2007, expanded. No. 41, 22 May 2007* amend. No. 53, 30 Jun 2007, effective from 30 Jun 2007. No. 113, 28 Dec 2007, effective from 1 Jan 2008. No. 110, 30 Dec 2008, effective from 1 Jan 2009, amend. and expanded. No. 14, 20 Feb 2009. No. 37, 19 May 2009, effective from 19 May 2009. No. 42, 5 Jun 2009, amend. No. 99, 15 Dec 2009, effective from 1 Jan 2010, amend. and expanded. No. 12, 12 Feb 2010, amend. No. 47, 22 Jun 2010, effective from 22 Jun 2010. No. 97, 10 Dec 2010, effective from 10 Dec 2010. No. 99, 17 Dec 2010, effective from 1 Jan 2011. No. 101, 28 Dec 2010, amend. and expanded. No. 28, 5 Apr 2011.

Digest – APIS, Book no. 12/98, p. 308; Book no. 10/2000, p. 108; Book no. 12/2001, p. 185; Book no. 12/2004, p. 247; Book no. 1/2005, p. 430 Law Library – APIS, Vol. 1, Section 1, no. 70

* Editor's note: Regarding the coming into effect of amendments and additions to the Law on Radio and Television with Darzhaven vestnik (State Gazette) no. 34 of 25 Apr 2006, see § 56 of the transitional and final provisions of the Trade Register Act.

Chapter I
GENERAL PROVISIONS

Art. 1. (Amend. – Darzhaven vestnik [State Gazette] no. 12 [2010]). This Law regulates media services supplied by providers of media services under the jurisdiction of the Republic of Bulgaria.

LAW on the Cultural Heritage

Published in Darzhaven vestnik (State Gazette) no. 19, 13 Mar 2009, effective from 10 Apr 2009; amend. by Resolution no. 7, 29 Sep 2009 of the Constitutional Court of the Republic of Bulgaria. No. 80, 9 Oct 2009; amend. and expanded. No. 92, 20 Nov 2009, effective from 20 Nov 2009, amend. No. 93, 24 Nov 2009, effective from 25 Dec 2009. No. 101, 28 Dec 2010, amend. and expanded. No. 54, 15 Jul 2011.

Chapter I
GENERAL PROVISIONS

Art. 1. (1) This Law regulates the preservation and protection of the cultural heritage of the Republic of Bulgaria.

Darzhaven vestnik (State Gazette) no. 54, 15 Jul 2011

Amendment to the Law on the Cultural Heritage

DECREE no 171

Pursuant to Art. 98, subparagraph 4 of the Constitution of the Republic of Bulgaria

I HEREBY DECREE:

publication of the amendment to the Law on the Cultural Heritage in Darzhaven vestnik passed by the 41st popular assembly on 1 July 2011.

Issued in Sofia on 8 July 2011.

Acknowledgments

I would like to extend my heartfelt thanks to the staff of the Institute for Culture Management and Culture Studies in Vienna and to my colleagues for their numerous helpful comments. I had the privilege of spending several years in a productive, absorbing and stimulating intellectual environment.

I am particularly indebted to Prof. Dr. Otto Hofecker, Prof. Dr. Andreas Schwarcz and Prof. Dr. Peter Bachmaier for their expert supervision of my research work. Lastly, I would like to thank my brother Dimitre Alexandrov and my friends Margret Gartz, Miroslav Semkov, Polina Bahrina, Elena Kislinger, Dr. Monika Mokre, Dr. Günther Perchtold and Dr. Martin Grünzweig for their faith in me and for their assistance.

Vienna, 2013

Miscellanea Bulgarica

hrsg. von Verein „Freunde des Hauses Wittgenstein Österreichisch-Bulgarisches Forum“

Andreas Schwarcz; Peter Soustal; Antoaneta Tcholakova (Hg.)

Der Donaulimes in der Spätantike und im Frühmittelalter

Der Donaulimes schützte die neuralgische Nordgrenze Italiens und Konstantinopel. Seiner Bedeutung in Spätantike und Frühmittelalter ist dieser Band gewidmet. A. Schwarcz illustriert die Entstehung des Donaulimes in der Spätantike. E. Weber behandelt die Tabula Peutingeriana als wichtigste kartografische Quelle zum Imperium Romanum. M. Konrad untersucht die Kontinuitätsfrage des Legionslagers Regensburg. Drei Beiträge sind Pannonien gewidmet: M. Mosser behandelt das Legionslager in Vindobona, M. Kandler das Carnuntum, Z. Visy die Villen in der Valeria. Sieben Artikel untersuchen die untere Donau: A. Poulter die römische Strategie dort, G. Kabakchieva die Oescus-Gigen in der Spätantike. G. von Bülow und L. Vagalinski debattieren die Grabungsergebnisse von Iatrus-Krivina. R. Kostova beschreibt die Siedlungstätigkeit in Nordostbulgarien. C. Olariu analysiert die Geschichte und Archäologie von Dinogetia, C.Kirilov das Hauptstadtproblem im Ersten Bulgarischen Reich. C. Stepanov vergleicht die Grenzen an der Donau und im Kaukasus mit literarischen Erwartungen.

Bd. 22, 2016, 318 S., 34,90 €, br., ISBN 978-3-643-50689-4

LIT Verlag Berlin – Münster – Wien – Zürich – London

Auslieferung Deutschland / Österreich / Schweiz: siehe Impressumsseite

Andreas Schwarcz; Peter Soustal; Antoaneta Tcholakova (Hg.)
Das mittelalterliche Bulgarien, Byzanz und Europa
Festschrift für Vasil Gjuzelev zum 75. Geburtstag

In seiner Einleitung zur Festschrift für Vasil Gjuzelev zum 75. Geburtstag öffnet *Johannes Koder* den Blick auf die Schwerpunkte im wissenschaftlichen Schaffen des Jubilars und dessen Wirken als Leiter des Bulgarischen Forschungsinstituts in Österreich (1984 – 1989). *Peter Schreiner* lieferte eine Tour d'Horizon zu den Verbindungen Südosteuropas mit dem Mittelmeerbereich. Stark vertreten ist die Geschichte der Genuesen und ihre Präsenz im byzantinischen Raum (*Michel Balard, Laura Balletto, Sergej P. Karpov*). Eine Studie zu den Anfängen der Komnenendynastie führt in das Byzanz des 10. und 11. Jahrhunderts (*Elena Koytcheva*). In die Sphäre realer und imaginärer Völker ist *Vasilka Täpkova-Zaimova* vorgestoßen. *Ivan Jordanov* befasste sich mit Titeln und Würdenträgern des Hofes von Veliki Preslav. *Ivan Božilov* schreibt über Franjo Račkis „Histoire de Bulgarie". *Peter Soustal* geht den Spuren slawischer Präsenz auf dem Heiligen Berg Athos nach. *Oliver Jens Schmidt* schließlich führt uns zu Skanderbegs Erhebung 1443 und den unterschiedlichen Ethnien und Konfessionen im westlichen Makedonien und mittleren Albanien.

Bd. 21, 2014, 128 S., 29,90 €, br., ISBN 978-3-643-50591-0

LIT Verlag Berlin – Münster – Wien – Zürich – London
Auslieferung Deutschland / Österreich / Schweiz: siehe Impressumsseite